Black Powder Hunting

Black Powder Hunting

Sam Fadala

bkl

Stackpole Books

BLACK POWDER HUNTING

Copyright © 1978 by
Sam Fadala

Published by
STACKPOLE BOOKS
Cameron and Kelker Streets
P.O. Box 1831
Harrisburg, Pa. 17105

Published simultaneously in Don Mills, Ontario, Canada
by Thomas Nelson & Sons, Ltd.

Jacket photograph by Kenn Oberrecht

Printed in the U.S.A.

Library of Congress Cataloging in Publication Data

Fadala, Sam, 1939-
    Black powder hunting.

    Includes index.
    1. Hunting. 2. Muzzle-loading firearms. I. Title.
SK36.9.F32 1978   799.2′02832   78-17940
ISBN 0-8117-0251-0

Contents

Preface

This book is about black powder hunting, a fast-growing sport in America. It is designed to help the newcomer get started, and I hope it will offer tips and challenges to the initiated black powder shooter as well. If a favorite black powder firearm type is not mentioned, the reader should not feel slighted. The author is aware of the effectiveness and beauty of the Kentucky (Pennsylvania) longarms with their graceful barrels and full stocks and he defends their use. The flintlocks of all types are revered, too, a reliable form, with some custom flinters and special factory offerings capable of an ignition time that rivals the best percussion guns.

If mention goes in favor of the percussion-type Hawken rifle, this is due to its popularity, as well as its excellence in the field. The Hawken dominates the black powder hunting scene today, in tribute to the American mountain man, who made the rifle famous in the opening of the Far West.

The word "primitive" as used in this book does not carry its normal meaning of prehistoric or ancient, but is meant instead to describe the type of modern hunting in which black powder arms of yesteryear's design are employed. Game departments the country over have used the term "primitive hunting" to describe these modern hunts in which black powder or archery only are allowed.

If the old-time buckskinners find room for argument with the ways and means described in this book, that is good, for it is a difference of opinion that not only makes the horse race, but also adds the spice to many of life's endeavors. Black powder hunting is an individualistic effort in which each person modifies a mixture of old and new methods into a unique blend that suits his personality, needs, and desires.

Finally, let none of the women readers be offended if the male gender appears so often, for it is only a writing expedient and does not infer or imply that black powder hunting is for men only. Women have every right to tote the soot belchers into the field in pursuit of all game from the tasty bobwhite to the ponderous moose.

CHAPTER 1

Why Go Primitive?

The metallic hand of the spacecraft vehicle reached out in robot fashion and scooped a chunk of dust from the Martian landscape, returning the prize to a compartment in its bowels. As the machine made its tracks across the face of the hitherto unreachable planet many thousands of miles from earth, back home an ever increasing number of sportsmen were tracing their own quiet paths through forest and backcountry, enjoying a rebirth in kinship with cultural and aesthetic ties belonging to another century. They were hunting with the tools of their forebears. Some dressed in buckskins, others in more modern attire, but all had one thing in common—weapons from an era gone by, the soot-belching single-shot frontloading rifles and shotguns of frontier times, as well as the one-shot pistols and the six-shooters of flintlock and percussion style.

Why, on the threshold of the twenty-first century, and in the face of the most advanced technology known to this planet, have hunters taken steps back to the past? In an age where science fiction becomes daily fact, something unique has happened.

Amidst radar cooking and computerized tax returns, along with a myriad of other contemporary complications, a desire has risen to become involved with simpler, less complex activities. Black powder hunting is one of these—a preservation of a labor of love which was a natural condition for America's pioneers, a rewarding satisfaction gained from hunting with the more primitive, basic arms that seem to bring us closer to nature, while at the same time giving a rewarding feeling of satisfaction gained from a greater challenge, a sense of deep accomplishment. There is quality fulfillment in a sport that gives the hunter just one chance to hit the quarry. The chances for a second shot become quite remote when that second ball or bullet has to be fed down muzzle first, one at a time.

Black powder hunters say they feel brand-new when they enter the sport, and a few quail or ducks in the hand taken in the atmosphere of acrid blue smoke from a double-barrel front-feeding shotgun render a greater reward than a full bag downed with a modern pump or auto scattergun. "I felt the same thrill I got when I was a kid," one newcomer to black powder hunting told me, "the way I felt when I brought home those first squirrels and rabbits with a .22 rifle dad gave me for Christmas." Plenty of the older hands of the sport are turning to the frontstuffers. Having pretty well mastered the techniques of using the modern firearm, they are adding a new dimension in terms of challenge and reward by going "backwards" to the older style guns. And many newcomers to hunting are beginning with the older arms. There is greater satisfaction in the simpler, more basic tool, in the methodical loading procedure, the do-it-yourself aspects of making bullets and black powder gear, and experiencing success the "hard" way, with the single-shot frontloader design, where the stalk must be efficient and the first shot true.

These are the prime reasons for modern black powder hunting—the sense of satisfaction, the involvement, the more basic approach. But there is a pragmatic side, too. In spite of the antihunter sentiment, nurtured by half-truth and lies, the ranks of the hunter expand yearly, while the habitat of game shrinks with the inroads of development. How can more hunters enjoy the field in safety, while assuring a continuing game supply? Primitive hunting methods can be one answer. A decent harvest is still attainable; however, the pressure on game is lessened when single-shot arms of relatively short range are employed.

State after state has offered the special hunt for the black powder devotee. These hunts are limited to muzzle loaders only, usually single shots, and those states which do not have special primitive weapons seasons allow the old-style guns during the regular seasons, Alaska being an example of this arrangement. The single- and double-barrel front-feeding scatterguns are also allowed during regular upland game and waterfowl seasons for those who wish to bag their birds in the framework of an older tradition.

Mississippi, Alabama, New Hampshire, Arizona, New Mexico, Oregon, Oklahoma, Washington, Idaho, Colorado—all of these, as well as numerous other states, offer special black powder only hunts, seasons set aside for the charcoal burners to enjoy. Kentucky has isolated 7,800 acres of its Daniel Boone Forest for primitive firearms only. Ohio has granted 49,000 acres for the same purpose. In Illinois a hunter is compelled by law to hunt deer with a shotgun only, rifles being outlawed, unless a hunter prefers a muzzle loader, and then he may use that form of rifle. Indiana has the same rule. So does Massachusetts. State after state grants seasons for the specially privileged hunt, the hunt where black powder only is allowed, and some states have begun to discuss the idea of more black powder seasons, even general hunts where muzzle loaders only are allowed, while making the use of long-range modern arms available only to special permit limited situations.

The only argument against widespread primitive weapons hunting is the sometimes *too little* harvest, in which the herd is not properly cropped and remains high enough in numbers to deplete its winter forage. Despite the argument that the old single-shot frontloaders are as efficient as modern arms, the fact is, there is indeed more challenge in taking game with the old guns. Range is one large factor. The average black powder rifleman should limit his shooting to the century mark. A hundred yards is plenty far under most conditions when the initial velocity is about that of the modern .22 Long Rifle cartridge. Looping trajectory is standard for black powder rifles, and stalking close is the byword for success. The muzzle-loading shotguns are less limited in terms of ballistics, being pretty close to their modern cousins in range and patterns; but they still must be loaded deliberately from the front, and taking more than two birds out of the air on a rise becomes virtually impossible.

This is not to suggest that hunters who elect to go black powder are doomed to eating canned soup. On the contrary, the practiced and patient black powder man can do well for himself indeed. Of course, he must sometimes settle for a lighter bag, but then a quail on the wing with a black powder scattergun seems like two with a modern pumpgun. The black powder shooter simply has to learn his sport thoroughly, including an adaptation to a different way of hunting, and that is the reason for this book: to promote the discovery of an alternate method, an older way that has newly returned to use.

What arms and equipment should be selected? How can black powder guns be personalized to shoot with more efficiency for the individual? What black powder hunting accessories are available, and how are they made? How does the hunter make good projectiles for his black powder rifles? How powerful is black powder? How are the best black powder hunting loads worked up? How does the primitive weapons hunter get closer to his game? How are loads carried for fast reloading in the field? How can perfect ignition be achieved? These, and many other questions, are answered in the chapters of this book.

The hunter is invited to return for just a little while to the riverbottoms, forests, fields, or desert with his fingertips touching a part of the past in the form of a Hawken-style rifle, a smooth-handling double-barreled black powder shotgun, a Colt or Remington six-gun—a firearm which, at least in spirit, matches those carried by the frontiersmen who made our history a century ago, and even more, the John "Jeremiah" Johns(t)ons, the Bridgers, the Boones, Crocketts, the famous, the little known. A rewarding experience waits for the modern black powder hunter, special seasons at particularly fortunate times of the year, more participation in the sport, with a lot of do-it-yourself action, some nostalgia, a sense of history, often a slower pace, and still the chance to bring home game from birds to bears.

The switch to black powder hunting does not require a great amount of new gear and gadgets. Of course, these are available in what seems to be an almost unlimited amount, with new offerings at least monthly, if not weekly. But the modern black powder hunter needs only his firearms to get started, and a fairly complete array consists of a good rifle, some kind of shotgun, and maybe a sidearm. More of this later. Bullet and ball can be bought today ready-made, though most shooters prefer to mold their own. More on that later, too. A man can go full primitive, with clothing to match and perhaps a hand-constructed Hawken or Kentucky which matches its earlier counterpart in almost every detail. Or, he can elect to stay in fairly modern dress and use a currently designed firearm. The choice is his. Either way will be enjoyable and relaxing—and memorable.

I still recall vividly my first black powder hunt for large game, over a decade ago. I will never forget it, nor have subsequent hunts proved less thrilling with black powder firearms. My partner, John Doyle, a taxidermist from Tucson, Arizona, and I set out to find a javelina in the mountains of southern Arizona. The little animals had been familiar to us for years, but on that trip something was new. I had along a .58 caliber Navy Arms "Buffalo Hunter," a percussion rifle with a 26-inch barrel, firing a 525-grain Minie ball at about 1,400 feet per second from the muzzle.

Javelina are easy to stalk once located, and I planned to get close enough to ensure a good solid hit. Frankly, I did not have total confidence in the smokepole I was carrying, having gotten all my game with modern scope-sighted long-range arms. My confidence was only partial that Thursday morning before sunrise when we left camp. The hunters had all gone home. Friday would be last day of season, and we preferred to hunt the quiet part of the season, rather than the all-too-popular opening day. The land we worked up into was a never boring mixture of rich grasses laced with green cacti, dotted with little oak trees, and dressed with a background of purple peaks that rose from a desert floor of about 3,000 feet to over 10,000 feet above sea level, appearing as huge cathedrals in the distance.

Our major concern was locating a hog "super market," the feeding grounds, which would be distinguished by rootings in the earth where the little peccaries had dug for wild onions, or uprooted cactus plants. There might be chaws out of the prickly pear cacti as well to mark the place where the pigs had recently eaten. If we could find their food, we had a good chance of locating the eaters by taking stands on high points and studying the area with binoculars.

By noon we had uncovered precious little sign, so we split up, John working one section as I worked another, thus doubling the ground we covered. I knew my partner would not stray far. I had all the food in my packsack. In fact, we did come together at the lunch hour, ate, and once again took our solitary ways in

Here are two javelinas afield. One of them turned out to be the first game the author brought down with a .58 Buffalo Hunter.

search of game. On a high ridge my large 10 x 50 Bushnells bit a chunk out of the landscape for scrutiny. I spotted a few deer feeding quietly on the opposite ridge. Then in a small basin the glasses picked up something that was neither plant nor mineral. It was a snout pointing out of the greenery.

The animal moved into view and the rest of the herd materialized almost out of the rocks, it seemed. Nine animals there, seven mature, two young, I counted. Since it was already afternoon, I had to work fast, finding my partner so we could begin a stalk. A half-hour later I found a hat bouncing along a ridge top and signaled in our own predecided sign language that I had found the porkers. John swiftly joined me and we proceeded to relocate the hogs. They had moved down into the basin and light was fast fading for us. Soon we were hunkered down in the grass belly-flat to the earth closing in on the herd.

Wind currents played capriciously upcanyon and I was afraid the herd would scent us and break for the thick brush that lined the bottom of the canyon. Hogs can't see well, but their sense of smell is good. Finally, I was in place. John had moved up higher on the ridge to cover the event and get a shot after I fired with the muzzle loader. At last things seemed right. A nice hog that turned out to be a boar was just in front of me, probably not more than twenty yards away, but there was a large cactus between us.

I cocked the big hammer of the soot belcher and checked to see if the tophat percussion cap still rested on the nipple. The sun was behind the mountain now. I waited for the pig to step out so I could shoot, and at last he did. A spurt of flame left the

In the center of this picture two javelinas (wild pigs) stare right at the hunter. See them? They are camouflaged by the grasses and cacti, but the barrel of the .58 Buffalo Hunter acts as a pointer to give away the larger of the two animals. Getting close is the name of the black powder hunting game.

muzzle of the .58 and the huge chunk of lead slipped through the boar like a silver needle through onionskin paper. The javelina stood perfectly still. Though it is usually difficult to get off a second round, I figured I might as well try, thinking I had missed my target altogether.

I flicked off the spent cap, dropped a premeasured charge of black powder down the muzzle out of my "readyload" container, rammed a new Minie home, and boom! Another spout of smoke and flame entered the canyon. The second bullet had landed less than two inches from the first, neither touching bone, and the boar was finished. He took one step and toppled over. My partner felled his animal as the herd raced up the canyon and in the quiet dusk we dressed our game.

A full moon lit the canyon and the last we had seen of the herd of pigs they were rooting up a hillside not 300 yards from us. Having never caught sight of either of us, the herd was not frightened. It was a good harvest and I enjoyed packing the bacon back to camp on the packframe. I must have inhaled too much black powder smoke that afternoon, because a good case of black powder fever, from which I have never recovered, set in—the kind of fever waiting to be caught by anyone who decides to become a modern black powder hunter.

CHAPTER 2

History of the Black Powder Hunt

In spite of the legendary magnitude of Boone, Crockett, and the other Tennessee-type heroes of America, it took the mountain man, his era, and style to capture the modern black powder hunter's imagination, and his influence prevails today. The man who goes afield with the frontloader now is probably emulating the tradition of the free trapper of the 1800s, and it is worth pausing for a moment to reflect on this special breed of American adventurer in order to gain a sense of his history and learn why we are hunting in the present with yesterday's guns.

It is likely that our modern black powder rifle for hunting will be a replica of the Hawken style or Leman trade model, for these were the favorites of the mountain man. He carried his rifle with him everywhere, for it often made the difference between living and dying, and death was a way of life with the frontiersmen who trapped and hunted the Far West of this country in the early days. In fact, according to history, the mountain man often lived a short, violent existence. James Ohio Pattie, a trapper of the 1820s, claimed that of the 116 men he knew who left Santa Fe one particular trapping season only 16 survived, according to the Time/Life text, *The Trailblazers*. Another frontiersman, Antoine Robidoux, stated that of 300 men he signed into service for fur trapping out West, he could account for the return of only three after several seasons. The rest had been killed by Indians, starved to death, fallen fatally in the mountains, died of disease or infection, or had wandered off into obscurity. Some had possibly even been blinded by the pure alcohol, or "Taos Lightning," served them at rendezvous where the mountain man gathered once each year to sell his furs, get drunk, partake of the ladies, and in short, get rid of all the money he had worked an entire season to earn.

Our current image of the mountain man is derived from books, from prints, such as those of Frederic Remington and other Western artists, and lately from a popular movie of a few years back, *Jeremiah Johnson*, a film based on the true story of John Johnston, Indian fighter and mountain man of the late 1800s, a real-life figure whose biography appears in the book *Crow Killer*. Johnston's way of life was not typical of the mountain man, but he was one of the more interesting and colorful figures of that era, and indeed a bloody one, who was known to partake of the liver of his Indian victims, thereby earning the nickname Liver-Eating Johnston, or The Liver Eater. On one occasion after a skirmish in which several trappers were present, a few doubters goaded Johnston about his liver eating; Johnston then demonstrated his talent, to the chagrin of the group.

"Jeremiah" was larger than life, a man who represented the mountain man at his best, and possibly worst, and whose life has come down to us in history as a trapper/hunter of early America, a Hawken-carrying explorer and wanderer who lived off the land by means of knowledge, wit, and courage. His body was exhumed from its grave in Los Angeles, where the man had gone to die at an old soldier's home when age prevented the continuance of his frontier life, and reburied in the man's mountain home country in Montana.

The Liver Eater represented the kind of man who set out to trap beaver in the west of the 1800s, the man whose style, of course in much modified form and in a special way, has returned today, exhibited not only by its supporters who come each year to rendezvous dressed as their counterparts of a hundred years past, but also by the modern hunter who goes for game as the mountain man did, with the single-shot muzzle loader. The mountain man was many things at once, reckless and often uneducated in terms of "booklearning," very often speaking a cross between Indian dialects and English mixed with words of his own invention. And he was brave, about as brave as any heroes have been at any time in history. In our imagination we can picture a mountain man entering the country of the dreaded Blackfoot Indian in search of that yet undiscovered beaver stream where the big fur bearers run free, easy to trap.

Aside from the trusted Hawken, he may have had a single-shot pistol stuck in his sash along with a tomahawk. He was on his own, self-reliant, self-assured, self-taught through experience. He had to rely on his senses, and those of his pack animals, to remain alive and out of scrapes that could cause him harm. Few made it back to civilization unscathed. What did he look like? How did he dress? What did he carry with him?

He came in all sizes, from the 130-pound Kit Carson, who was able single-handedly to tackle a grizzly that could make a meal of him in a couple bites, to towering men like Joe Meek and Johnston, the latter known to be deadly in hand-to-hand combat, in which more than one man was disabled, even crippled with a swift kick, or killed by means of a broken neck. At one rendezvous the Liver Eater was appointed policeman, and doing his duty he crunched the vertebrae of one troublemaker, killing him bare-handed.

According to the research of Sabin from his fine book *Kit Carson Days*, the mountain man, who incidentally both predated and postdated Lewis and Clark, came in three main classes, the hired trapper, the skin trapper, and the free trapper. The hired

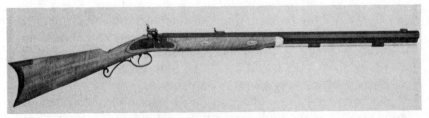

The mountain men of the 1800 era preferred the heavy Hawken rifle made in St. Louis. Today, most of our "Hawkens" are only replicas in general contour and intent. However, the Browning Arms Company is now offering their Jonathan Browning Mountain Rifle, an attempt to reproduce the Hawken.

This print by renowned Western artist Frederic Remington gives a good idea of the appearance of the first black powder hunters. Notice that all of this mountain man's apparel seems to be made from game he encountered on the trail.

trapper earned yearly wages from the fur company, often by accomplishing such menial tasks as camp cleanup. The skin trapper went along with the company, too, but was not under a wage agreement. He was fitted out to trap and had to share his catch with the business. Then there was the free trapper. He was the mountain man personified; attached to no one, his cause was his own, his furs belonged to him, his life was his to do with as he willed. He loved to be called "White Injun" and was pleased when referred to as an Indian.

His hair was long, hanging to the shoulder, combed out when conditions allowed, sometimes braided, perhaps tied with colorful ribbon on the way to rendezvous. He wore a leather shirt that was rough cut and long, its uneven pieces hanging well below the waist. His pants were also leather, tight fitting, called leggins by some, often tied together rather than sewed. On his feet were moccasins, sometimes carefully beaded and decorated by his Indian woman, very comfortable and suited especially to feeling the ground that he walked upon, unlike the heavy walking boots of the white people that parted them from the ground with a thickness of heavy leather.

He might have a stout blanket, preferably a red one, hung over his shoulders for riding, and a red sash tied around his waist, which held the loose shirt tight, as well as gripping his pistol and 'hawk. In the sash would be a butcher knife, a cheap but functional blade that did all manner of work from camp chores to scalping. He might also have an Indian pipe, either stuffed in the sash or tied on himself somewhere. For rendezvous he looked this way, and he looked this way whenever it could be managed.

Out on the trail, his clothes became worn and showed the hard use given by their wearer. He then packed along an extra blanket and spare moccasins. In a sack were his beaver traps, usually about six of them. He wore a powder horn both for show and utility, and he had a leather pouch handy for carrying ball. The bright sash may have been a leather belt, again holding the butcher knife and pistol, and the shapely tomahawk might be a heavier hatchet, called a "Squaw Axe," for wood and meat cutting or to cleave a man's skull in half during battle. There was a wooden box on the horse or mule; the trapper usually had both, the first to ride, the second to carry. In that box was the beaver lure, the smelly stock used to bring the fur-bearer into the trap. The tobacco sack was still present, along with implements for making a fire—flint and steel.

If the tomahawk were not riding in the belt, it might be tied to the pommel of the saddle, and it could be decorated right down to having a hole up through the handle and a bowl on the end so that it could be ceremoniously smoked. The working trapper still had his leather britches in the field, but quite often covered with heavy buffalo skin leggings to ward off the brush. And he might also own a greatcoat or robe of buffalo hide. His hat was often of wool, but could be otter or buff or even handmade of beaver by a St. Louis shop. In cold weather he had a blanket or parts of a blanket with which he wrapped his feet and hands to ward off the chill.

The hat might also be decorated with horn or made from an animal hide so that the critter appeared to be riding atop the head of the mountain man. He might own a shirt stained orange or red, or buff-skin mittens, or a buff-hide knife sheath. And he had his precious whetstone in a cherry wood case along with a small awl with a deer horn handle used for mending leather clothing. He had a cleaning kit for the rifle, and a screw for extracting a ball misloaded, plus a cleaning jag tip. And there was the wiping stick, a wooden ramrod used for cleaning, especially between shots when he wanted to extract every bit of accuracy from his rifle. There was the now famous possibles bag, named because it was "possible" to find about anything in it. Actually, it contained spare ball and powder, along with essentials for making bullets—a mould and some lead.

However, as cavalier as his dress and accoutrements were, there is another side to the story. As Billington, in *The Far West*, says: "Romantic as these clothes were they could best be appreciated from a distance, for they were never removed from the time they were put on until they were discarded, except, perhaps, when their owner laid them across an ant hill for those busy insects to eat some of the lice." Not an easy life was the mountain man's.

Most of all the mountain man prized his rifle, the Hawken made in St. Louis by the shop of the same name. He carried it unsheathed in dangerous country or when hunting, resting in front of him on the saddle ready for use. The rifle may have been fitted with brass tacks to show coups, and it may have worn the signs of field repair, where strips of wet rawhide were wrapped around a broken place and left to dry hard and strong after a rifle was used for other than its intended purpose, usually in a battle with an Indian foe or a grizzly. When riding to rendezvous, or in the company of many other trappers, the rifle might be encased in a smooth buckskin scabbard ornamented with feathers, beads, or quills, the strips of hide hanging down in frills along the trailing edge of the case's bottom.

The Hawken had been invented for use out West, where the game was the elk and the grizzly rather than the little eastern deer and the black bear. The caliber was larger than found in eastern rifles, and the piece was heavy to assure both steadiness in shooting and absorption of recoil. She cost a man $40 when St. Louis was the drop-off point for the boys going West, and when a "fusee," or smoothbore musket, was priced at $12. Her kind has been revived today for modern black powder hunters, as discussed in Chapter Three.

How did the mountain man hunt, and why did he hunt? First, we have to understand that he hunted akin to his everyday nature, which was indeed a strange one. His attitude was one of living for the moment, for he might be dead the next. He exhibited a bravado that we would call foolhardy today. One tale that exemplifies his attitude recounts a rabid wolf coming into a camp of mountain men on a fall night in the backcountry. The men knew the consequences of being bitten by the mad animal, but still they lay under their blankets and buff robes shouting "Hey, it's over here now!," and then laughing at the joke they had made knowing that the wolf was on the other side of camp. Then, "No, over here! Ha, ha, ha." As the men teased each other and made sport of the situation, two of them were bitten by the animal, both doomed to a death by hydrophobia.

During a skirmish with Indians one trapper was hit by a ball. He shouted out to his comrades, "I'm hit!," at which they merrily chided, "Hey, he says he hit one of 'em." "No, I got hit," the man repeated, at which his friends jeered back, "Where'd you say you hit 'em at?" Luckily, the wound was not serious, and the man survived, but the men who faced death daily could not find it in themselves to take life too seriously. Perhaps they took at least some of their hunting the same way, not too seriously; however, from accounts out of history it seems that only some of their hunting was for sheer fun, while most of it had both a deeper meaning for the men, as well as the important function of providing food.

The black powder hunter of yesteryear went on horseback for the most part. Although he was known to take off cross-country afoot, sometimes with a pack of sorts on his back, the mountain man was not really prepared to hunt this way often.

His footgear was designed for the saddle, not for long hikes, and his rifle had no means of being slung, but was meant to be carried across the horse's shoulders instead. When forced to go on foot because of accident to animal or other necessity, the mountain man complained bitterly about it. Yet, the same footgear served better than boots when a stalk was necessary. Assuming, again, that game was seldom frightened by a horse, still there must have been times when the mountain man had to force a stalk on foot, and then the quiet moccasins with their kinship to the earth allowed the feel of every twig and rock in the path.

We know one thing: the mountain man considered his shot.

He got close, a lesson which has come down to us today, when the velocity of black powder arms is recognized as being quite slow. This, then, is the first point we learn from the original black powder hunters. We must get close for that truly effective, humane kill.

Firepower, the ability to get off large numbers of shots, was nonexistent by our modern automatic weapon standards. In the heat of battle when life itself was at stake, it is said that a good mountain man could get off as many as five shots in a minute. Obviously, it only takes seconds for a wild animal to be completely spooked away after a missed shot. In other words, the mountain man may have hunted, and probably did hunt, in such a way as to put that first shot to best advantage, by getting close, maintaining a steady aim, and placing the bullet just right. This style has been inherited by the modern "downwind" shooter, too. Get close, steady up, and put the first ball where it counts.

Another part of the mountain man's hunting style has come down to us, and that is the idea of staying out on the trail for a time. Of course, he lived there, in the woods, mountains, and along the streams. We can only be visitors for the most part, with our jobs calling us home on Monday morning. However, we can spend some time in the wild by using vacation and holidays to best advantage. And we can go back into the country off the roads still. Of course, our horse and mule have been traded for a four-wheel drive vehicle, and when we want to go back in where roads do not exist, we have become backpackers, using the modern frame and pack to hold our "possibles."

The mountain man camped differently, of course. He did "bush up" for the winter instead of looking to the comforts of town, however. His best bet would be a snug cabin, but often he lived in a wall tent shelter, or better, a tepee of thick hide. His fare was undoubtedly a supply of meat, both dried and fresh, along with pan bread or biscuits until the flour ran out. So it was that, as it is for us, camping was a part of the mountain man's life and his hunting style.

But there is another and even more important likeness between the old and new black powder hunters. The mountain man did not hunt for the sake of meat alone, although he prized such food as the best in the world, as many of us do today. He hunted also for intrinsic reasons, out of a deep desire to *be* a hunter. He responded to a challenge that has not yet died, and which will probably remain until the last patch of wild animal habitat is bulldozed over, the contest of going into remote territory, upon grounds that are less than familiar to us, and coming out in possession of wild game.

Naturally, today's black powder hunting has been modified greatly. The modern hunter spends far, far less time in the outdoors than his forebears did. Still, the basics remain intact. Trying to establish each psychological reason for the tremendous growth of modern black powder hunting is impossible, but it seems that as man becomes more and more technological, more materially advanced, he, at the same time, requires at least a fingertip touch with the past and a feel of some sort of roots underfoot. The hunt with the old guns brings a sense of these back.

Meat harvested with the one-shot, slow-loading method seems to taste especially good. In fact, there is seldom a tremendous shock to the tissue, and often the meat itself is more palatable after being taken with the all-lead projectile of the older guns. But mostly it is that puff of smoke that pours into the air, with its attending aroma of the past, that satisfies the modern shooter. Usually, he has had to do at least some stalking, getting close to his game instead of lowering the boom from as much as 300 yards and more, and there is a sense of reward in this, too. But trying to label all the reasons for going black powder hunting is still difficult to do. Each man who goes would probably have a slightly different reason for having turned back to the "obsolete" guns, the basic tools of the last century. It is a personal thing, accomplished in a personal way, and that is a good part of the attraction.

Finally, aside from having to get close and having, basically, only one shot, there is further kinship with the old-time hunters because the modern man often chooses to use self-made gear in part, just as the mountain men did, from gadgets and clothing to self-moulded bullets and ball. This represents a basic desire to get down to the roots of the matter and obtain a hands-on experience with each missile loaded deliberately down the barrel and each barrel deliberately cleaned by hand after the shooting is over for the day. Also, the modern black powder hunter modifies his gear and even his weapons, just as the old-timer did, personalizing the whole affair, choosing what suits him best, what works best for him, what fulfills his desires most completely.

CHAPTER 3

Selecting Black Powder Arms

A complete battery for the modern black powder hunter can range from a single firearm loaded differently for different game all the way to a host of guns selected for special purposes. The choice is predicated on the game being hunted, of course, but even more important are the personal desires of the hunter, how deeply he wishes to immerse himself in his sport, and how much he cares to invest in time and money. He may elect to hunt close to home for familiar game or roam the continent in quest of black powder trophies.

When a modern hunter chooses only one black powder weapon, his choice today is a rifle. That is statistical truth, not an authoritative suggestion, for a double-barrel shotgun could serve very successfully as the one-gun-only black powder battery. But America is a nation of riflemen, and it is the rifle that sells best in muzzle loader form. Many decisions face the modern black powder hunter, and the paths lie before him like the passages in a maze, which way to go, which types of arms to choose, and which reasons for choosing them.

The first criterion probably centers around lock type, which will be either flint or percussion in tophammer or underhammer form, with the sidehammer another possible addition to the list. Flint is the older style, and when the rebirth of black powder occurred flinters may well have been elected the vanguard arm since they were romantic and historical locks. But flint was forsaken for the later percussion, or caplock design. Of the hammer configurations, the basic tophammer model has led the way, with underhammers selling well enough to remain in contention and the interesting sidehammers gaining a small, but significant, following among bench shooters as well as among some hunters who like this mostly custom-offered percussion.

Should the modern downwind shooter go flint or caplock? Turning back to our mountain man, we can be assured that most of his rifles were flinters, a reliable form of the day, popular not only because it worked, but even more because it was about the only style around. Modern flinters still follow the game trails today, and some aficionados of black powder hunting are adamant about their use, insisting that this is the true sporting way to go and that the percussion guns are too modern for "real" primitive hunting. This is, of course, a narrow view, and in fact, the "flinchlock," as it is affectionately called by some, has lost sway to the more modern capshooter.

The flintgun can shoot very reliably and with surprisingly short ignition time. Still, there is that "ftttt—boom" idiosyncrasy that can make fidgeters out of normally steady shooters. The delay between the sparked igniton of the pan powder and the main charge which propels the missile can be very disconcerting, and this is the reason for the "flinchlock" epithet, for the modern smokeless shooter used to instant ignition is not accustomed to pulling the trigger, holding steady on target while a puff of smoke jets off just ahead of the right eye, and then continuing his hold for the milliseconds that seem like minutes until the gun goes off, sending its ball downrange. The tendency may be to flinch with the old spark tossers. So today the modern black powder shooter is generally a caplocker.

The percussion design uses what we recognize as a type of primer, and it comes in two general cap sizes, the smaller 11 and 12 fittings, and the much larger musket cap, also known as the English tophat cap. The 11 and 12 sizes are more popular than the musket cap size, but the latter carries a proportionally larger amount of detonater, and it makes a very reliable ignition spark. More modern arms are now being fitted with nipples for the tophat than ever before. The percussion rifle is a bit more surefire than its flintlock cousin, and it is certainly better understood by us today. Of course, there are some flintlocks that are particularly good about going off with a minimum of delay, but out in the field the shooter will be more content knowing that when he touches off a boom will quickly follow.

If the choice is the percussion, the hunter must then decide upon a variety of other things. The first is what hammer style he wants. The tophammer is far and away the most popular and it will remain so because it follows a long history of tradition in rifle design set down by the old-timers and passed on to the generations that followed. It is not, however, necessarily superior to either the underhammer or the sidehammer. The hammer sits on top and the thumb reaches forward, brings it back to the full cock position, and the piece is ready to fire. We enjoy both the simplicity and the familiarity of this hammer style, and are already used to it, for most of us have either owned, or certainly fired, a hammer gun which operated exactly the same way, right down to the half-cock safety feature. So the tophammer is king. It is fast, easy to use, reliable, and most of all, familiar.

The tophammer does have two faults. First, rain, snow, sleet, or any other drenching agent can land up on the nipple opening and sneak down into the powder charge, setting up a certain misfire. The second fault of the tophammer black powder design is that should any sparks or cap debris fly away from the nipple, this smoke and soot could end up in the shooter's eye. Of course, it is widely and wisely recommended that shooting glasses be used at all times, but sometimes we forget and then these particles must be directed away from the shooter. By using a deeper hammer nose with a prominent V-slit cut in it, most gasses and cap parts can be directed down and away from the shooter in the tophammer design. Still, the up-on-top hammer does explode its cap on the same plane as the shooter's eye.

The sidehammer is better about keeping the elements out of the powder charge, with its hammer appearing right where the term suggests, on the right side of the lock. Also, if any debris should fly out and away from the rifle on firing, the direction will be off to the right and away from the shooter. The sidehammer has another advantage. The spark from the cap is transferred from the nipple in a straighter path to the main charge and

The tophammers and underhammers are seen often enough, but the sidehammer, shown here, is a bit more rare. It is a fine action, sending its spark directly into the main charge of powder, making for a fast lock time. Also, any spark and cap debris are showered away from the shooter, not back at him, a feature shared with the underhammer.

ignition in the sidehammer is usually a little faster than the tophammer. Again, there are some tricks which will quicken the ignition time of the tophammer, and these will be revealed later. While sidehammers are not terribly popular, custom locks are becoming more prevalent and the type bears not only mention but possible consideration.

The underhammer, with its simplicity of design, wears its striker directly underneath the rifle. Some shooters have learned to operate this style about as quickly as the overhammer by swiftly rotating the rifle in the hand, then earing back. With a quick rotation back to the original position, the underhammer is cocked and ready to shoot. The underhammer is uniquely American in design, and unlike the sidehammer, is available commercially in a finished firearm called the Hopkins and Allen, after the great old arms firm of the same name. Today, the underhammer appears in many models, from a dainty Buggy Rifle of caliber .36 or .45 weighing about five pounds, up to a long, barrel-heavy .58. The H&A makes a strong hunting rifle, especially appealing because of its modest price tag.

The modern underhammer is easy to clean, quite free of maintenance worry, accurate, sure-firing, and a good choice for black powder hunting. The hammer is well away from rain and snow, and the line of ignition is directly into the barrel, the spark hitting the main powder charge rather than powder contained in a lock. Ignition lag from trigger pull to detonation is minimal. Sometimes the big .58 underhammer is modified into an even better hunting rifle.

There are far too many lock styles and variations to go into here, but the previously mentioned locks constitute the bulk of the choices. One other type does bear consideration, however. If a good reliable firearm is needed and the pocketbook is as empty as Mother Hubbard's cupboard, there are modernized versions of black powder smokepoles that get the job done for a minimum of cash. One such is the Harrington and Richardson, which is essentially the faithful Topper design switched over to hold a swing-down rifle or shotgun barrel in various calibers and gauges. The H&R in .58, for example, makes a sturdy big game rifle, especially practical with some minor modifications, as discussed in the next chapter. Capable of handling decent powder charges, it will drive a big ball or bullet downrange at hunting

Three different types of nipples are shown. On the far left is a special nipple that fits into the standard musket thread, but accepts the number 11 percussion cap which appears in front of the nipple. In the middle is the musket nipple which uses the big English tophat cap, shown in front of it. And on the right is the Flam-N-Go device, a fusil patterned after old-time devices, which uses the modern primer for firing, such as the standard small pistol primer shown. The Flam-N-Go accepts the primer in the upper threaded portion, then the cap section, on the far right, screws down in place over the primer, with the upper section acting as a firing pin.

velocities, and its sights are better than average, assuring good aiming prospects and successful ball placement.

Aesthetics play a major role in the selection of a black powder hunting arm, as well they should. After all, a main reason for turning back to our ancestor's shooting tools was to enjoy a more basic form of hunting, with the "feel" of the chase being a large part of the attraction. A great part of that sensation comes from the handling and style of the black powder guns we use, the way these firearms look, and the way they shoot. The feel of the old guns, so important to total reward in black powder hunting, has greatly promoted what we refer to as the "plains" rifle, that graceful, good-looking, half-stocked longarm of heavy barrel weight and large-caliber-percussion design we call the "Hawken." The Hawken has attracted the twentieth century buckskinner pervasively.

Even though our Hawken types are not true replicas of their forebears, it is the tradition of this style that carries the force, and it is worth our while to see just what the Hawken meant during the Western movement. Jacob Hawken, a young man when he moved to St. Louis in 1815, had a goal—he wanted to handmake the best rifles in town (St. Louis was a drop-off point for the boys going West). His brother Sam joined him soon and together they built the thriving enterprise which survived both of them by many years. They were successful because they had "built a better mousetrap," a heavy, reliable longarm capable of getting the job done out west.

The old mountain man came to love his Hawken. A passage from a book dated 1884, but describing a time about fifty years earlier, tells of the trust that the mountain man placed in his special rifle. The writer said, ". . . a Rocky Mountain trapper, in moments of peril, grasp(s) his trusty rifle. It is his companion and truest friend. With a Hawkens rifle in his possession he feels confident and self-reliant, and does not fear to cope with any odds, or encounter any danger."

First loads for the Hawken were worked up by the gunsmith himself, and our hardy mountain man received with his rifle a brass charger that held the correct amount of powder for the particular caliber and ball size, as well as barrel stoutness, of the rifle. The rifle was purchased by the mountain man originally in a modest caliber, the most popular range being about .50 to .53 bore. And later the bore size was increased as the rifle was "freshed out," or rebored. Apparently, the mountain man "warn't as keerful as mebbe he oughter have bin" in cleaning his Old Betsy after shooting it, because the freshening out process was said to have taken place about once a year on the average. Of course, out on the trail under harried conditions he probably did the best he could.

(Photo by Kenn Oberrecht)

A few modern hunters may have the chance to use an original firearm. The author displays a full-stock rifle owned by Charles J. Keim of Fairbanks, Alaska and carried by Mrs. Keim's grandfather in the opening of the West. Professor Keim has used the rifle in Alaska for hunting.

The mountain men were round ball shooters. Patch 'n ball was the byword, and the larger calibers had plenty of snort when tight patches were used with ball of .50 and up to even .60 plus calibers, especially if the powder charge were fresh and good and compressed tightly with the ramrod. A ball of over a half-inch diameter with a heft of about a half ounce, when pushed at decent initial velocity, possessed a large authority. The Hawken, then, was prized for itself as a rifle, but also was valued because of its good caliber size and power.

These rifles were fairly plain, normally with two pins holding barrel to stock and all metalwork of iron, rather than the ornamental brass used on most of our replica Hawkens. Patch-boxes were not prevalent. The black powder hunter of current times does not come up with exact replicas of the Hawken because, after all, each was handmade in the old days and an exact type did not emerge as it would have from an assembly line factory. Today's replicas of the Hawken are generally good ones in terms of function, with the original choice of patch 'n ball being the modern choice as well, even though the ball, in all truth, is a ballistically inferior missile when compared with the conical slug.

About 1835 this country saw experiments underway to produce a bullet, because the ballistics experts of the day knew it would retain its velocity and penetrate better than a ball. Later, a type of sabot did emerge, but the original bullets left an awful lot to be desired. They were first in an acorn shape, and they failed to outdo the ball in any sense. Again in 1835 a new invention called the "sugarloaf" or "picketball" emerged. They were better than acorns, but still could be loaded crookedly, were harder to cast up than ball, and were not as accurate. Much later the more efficient and now popular Minie bullet arrived on the scene, invented when a French Army captain named Minie perfected a hollow-base bullet design.

This is all very important to rifle selection for the modern downwind shooter because current arms manufacturers are trying to build their guns for both bullet and ball shooting. Since we are visitors to the hunting grounds today, and since we will generally not have the time to spend hours getting that perfect shot, it is imperative that we obey a strict code of ethics which says "shoot a load that will be clean and effective." That load has to be, first of all, accurate. The crossbred twists and riflings do not always give us this accuracy.

Therefore, we should buy our rifles based in part on what the manufacturer has done to insure accuracy. The ball shooter requires a fairly deep rifling in order for the patch to act as a guide to the ball itself. Also, it does best with a slow twist. The 1-66 twists are good for ball in most calibers. On the other hand, conical slugs require more twist for stabilization, and a more shallow rifling so that the soft lead is not mangled. The 1-48 twist, popular today, will allow for fair hunting accuracy with the bullet and pretty decent accuracy with the ball, and it is an acceptable choice. Some custom riflemakers are experimenting with shallow-grooved barrels of unique twists designed to shoot heavy bullets with accuracy. One such experiment centers around a caliber .54 custom rifle with a twist of 1-32, and preliminary tests are encouraging.

If the shooter goes with ball, he is best advised to pick a rifle with deeper grooves and slower twist. If he goes with the compromise twist, then for accuracy he will have to load the bullet down with rather weak powder charges, because as the powder charge increases, accuracy generally decreases. Patched ball will shoot straight enough to bring home the venison steaks, but may not deliver the precision that lets you "bark" a squirrel off a tree limb. Finally, if shooter preference for slugs becomes large enough, the manufacturers may give us a faster twist choice as a production option.

Caliber choice is another decision the black powder hunter has to make in arms selection. Each devotee will argue his own cause, but because of the ballistics of black powder, the ball shooter will simply have to go to a large bore in order to gain any real power for big game hunting. Generally, the .50 is extremely popular, as it should be. A ball of .50 caliber will weigh in at about 177 grains in .490; since it is a half inch wide, it will open a good hole in game and render a fair and humane kill when the range is close. Still a ball is a ball, and the sphere loses velocity rapidly, making shots on really large game a close-range proposition.

Going down in bore size means a much lighter ball. Since velocity is minimal in black powder shooting, compared with modern cartridges, mass is very important to power. In caliber .45 the ball weighs only 133 grains, for example, which would be ample if velocity were high, but it is not. When the smaller calibers are reached, ball weight is very light, down to only 71 grains in a .36 caliber, for example. At the same time, a Minie bullet in .45 can weigh as much as 300 grains, as compared with the .45 ball of only 133 grains.

If the hunter has elected for one rifle, and if he prefers the smaller calibers, he will have to go with a Minie if he takes on the larger game, or he will have to be content with getting very close and putting the ball precisely on target for a quick kill.

Supposing that caliber .50 has been opted for, an efficient load with a ball is very easy to determine. Since the ball will weigh-in about the 180-grain category, then 180 grains of black powder will give it about all the velocity that can be obtained. Going to a full 200 grains will improve the speed by so little that the extra is not worth it. A muzzle velocity in the neighborhood of 2,000 feet per second will be realized with the 177 ball and about that much powder in grains of weight. This principle is a rule of black powder ballistics that holds true—powder and ball weight should be about the same for maximum efficiency.

A real beauty of black powder shooting is that each round fired is a special hand load, and such loads can be changed in the field by the hunter. This is what makes the one-rifle-only proposition a sound one. The same .50 that was loaded with ball and 175 or 180 grains of powder for deer hunting can be immediately changed into a reasonable small game round by using the same ball, but only 50 grains of powder. Up close the sights will still be on target, and the velocity will drop to 1,300 feet per second, adequate for clean, quick kills on smaller targets, but not heavy enough to destroy meat. Naturally, the ball will flatten and increase its own caliber on impact, thereby exiting with a larger hole than its entrance hole and conceivably destroying meat. The low velocity prevents this expansion, and preserves tender edible tissue.

The old-timer did not have a grasp of ballistics, not having a chronograph to show him what was happening when powder was added to the load. Although a tad more velocity may have been gained with maximum powder charges, what was actually happening was an increase in recoil, soot, smoke, flame, and precious little else. We forever hear about the huge gulps of powder forced down the barrel, with our shooters from yesteryear gauging the power "by guess and by gosh." The bigger boom and copious quantities of smoke gave the impression of heap big power, with the final convincer being a bruised shoulder after shooting. Actually, there was more junk being forced out the barrel, which added to the pressures and recoil, but not more power after the nominal charge was reached.

The black powder hunter decides on caliber commensurate with his game and the power he thinks he needs. By finding that rifle with the proper twist and heavy-walled barrel he can shoot big charges behind long and heavy Minie and Maxi bullets—real black powder power—as discussed in Chapter Five.

The modern black powder hunter wants what his predecessor wanted, an accurate rifle with adequate power, balanced, easy to pack around, not too long of barrel, but long enough to gain good holding weight out front and a decent sight radius, in a caliber large enough to get the job done. Our 1800 frontier brothers found all of these attributes in the Hawkens, as we are finding them not only in our Hawken replicas, but also in the fine Indian Trade Rifles and in many, many of the muskets and modernized versions of the front-stuffing rifles.

One of the most sensible roads to the selection of that black powder rifle is a visit to the local black powder club's shoots, where the newcomer can try many different models, deciding afterwards which he can handle and shoot best before investing his cash. Black powder shooters are normally delighted to help a newcomer get started right.

While it would seem that the air has been cleared concerning the selection of that personal hunting rifle for the modern black powder shooter, there are at least two stones yet unturned. The two remaining areas of consideration are the kit and the custom, further avenues to the selection of that personal rifle that may be the sole actor on the stage of black powder hunting. The kit can be a means of arriving at a fine rifle without having to pay full price for it. Kits are gaining in popularity daily because of the do-it-yourself aspect that is so widespread now. In fact, black powder kits are being built by hobbyists who do not even shoot. The kit can be put together with a minimum of tools, and a handy person will arrive at a beautiful and functional product. A few of the trickier details can be turned over to professional hands, of course, still resulting in a good rifle and a good savings, as much as 50 percent in some cases.

Finally, there is the custom. This is the handmade firearm put together by a master, and anyone who has held one in his hands knows the quality that it radiates. The custom can be anything from a fairly exact replica of a specific old-time rifle

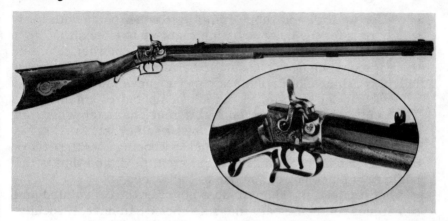

An accurate and handsome rifle was the Wesson, reproduced today by Richland Arms. The modern black powder hunter has many fine arms to choose from, or he can have a personal hunting arm made up for him by a custom gunsmith.

all the way to a modernized version designed for the shooter in every detail, with a straighter stock than usual to put the recoil into a better pattern, and a thicker butt to absorb some of the kick as well. Some may have special barrels with exotic twists and riflings.

The custom twist mentioned earlier for the caliber .54 handmade rifle, 1-32, will be a part of a rather plain, though beautiful, rifle designed to hunt large game, shooting 400- to 410-grain bullets in the 1,700-feet-per-second domain. The 30-inch barrel will be heavy for safety in big loads and long enough to have an excellent sight radius. It will be heavy by modern standards, about 11 pounds, but that weight, which will be carried via a rifle sling, will create a rock-steady holding situation, and it will also help in reducing recoil. In spite of the long barrel, the rifle will not be unwieldy because, since there is no actual action, such as a bolt, the overall length is reasonable. This is the apex of rifle selection for the black powder hunter, the custom.

Because of its chameleonlike nature, the lone black powder rifle can serve as many rifles in one since it is handloaded for each shot. The round can be a little popper load or a big boomer, depending on the needs of the moment. Still, the battery can be extended by adding more rifles for specialized needs, small bores for squirrel and rabbit hunting to super bores with massive barrels for the heaviest game, right up to elephant.

A man could get by with only that black powder rifle, but there is too much deep pleasure to be gained from the field on a fall day pushing clouds of black powder smoke into the air from a black powder shotgun in pursuit of upland or small game. That same shotgun takes on a different character when the skies cloud and darken and waterfowl weather sets in. There is only one grander thrill than the ducks swooping over the decoys or geese grinding to a halt in a cut-grain field, and that is the addition of black powder smoke to the scene.

Fortunately, the shotgun does not offer the convoluted and sometimes confusing path that rifle choice can have. Basically, there are two main types, singles and doubles. The double is the prince of the two, but it costs more, and a patient man can bring home a very plump game bag with a single in his hand, such as the Morse by Navy Arms, which will run about $125. Should a black powder hunter own a Zouave or Buffalo Hunter, Navy offers an additional shotgun barrel which sells in the $50 range, another thrifty way to go.

The double, aesthetic and fine handling piece that it is, costs more, up to $225 and more in the case of the fine imports of English design that are now being offered. These fowling pieces are available in full/full and in improved cylinder/modified, and the chokes are functional, not cosmetic. They come in true 12 gauge, which is a large plus. The other black powder gauges, such as the 11s and 24s, are good, but the modern black powder hunter will enjoy the ease of buying wadding that fits his scattergun without having to cut wads for a 15-gauge.

Tingle Manufacturing Company does offer precut wads of good quality for the individual gauges for those who own, or would like to own, the 11s, 15s and the like. But it is especially nice to purchase a box of wads in 12 gauge and find that they work adequately. They will not, in some cases, give top velocity because the 12-gauge wads being purchased are made to fit inside of a shot shell. In other words, they are smaller than 12 gauge so that they can fit into the hull of the plastic or paper shot shell itself, thus allowing gasses to escape around them inside of the 12-gauge tube of the black powder shotgun.

Regardless of this, the standard 12-gauge wads still put on quite a show of performance, and the one-piece plastic wads will also work very well. Again, this is business for later discussion, but in the selection of a black powder shotgun the hunter must be aware that if he selects the odd-sized gauges he may have to do a lot of wad cutting. The old-timer may have had the time to sit by the hearth in the evening hewing out wads to fit his shotgun, while the modern downwind shooter may be simply too strapped for such work. If he is, he can put down a simple plastic wad and still get adequate, though perhaps not full, performance. Losses go up to 125 feet per second with loose wads. These losses, in terms of bagged game, have proved of little practical effect.

The shotgun was the tool of the common man out West. It cost less than a good rifle and with "buck 'n ball" loads—that is, a round ball loaded in one barrel and buckshot in the other—it made a terribly destructive close-range weapon. Earlier, the choice of a single rifle was made for the one-gun-only black powder hunter. This was fair because the black powder rifle is allowed even in parts of the East where modern rifles are outlawed and shotguns only are legal for taking deer. Also, the rifle seems to be the choice of the general public today. However, the 12-gauge shotgun, in tight forests or where the range is going to be short, can prove itself extremely adequate for all game—from the smallest cottontail to the biggest buck in the woods.

The basic battery has sifted down to a rifle of the half-stocked plains type, or a musket, underhammer, custom what-have-you, and a shotgun—the latter for taking the small game and birds, preferably in true 12 bore. The rifle might be of .45 caliber, .50, .54, .58, or even larger shooting ball. But the shotgun is most likely a 12, and hopefully a double-barrel choked modified and improved cylinder or full and full. The good ones, such as Navy's "Magnum" and the fine double being imported by Dixie, will handle large shot charges with heavy doses of powder. In fact, these 12s are, unlike the black powder rifles of the day, very much on par with the ballistics of their modern cousins. A full ounce and a half of shot can be propelled at velocities in the neighborhood of 1,200 feet per second, and that will get the job done, whatever the job may be, including geese.

An addendum to the standard battery is the handgun. This addition rounds out the weaponry, giving an enjoyable pack-along gun for informal plinking or a hunting arm where allowed by law. Although the fact has not been widely recognized, there are a few black powder six-shooters and single-shot pistols that will stay right with, even surpass, many of the modern cartridge-firing handguns. Again, where legal, these can bag small game for food, and could take larger animals if they may be used on them. An example of big black powder power in a handgun is the Walker. This nearly five-pound six-shooter will hold almost 60 grains of black powder and was designed to blast a .45 caliber ball (although termed a .44 caliber) at nearly 1,500 feet per second at the muzzle. Even more impressive is the huge Harper's Ferry 1858 model, which will shoot the massive .58-caliber 500-grain Minie at 800 feet per second with appropriate charges, and has been chronographed at 900 with special triplex loadings of black powder. In terms of momentum, and not kinetic energy, the "horse pistol," named so because its 11-inch barrel was unhandy strapped to the side of a man—hence it was carried on a horse instead—outstrips even the modern .44 Magnum.

Although it is an anachronism, the combination that seems very useful is the Civil War Remington Army .44 sixgun, along with one of the good rifles and a 12-gauge English-type shotgun as a complete set of hardware for the black powder hunter of

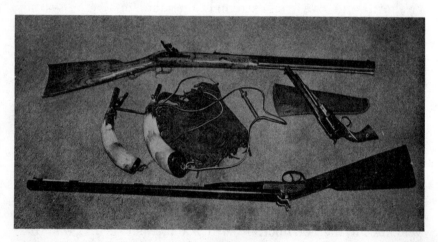

A fine black powder battery consisting of a well-constructed Navy .58 rifle capable of handling all big game from deer to moose—in fact, this rifle was used in Africa with success. The handgun is the Civil War model 1858 Remington, a .44 six-shooter that is quite accurate and powerful. The shotgun is a Magnum 12 gauge, which will handle heavy charges of shot and powder for all game, be it upland or waterfowl. The matching powder horns are homemade shotgun feeders, the left horn for shot, the right for powder. Set up with long throw tubes, they will put out a hundred grains of FFg black powder and a 1½-ounce shot charge.

today. The '58 Army is a superb handgun, extremely accurate with good sights fitted, and powerful, especially with the Lee moulded 200-grain bullet and top charges of FFFg powder or Pyrodex. Where allowed, this graceful, fast-pointing beauty is a companion on the trail, and will pick up some side food, as well as offering the comfort of added shots if one round is not adequate for some reason, such as signalling to other hunters, or answering such signals.

A logical move for the beginner to black powder hunting would be a look into Chapter 21, where lists of black powder companies will greet him, along with addresses to write to for free, or very reasonably priced, literature that will dazzle his eye and show him exactly what is available for what price. As for the old grizzled buckskinner, well, he probably hasn't listened to a word anyway, or if he did, he was patting his old .40 caliber in reassurance that it would harvest all the game that it would ever encounter, or gently stroking the side of the old 14 bore with the same reassurance.

CHAPTER 4

Modifying and Tuning Your Arms

Dedicated hunters seldom leave a favorite firearm in factory standard condition, and buckskinners are no exception to this rule. The black powder gun is open to a great deal of sensible modification, usually to a greater extent than its smokeless powder counterpart. The black powder hunter modifies his arms because he is normally using a replica of an old-time piece, but he is hunting under modern conditions. Generally, the changes are made in order to tailor the firearm to the shooter, and normally these changes do not, in effect, render the old-time gun modern, nor do they eclipse the joys of hunting with the more basic weapon. The rustic effect embodied in the smokepole remains intact. The traditionalist may balk at a few of the adjustments, and in fact, may wish to apply only those which tend to push the replica closer to the original, perhaps removing a blued finish in preference for a browning application to the steel, or changing a more modern sight to a cruder original style, or cutting the bright metallic brass in favor of a more drab hue. All of these modifications tend to personalize the frontfeeder;

however, they are not things the average black powder hunter will be doing.

The major aim of personalizing the black powder shooter is to gain a degree of efficiency from the arm commensurate with the much more difficult conditions of today's more crowded woods, and far shorter hunting seasons. The man feels he cannot afford to stalk close to his quarry only to be rewarded with a sputter upon pulling the trigger. Hence, ignition modifications might be in order. He has less time, probably, than he would like to afford to his sport; so he welcomes tricks that make cleanup easier. He insists, not only for his sake, but even more for the sake of the game hunted, that the piece shoot accurately, and that he can aim it accurately; hence sights are often modified to the personal desires of the shooter.

The atavistic urge to hunt with the black powder gun often goes up in smoke when success is thwarted time and again, and instead of participating in one of the most fascinating and rewarding outdoor sports in the world, black powder hunting, the frontloader is relegated to the prison of a dark closet, seldom to be carried afield. There is a sensible middle ground, where all of the historic spirit of the hunt is held captive and at the same time the hunter has ultimate confidence in that single-shot piece that loads from up front, a happy marriage of romance coupled with success, what might be called functional aesthetics.

The black powder battery can be personalized tastefully and profitably by the shooter himself. When he does the work, it is even more rewarding for him to see workable results. Most of the changes can be done with simple tools in the home workshop. A few of the operations, however, are best left to the professional gunsmith, and these will be cited. Original grace remains intact, while reasonable efficiency is gained. That is the goal of personalizing the black powder battery. Furthermore, there is very strong evidence to show that the old-timers personalized their shooting battery in order to arrive at a set of "shooting irons" which stood for two things: confidence and efficiency.

It is no breach of black powder ethics to be able to hit what is being aimed at, and this is why many modern shooters modify the sights on their replica guns. Not that the sights which come on today's firearms are poor, for they are not; but they can be crude enough in design to be very unfamiliar to the modern hunter who has used either refined metallic sights or scopes most of his outdoor life. Some shooters feel more confident with a peep sight, and while this is not the normal aiming device used by our mountainman, more than one fairly old smokepole has been found with a type of aperture sight attached! Some shooters benefit from the fact that the peep sight requires less eye accommodation in the aiming process. The correct use of the peep is responsible for this fact. Also, as eyes get older it is harder for them to focus on the three points of the open sight.

The shooter looks *through* the hole, not at it, ignoring it completely and only lining up the front sight on what he wants to hit. If that bead is on target when the squeeze is finalized, there is going to be a hit registered, for the eye *naturally* centers that bead in the peep since the eye seeks out the point of most light in the hole, which happens to be dead center. There is no need consciously to focus the front sight into the middle point of the rear sight. The man who recognizes this relaxes, looks through the aperture, and lines up the front sight on what he wants to hit, carefully squeezing off the shot, which is usually his one and only shot in black powder hunting. If the range has been properly judged, chances are excellent for a clean harvest.

Although the eye must focus between three points instead of two with the standard open sight, this type is still extremely useful, and most shooters can make both types work well for them. It is a matter of which works best for the individual. If the peep is preferred, it may be fitted specially to almost any of the black powder rifles of the day, and some arms, such as the Thompson models, are already tapped for receiver sights, such as the vernier tang, coupled with a front globe or standard blade or bead. Since the holes are in place, this conversion is a screwdriver operation. Lyman makes quality adjustable peeps for the Thompson, too.

Going in the other direction with the same rifle, the Thompson may be fitted with the primitive sight, a cruder open model with blade-front combination. (Some B.P. clubs allow only the open fixed sight for competition.) The fixed sight can work fine, but often it might be a matter of adjusting the load to suit the sight, instead of the sight to suit the load. For example, a modified version of the H&A Underhammer in .58 wears a fixed front *and* back sight, and it shoots right on target at 100 yards. Fortunately, the fixed sight is the right height to put the 600-

grain Lyman minie at 1,300 muzzle velocity on the money. The much lighter 460, however, shoots too high.

Existing sights can be tuned to shooter preference, too. On the Thompson, the factory rear sight can be tightened in place with a drift punch and hammer, making it stay in place after sighting in. Sometimes, only one sight requires changing, such as on the Navy Hawken Hunter/Hurricane series, where the very efficient Williams adjustable rear is coupled with a simple blade. For some shooters, this is not a match-up, and a fine bead-front sight seems more compatible with the notch on the Williams rear. Front sight options are easy conversions and they come in dozens of choices, not only in the height of the sight, but also in the bead size and color. It is a simple trick to drift the front sight out of its dovetail and replace it with another, remembering that the taller front sight will move the point of impact lower, while the shorter front sight will cause a higher strike.

A few shooters will even prefer to make their own sights, hewing them out of moderately soft metals with file and emery cloth. Or existing sights can be operated on, such as slimming a fat blade-front sight, or carefully widening a rear notch, or flattening off some of the "buckhorn" effect of the rear sight, which obliterates the target. These hacksaw jobs can turn out only if the shooter has a preset idea of how he is going to improve his sights, and does so with patience and care. Often, the results can be opposite of what was hoped for.

Rifles are peculiar when it comes to fitting sights, for the sight must not only match the shooter, it must also conform to the style of the stock cut. On the Thompson, for example, very low sights can be a problem and the Sharon Company has provided special sights to accomodate this comb configuration. On the other hand, a rifle such as the Hunter/Hurricane models from Navy seem to have drop that will marry with a host of sight heights while still allowing the shooter to adjust his face properly on the stock. Personal experimenting is a must for shooter satisfaction. Generally, the shallow V sight is best, allowing light to enter on both sides of the bead, which means easier alignment. The buckhorns can be pretty bad, covering up a good deal of target with their outrageous horns projecting up on both sides of the bead.

Sights on handguns can be modified, too. Dovetails have

been milled into topstraps of some black powder six-shooters so that usable rear sights may be installed, replacing the somewhat crude, and sometimes useless, sighting channel found on these guns. Full target sights are usually optional on the topstrap revolvers, but some shooters do not like this departure from clean lines. A good compromise is the fitted rear sight. Also, some models will allow for the fitting of the small, unobtrusive .45 auto rear sight. When the design of the handgun precludes changing the sights for best advantage, then there are two other modifications that may be in order. First, the load can be adjusted to hit point-of-aim if the sights are immovable. This might result in decreased velocity, but it will improve your ability to aim. A second way to adjust the "unadjustable" fixed sights on the revolver is to have a gunsmith soften up the front blade and bend it in the direction that it must go, rehardening afterwards. Also, the front blade can be cut down if the gun is shooting too low, or a piece may be soldered on if it is shooting too high.

As for the scatterguns, the single bead found up front between the barrels or atop the single barrel is not a sight, and is used as an aiming device only when a ball or slug is fired from the tube. Mainly, the bead serves as a mental pacifier, since the shotgun is pointed, not aimed, and shooters have gotten several limits of birds only to discover that the bead is missing or broken on their shotguns, and who knows for how long? Still, a bead is comforting to have up front, and it should be left intact. With some very large beads there could be a pointing advantage, and if this is the case, then the shooter may wish to have such a bead attached to his shotgun. In short, there is seldom much justification in tampering with the bead on the black powder shotgun. The factory original usually makes sense just as it is.

Wood changes can range all the way from rasping material away from the stock for a better shooter fit to full restocking. But cutting wood off a stock should be done only after consultation with a gunsmith. While cutting is dangerous, finishing is not, and few stocks from factory guns will be truly finished when the shooter buys them. This is not the fault of the manufacturer. If any further handwork were incorporated on the firearm, its price would increase.

In spite of the adequate, but unexciting, stock finish found on most of today's muzzle loaders, the wood on these arms is often superior to that found on many other guns, and refinishing is in order. The refinishing of a stock is cosmetic and functional. The stock will not only look and feel a lot better after refinishing, but it will also be more impervious to the weather. If you refinish the gun properly on the inside as well as the outside, it will also shed water instead of swelling up should liquid reach the wood during cleaning. And black powder soot and residue have much less effect on a finished stock than on a standard factory-finished stock.

Stock refinishing is easy. There are kits on the market today which not only contain all of the necessary materials for a new finish, but also have instructions to boot. Or, the black powder man can do it on his own. First, the old finish has to be removed. This is best accomplished with the painting on of a strong varnish remover, which will allow the old seal to be peeled away. If the old finish is stubborn, a piece of broken glass used as a scraper will get rid of it in a hurry.

The stock is rough sanded next, and then warm water is applied directly to the open wood, either directly from the hot water tap or with a sponge or a cloth. This process raises the "whiskers" of the wood, in other words, the soft grain that exists with the hardwood of the stock. The whiskers can be felt after the washing process. They must be sanded smooth and more water applied. After two or three applications of water and sanding, the main whiskers will be gone. The hot water treatment is also good for removing any dents in the stock, but the method of application is different. A small rag well soaked with water is placed directly on the dig and a hot iron is held on the piece of rag, thus steaming the dent right up out of the wood. All but the largest caverns will be removed by repeating the wet-rag hot-iron process followed by sanding.

By using finer paper each time you sand the stock, you will soon create a very smooth stock. A final going over with steel wool will result in that glass-smooth finish that means the wood is ready for oil. The oil, available in gun shops, is warmed first. Some prefer to add a bit of thinner to the oil to allow it deeper penetration. The warm oil is applied directly with the fingers, rubbing it into the wood. After thorough drying, a light sanding is in order, followed by another coat of oil. Three or four of these alternations of sanding and oiling will be sufficient, but six will put plenty of oil on the wood. The last coat is allowed to dry hard, and then the glaze is cut down by rubbing with a compound such as rottenstone, which leaves a soft lustre, rather than a glaring hard finish.

The shooter who wants a really personalized finish on his stock may use stains on the wood to bring out various tones and help to blend the sapwood in walnut; or he may use a blowtorch, with great care and caution, to "feather" the wood, bringing out the darker swirls of grain. This staining or burning takes place during the sanding process, and before any oil application.

About three coats of oil are applied directly to the interior of the stock, without any sanding. This allows for an all-around seal of the wood, and since black powder guns are subjected to a lot of corrosive materials, as well as cleansing water, this inside finish is well worth the trouble.

Naturally, any stock cutting takes place before finishing. Should the face be hitting too high above the aiming plane, judicious removal of wood can result in a comfortable fit. Of course, any real changes in the pitch of the stock are strictly work for the gunsmith. Also, glass bedding of the tang area may be in order on either a hard-kicking shotgun or rifle. The handyman can do this. But if you have any doubts about the process, a pro should be hired for the job. The result is added strength in the vulnerable tang area.

For the home shopworker who got high marks in shop courses an inlay is a very fine personal touch to a black powder gun. The process requires a minimum of tools, and tricks of the trade can be picked up either from books or the local gunsmith. The main danger with inlays lies in their size. Gaudy lions, tigers, and unicorns leaping and cavorting all about the stock remind one of a nightmare in the zoo and should be avoided. One simple impression of a Remington mountain man, however, can result in an enjoyable and interesting conversation piece. The mountain men, by the way, were known to carve and cut up their stocks, not always with refined taste, however.

Brightwork in the form of patch boxes, toe plates, and fore-end caps can be polished nicely with Brasso, and then heavily waxed over to avoid early oxidation. This personal touch is for cosmetic reasons only, naturally, but it does show pride of ownership in the firearm. On the other hand, some of the brightwork may be removed in favor of iron replacements, which are much more akin to those found on the original Hawken rifles. A toe plate can be added to a stock that does not already have one.

This functional piece of brass, steel, or other metal is inletted on the toe line of the butt plate itself, and it will alleviate stock splitting during the loading process, since a great deal of pressure is often exerted when trying to ram down a stubborn ball and tight patch or a Maxi ball after the barrel has been fouled by a few shots. Since some stock cutting is necessary for this modification, the gunsmith may be called upon to do the chore.

Recoil pads may be quite a comfort on real black powder busters such as the lighter .50 calibers, and the stout .54s and .58s, the latter burning as much as 175 grains of powder behind Minie bullets that tilt the scales at a full 610 grains. These rifles that gulp down huge doses of black powder, and belch out copious quantities of soot and smoke along with their artillery-like bullets, kick like frisky colts. Still, in spite of the recoil, pads somehow do not suit black powder guns and most shooters prefer to leave them off, using reduced loads for extended target practice, padding at the benchrest for sighting in, and a reasonably heavy shooting coat for the field. Also, in the heat of the chase most hunters can't remember whether the rifle kicked like an antitank gun or a cork pistol.

A stock that is without cap boxes, patch boxes or other metalwork can have these added should the hunter so desire in his personalizing campaign. Many of us prefer these cleaner models, such as the Navy Hawken series and the Thompson Renegade; others do not. The addition of the boxes means inletting, but this can be accomplished with a lot of care, templates, a few simple tools, and some basic instructions. A metal cap can be added to the fore-end of the stock, too, or conversely, a metal cap can be replaced with a rosewood tip. It is a matter of taste, after all.

Simple checkering goes well on a shotgun, and can be accomplished by the careful novice as long as the panels are simple and the lines per inch not too demanding. Historically, the old double shotguns often had tasteful checkering along the wrist and forearm of the stock. For the modern downwind shooter who does not adhere strictly to propriety, checkering on the rifle is all right, too, though the kind of checkering seen on some of the originals more closely resembles idle campfire scratching. Handgun grips can be carved, too.

Slings may not complement a graceful black powder rifle any more than rubber recoil pads do, but their utility normally supersedes their lack of prettiness. If conditions were those of

100 years ago, a sling would be unnecessary on the black powder soot belcher. After all, our Western mountain man was on
horseback most of the time, his trusty steed doing the rifle totin',
and the eastern forest tromper often had a pack animal doing his
carrying. Most of us, after we leave the sides of our iron ponies,
have to do our own mule work, which means carrying the rifle in
hand, and black powder rifles are not usually lightweights.

A sling becomes a terrific boon to the modern black powder
hunter afoot in forest and mountain. The sling swivels can be
purchased commercially or be homemade. The former are excellent, and a quickly detachable sling can be taken off for most
shooting and put back for hunting. A hole may be drilled in the
ramrod guide and the attachment base screwed into place.
Since the ramrod guides are usually thin, very little metal is
available to hold the base piece and the screw has to be cut
short. Since the base will only screw in a couple of turns, it is
best to apply a coating of Loctite to the threads. Also, it is wise
to use a rawhide retainer in case the base work loosens during a
hunt.

The rawhide retainer is a piece of leather shoelace tied
snugly around the barrel of the rifle so that it does not interfere
with the sights. The lace rides inside of the sling itself, and
should the screw work loose, the rifle will catch up on the retainer, instead of smacking the hard earth. There are other al-
ternatives to slings, including commercial black powder slings
for some black powder rifles, as well as the homemade option,
which might be a crude and rustic affair merely slipped over the
barrel and tied to the stock, some sort of tanned hide-cut narrow.
However, these tend to rub the finish off stocks and barrels.

Ramrods often need personalizing, too. Normally, the
somewhat flimsy hickory rod that comes with the firearm, be it
rifle or shotgun, is adequate—but only that. It is breakable, and
a broken rod can mean more than consternation in the field; it
can also mean a piece of wood rammed through the hand. Some
of the commercial rods of the day are now metal. These are
normally tapered and very serviceable. While they are not necessarily pretty, they are better than wood for the sake of utility.

Metal rods can also be made by hand. They may be either
solid stock, or hollow. Both work well. The rod is cut to length
and the end cup is pinned in place by drilling a hole and running
a length of brass through it, pounding the ends of the brass flat,
and polishing for appearance. Of course, it is even easier to

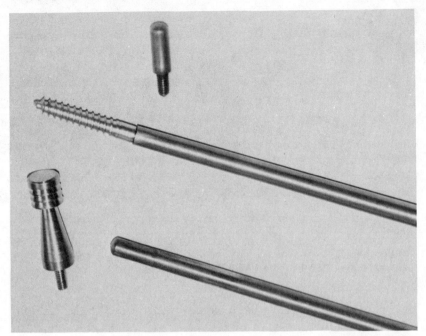

Versatile ramrod: the tip, which is shown screwed in on the lower rod, is removeable, as shown in the illustration. Two of the many accessory parts that can be screwed into the open end of the ramrod are shown. On the far left is a cleaning jag, which screws in place for holding patches, and a screw, which will remove a stuck ball or bullet, is shown in place on the upper rod.

make fiberglass ramrods, but they have proved very abrasive to gun barrels, especially eating away at the crucial riflings at the muzzle of the barrel. At the same time, the fiberglass rod works very well with the shotgun, for it need not rub the walls of the scattergun's barrels. Handsome it is not, but durable, yes, and strong. These rods won't break.

Another modification of the ramrod is to drill the tip for acceptance of a metallic end that will take a cleaning jag, worm, and screw. The jag is perfect for field cleaning, where a patch saturated with solvent, such as "moose milk," can be run home several times between shots or after shooting. The worm is good for freeing a stuck patch or removing a faulty shotgun load, and the screw is good for pulling out a ball or bullet. These accessory parts are handy and can be carried in the possibles bag, ready to screw into place on the tip of the ramrod. The threaded piece

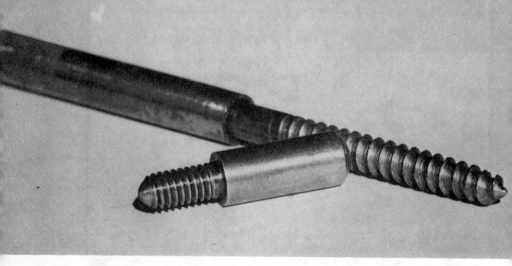

An excellent ramrod for heavy duty, though not as aesthetically pleasing as the wooden model, is this all-metal unit. The hunter never need worry about breaking it in the field. Also, the cap of the rod (small end) unscrews and many different fittings may be inserted, including cleaning jags. Here, a screw is shown in place, and the cap rests beside it.

that accepts these three devices can be attached to the rod end with a brass pin.

After a ramrod is purchased, it might fit too tightly in its guides. Also, a factory ramrod may be too tight. A good way to fit either is first to sand the rod until it fits fairly well, then wax the stubborn end and chuck the other end into a handbrace. By inserting the rod, waxed tip first, and turning the brace by hand, a burnished smoothness, and excellent fit, will be the result.

Locks can be a tinkerer's delight and are modifiable in a host of ways with wonderful results. Some of these operations are home workshop in nature, while a few are best left to the competency of the expert. Sear adjustments that require cutting are expert's work. But a sear can be carefully polished at home, which will render it much smoother in let-off. Honing will mean a cleaner break of the sear, hence a better trigger pull.

A gunsmith can work the trigger by cutting the sear even lower; however, he may have to make an addition to the lock's tumbler if the lock does not already possess what is known as a "fly." If the sear is cut too low, it will catch in the half-cock notch on the way down, meaning either the rifle won't go off or will be erratic in firing. The fly overrides the half-cock position and prevents this problem. A gunsmith can drill a hole in the tumbler, threading it, and then adding a small screw. The screw serves as a sear-engagement adjustment only and can improve the trigger. The screw can be turned to fine adjustment, and it is a joy to shoot a trigger that has been tuned in this manner.

A careful amateur can disassemble the lock and polish each interior part that has a bearing surface, stoning away all casting marks. By making these surfaces smooth and more squared up, the hammer comes back with a "snick! snick!" into the half and full-cock positions. The tumbler may be polished with a fine rubbing compound until all tool marks are obliterated.

An important modification on a rifle that has a flat hammer nose is to drill that nose out with a Dremel tool. The drilled nose will aid in the prevention of cap debris scatter, containing the particles of the cap and forcing them to be expelled downward. Naturally, shooting glasses are highly recommended all the same, but the recessed nose is a wise modification.

Sometimes parts of the lock may have to be softened so that drilling or other work can be accomplished. This work is for the gunsmith or knowledgeable amateur. After softening, and consequent modifications, the parts are rehardened.

A very good modification can be deepening of the hammer nose cup, a job for anyone who owns a Dremel tool. Some rifles have hammer noses that are too flat in the cup area. When the rifle goes off, pieces of exploded cap are allowed to blast off in all directions, especially back toward the shooter. By deepening the hammer nose cup, the debris is better contained, blasting downward instead of outward. Further direction can be given away from the shooter by cutting a V-shaped notch in the front of the hammer cup. This allows the debris to take the path of least resistance, away from the shooter.

If the hammer spur is smooth, it can be serrated very easily with one of two tools: a serrating file or a three-cornered file. Serration of the hammer spur offers a better grip for the thumb in earing the hammer back into the shooting position.

Sometimes a trigger will make contact with the guard on the rifle, especially if the guard is made of springy metal. What happens is: the shooter squeezes down on the neck of the stock during the firing stage, thus depressing the springy trigger guard, making contact with the trigger, resulting in a no-fire, or a very coarse trigger pull. The problem is easy to remedy in at least three ways. First, the trigger itself can be filed down. Second, the trigger guard can be bent away from the trigger, and third, trigger guards can be replaced entirely. These slight modifications make the rifle more fun to shoot, but more important, they make the rifle efficient in the field. After all modifications, emery cloth is used to repolish the parts. Home blue can then be applied as a touch-up measure.

A home blue may be applied to a barrel that has been worn from a scabbard, carrying case, or sling. These blues come with full instructions on the bottle and are easy to use. Then there is the browning compound for those who wish to "antique" their arms. Both blues and browns can be bought in kit form from the local gunshop. Sometimes the brightness on certain parts of the gun can be cut with emery cloth, smoothed up with rubbing compound, and then blued or browned for a more pleasing effect.

The very handy can do a touch of engraving on their guns.

Any intricate patterns, though, are best left to the expert. Practice sessions before diving into the real thing are well advised.

The ignition system can be modified, too. This is a very substantive change, and can prove vital to the hunter. Cook-offs and misfires are absolutely disheartening as a conclusion to an arduous stalk, and can be a turn-off for a would-be black powder hunter. My son made a nice stalk to within 30 yards of a good mule deer buck, only to be rewarded with a poof! instead of a bang! when he pulled the trigger. A mashed nipple cone coupled with a hard-to-ignite propellent was the problem. Others, in times both past and present, have had more serious problems when their guns failed to go off. Big Joe Meek, the mountain man who ended up an Oregon state official, was face to face with a grizzly when his rifle misfired. Joe had decided to "throw" the old girl, and he had closed to within 40 yards of her. Levelling his rifle, he pulled the trigger to be greeted by a ftttt! and a fizzle when the cap failed to fully explode. The bear turned and charged the sound, and Joe barely escaped with his own hide intact.

Personalizing the black powder battery can include changing the ignition system by first replacing the factory nipples with stainless steel models. These last longer and do not easily deform. Another possible change is to the nipple replacement known as the Flam-N-Go, a device which uses modern primers in the place of caps. In case anyone feels this is too modern a change for the old sport of black powder shooting, let it be known that Ned Roberts, in his long out-of-print book *The Muzzle-Loading Cap Lock Rifle,* dates these devices into the last century. The Flam-N-Go can result in 100 percent ignition, nice if that long stalk happens to be on a game animal that is difficult to hunt.

The musket system, with its large cap, has proved very efficient, and so have all the other caplock designs. Sometimes, especially when very cheap practice shooting is the goal, a musket shooter may wish to use the No. 11 cap. You can buy a musket size nipple that is designed to take the No. 11 cap. The advantage here is that extremely cheap shots can be fired by first scrounging the lead, instead of buying it, and then making up homemade caps via the Forster cap-making tool, which turns old beverage cans and toy caps into No. 11 percussion caps. With ball and light charges, the muzzle loader becomes cheaper to shoot than a .22 in some cases.

Further personalizing may come in the form of changing barrels on an arm. For example, a Zouave may be fitted with a shotgun barrel, or barrels may be removed from standard factory rifles and replaced with different calibers, if so desired. On a shotgun, the shooter may wish to have his bores chromed. This will enhance clean-up quite a bit and deter fouling, but naturally the patterns will be changed, sometimes for the better, but not always. Chokes can be modified by experts, too.

Bullet moulds may be slightly modified by an expert by having the hollow base pin turned down on a lathe. This will allow for a thicker skirt on the Minie bullet, a real plus when the original thinner skirt is blowing out when top charges are used. Any other mould changes may result in a ruined mould.

The short starter can, and should be, modified. A hole is drilled in the wooden ball of the starter, opposite the longer starter rod, or in other words, right on top of the ball section of the short starter itself. This hole is just a bit larger than the diameter of the regular ramrod tip, so that the tip will run up into the short starter. After the ball or Maxi has been started home down the barrel, the short starter is placed right on top of the ramrod in order to continue forcing the projectile home. This saves the hand from being bruised, and adds power to the thrust, seating the bullet or ball properly on the powder charge, which is a must because poorly seated loads can result in a bulged barrel.

The addition of telescopic sights to a black powder rifle is acceptable when the arm is going to be used for benchrest fun, or if it is going to see action in the field during the regular season. Most of the primitive hunts disallow scope sights. Bushnell makes long eye-relief scopes that work well on black powder arms, incidentally, and a shooter who is hunting during a regular season where long-range, flat-shooting, metallic-cartridge rifles are being used need not feel that he is fudging because he has a scope on his short-range, single-shot, slow-loading frontloader. It is a matter of personal choice.

Finally, there is the total arms modification, which usually begins with a plan from the shooter himself, but with full execution by a gunsmith. An example of a full modification might be the H&A Underhammer in .58. This rifle, with its nose-heavy weight, can be trimmed up by cutting the barrel to 26 inches. Also, the stock neck can be more permanently attached by welding fins of metal to the tang. These fins prevent the stock from turning on the tang after heavy charges. The H&R Huntsman can be modified in a variety of ways, too, including the revision of the plug to accept a Flam-N-Go for full-service ignition. By putting their heads together, a hunter and his smith can change a black powder gun from muzzle to butt plate.

The idea is to personalize the black powder battery to the satisfaction of the hunter. The result should be a more service-able firearm that retains all of the historical significance of the past.

The black powder battery has been picked out, modified, and the hunter is ready to go afield, but several questions still remain, not the least of which is, how much actual power does the black powder firearm exhibit? Just how does it stack up against the game it will be used on? Some of the answers are surprising. Black powder power is the topic of Chapter Five.

CHAPTER 5

Propellents, Ammunition, Ballistics

The modern black powder hunter, accustomed as he is to a high-velocity, high-kinetic-energy big game kill, may give pause to wonder about the actual game harvesting effectiveness of the old black powder firearms. In terms of sheer power, and no one has yet explained what ballistic "power" is nor given an acceptable formula for it, the black powder arm reveals itself differently from the smokeless. The authority is there, and the black powder hunter soon gains full confidence in his smokepole when it is "loaded for bear," but he cannot expect to have the same *kind* of kill he was used to with modern high velocity arms.

We are talking about rifles. In actual practice, the black powder shotgun, and most of the black powder handguns, can be eliminated from this discussion. The old-time shotgun, when properly loaded, is right on par with its modern cousin as far as game-taking is concerned. Except for the few handguns which use modern high-intensity cartridges, the same can be said for black powder six-guns and single-shot pistols, which stay pretty much on the same ballistic level as modern handguns. Anyone seriously doubting this is advised to pick up a .58 Harper's Ferry single-shot, feed it a full charge of black powder and a 525-grain Minie, and try it against even the modern .44 Magnum powerhouse.

But the rifle is different. There is a pattern or style in the effect of a black powder ball or bullet on big game. A compilation of the results of dozens of black powder big game kills has shown this style to manifest itself in two categories: the ball or bullet that strikes bone, and that which does not. Keeping records of kills on game from antelope and deer all the way to elk and moose, the two trends have become fairly clear. Of course, there is always that maverick kill, the one that defies the norm in every way. But usually, the black powder big game kill takes one of two paths.

First, the bone hit. This kill is related to a jacketed bullet hit more than the boneless category explained below. The very large caliber black powder bores shooting bullets of 400, 500, and even 600 grains weight seem to exhibit what some call "knockdown power." The term is used advisedly, for it does not mean "knock the animal down." No round does that. Cars and trucks knock animals down, not bullets, for the bullet from a rifle, modern or old, does not cover enough surface on the game animal to actually cause it to fly through the air, even though energy is measured in tons expended. But the bone crushing effect of a 600-grain chunk of pure lead does give the type of smashing results that bring an animal down in short order. However, because the shock transmitted is not of the great tissue destruction variety, the animal is often seen struggling to its feet after the hit, though unable to go anywhere. Nor is it alive in the sense of trying to consciously escape. In fact, the buck or bull usually tumbles a step or two forward only to expire in a few seconds. The kill is, by all indications, very humane, as we might expect from a load that delivers such force.

Momentum, a contrived term, is the kind of striking force black powder shooters talk about. In practice, momentum is construed as the power attending large bullets or balls of medium velocity. Velocity is still of great importance here, but mass is given equal sway. Mass in formula is the weight of the projectile divided by 7,000, which reduces the figure to grains, and multiplied by the acceleration of gravity, a constant that has been calculated at 32.174. Later, in the formula for momentum, mass will be as important as speed.

Also important to understanding the type of kill delivered by the black powder rifle is the actual performance of the all-lead missile. Aside from the property of momentum attached to these often large bullets and balls is the fact that an all-lead projectile is wonderful for taking game. It mushrooms when it meets with sufficient resistance, but it does not fly apart, not even when it strikes bone. Rather, it remains intact, a solid uniform chunk of material that drives deeply through a great amount of tissue, never exploding, never fragmenting. The cohesive force of the lead molecules is remarkable, for Minies taken out of moose, even elephant, show deformation, but precious little loss in weight as compared with modern bullets other than "solids."

So the black powder hunter can expect his game to drop to the forest floor quickly when a bone is hit, though the animal may rise to its feet again. If the hit is proper, the animal will not go far. Of course, a bad hit with any form of rifle, new or old, is a

Recovered from a damp clay bank, the 460-grain Old Style (Lyman) Minie shows its ability to upset. The slug was fired from 125 yards out of a 26-inch-barreled underhammer by Numrich Arms, and backed up by 130 grains of FFg black powder. A pure lead projectile, both in ball and bullet configuration, is a very efficient game-taker, often upsetting and creating a good wound channel without undue destruction of the valuable meat.

bad hit. A properly placed bullet or ball out of a large caliber black powder rifle, when it strikes bone, results in an often spectacular kill—humane and worthy of the game that the rifle is used on.

The other general category of black powder rifle kills is the no-bone-hit. Here, a strange phenomenon takes place, and an illustration may reveal more about the nature of this type of kill than a mere explanation. A typical no-bone-hit kill was a very large black bear sow taken on a Colorado hunt. I had looked for a big black bear for years, and finally, after some carefully planned strategy, a large old sow was only 30 yards in front of me. The ancient matriarch, although hampered by teeth worn to the gums, as proved later, had just taken a mule deer with a crushing spinal smash and she had eaten the entire hind quarter. Being full, and due to my rushing up the hill at her, she had treed. The mad dash at an altitude of 8,500 feet had burst a few small vessels in my lungs and I was totally bushed and coughing a fine rosy mist when I got to the bear.

I could see that at last I had a "real" bear at bay, not the rubbed ones I had encountered in the past, or the half-grown youngsters. My hunting partner, John Kane, primitive hunting enthusiast, finally puffed up beside me. Boom! The .50 Hurricane echoed in the steep canyon as only the old smokepoles seem to do, a throaty roar that lay over the land like a thick wool blanket. Looking through the cloud of acrid blue smoke, there stood the bear, seemingly unaffected, typical of a hit where all bone has been missed. My partner feared that I had shot wild because of my breathless state; but I had calmed and the bullet was well placed. All the same I popped the top from a Readyload, poured the powder charge home and rammed another 367-grain Maxi down the barrel. Boom! Pushed by 140 grains of FFFg the Maxi bullet landed right next to the first. The bear held fast. Then, suddenly, she toppled down dead.

Often that is the pattern of the black powder kill where no bone is touched. My first black powder big game had acted precisely the same way, a boar javelina, standing in its tracks after being "run through" with a .58 Minie that weighed 600 grains. A friend had taken his first black powder elk with the same results, a good solid hit that missed bone. The bull walked 30 yards, apparently in a daze, and then dropped down. A good rule of thumb, with either black or smokeless powder, is to shoot again if an animal has not responded to a first hit. However, the

Here are three .50 caliber black powder projectiles. On the far left is the Maxi ball, weighing in at an average of 367 grains. The next shown is the .50 round ball, this one in .490 size weighing 177 grains. Then comes the .50 caliber Minie, this model weighing 360 grains; and on the right is the .30-caliber, 150-grain modern bullet shown for comparison.

black powder hunter often may not see results from a good hit. The animal is apparently in a stupor after being smacked with a large-caliber ball or a huge bullet like the Maxi and Minie. But lacking what is often called "hydrostatic shock," that property which says the explosive force of the bullet is destroying blood vessels, the animal is in a state of nervous shock that does not manifest itself overtly. At the same time, an example of a bone-hit black powder kill was a huge bull moose that took a .58 610-grain bullet smack in the shoulder. The immense bone was broken and the animal flopped to the ground like a .22-hit rabbit, getting back up, taking a few steps, and then going down for the count.

The high velocity bullet imparts its energy dynamically, almost explosively as the jacket peels back, a distinct shock wave being set up well in front of the bullet itself. Obviously, it is this shock wave that makes the large exit holes often found in big game, for the bullet is expanded to only a half inch or so, yet the hole could be three inches or more in diameter. The shock wave makes the hole, and the bullet itself flies out of that hole. The black powder bullet or ball also sets up a shock wave in front of it, but not of the type seen in high velocity loads.

Because of this high intensity, the kinetic energy formula, used by all of the cartridge manufacturers to suggest power, is of good value. This formula is also applied to the black powder rifle, but often to the detriment of the latter. Because of the lower velocity, the kinetic energy formula, which squares velocity, favors the modern round by a good margin. However, a modicum of common sense will show that this end result, related in "foot pounds of energy," is perhaps inaccurate in expressing the real oomph possible from big black powder guns.

An example of KE (kinetic energy) weakening a black powder round may be seen in a comparison between the big .58 Minie and a 6mm Remington. KE is found by first squaring the velocity, then dividing by 7,000 to reduce to grains, again dividing by twice the acceleration of gravity, or 64.32 for short, and finally multiplying the resulting figure by the weight of the bullet in grains. If we have a 6mm Remington firing a 100-grain bullet at 3,200 feet per second from the muzzle, this results in a score of 2,274 foot pounds of muzzle energy. A big 600-grain Lyman-moulded Minie out of an H&A underhammer developed a muzzle velocity of 1,300 at the muzzle. Using the KE formula, this is worth a score of 2,252 foot pounds of muzzle energy. Is a 6mm really more potent than the .58? According to the KE formula, it is. But many who have used both on large big game would probably go with the .58 in terms of sheer "power."

A few of the projectiles that belong to the .58 caliber family are shown. On the extreme left is the .58 ball, this one a swaged number from Hornady that weighs a full 280 grains. The next missile is Lyman's 570, which comes from the mould weighing a full 600 grains. In the middle is the 150-grain, .30 caliber bullet for comparison. To the right of the .30 is Shiloh's big 610 Stakebuster, which emerges from its mould weighing 625 grains, and on the far right is the .58 500 Lyman, which weighs in at 525 grains of pure lead.

Because of this, other formulas have been applied when discussing the force of black powder ballistics. One of these is momentum, for lack of a better term. This is a simple formula. The weight of the bullet is multiplied by the velocity and that figure is then divided by 10^4 so that a nice small workable number will result. Another way to measure which tends to lean more toward the big bullet is called pounds feet. Here, the weight of the bullet is multiplied by velocity, but then divided by 7,000. The actual numbers mean next to nothing. It is only the *comparisons* that count. Below is a small table showing comparisons of some modern rounds, along with a few old-time loads.

				KE	Momen- tum	Pounds Feet
1.	.270 Winchester	130-grain bullet	3,200 fps	2,957	42	59
2.	.30-06 Spring.	180-grain bullet	2,800 fps	3,134	50	72
3.	7mm Magnum	175-grain bullet	3,040 fps	3,592	53	76
4.	.54 Minie	410-grain bullet	1,700 fps	2,632	70	100
5.	.58 Minie	525-grain bullet	1,450 fps	2,452	76	109
6.	.58 Minie	600-grain bullet	1,300 fps	2,252	78	111

While the whole issue of firearms power is akin to opening a can of worms, the fact is, bullet placement is the important thing. The black powder rifle, with its looping trajectory, is a shorter range arm. Getting close is the ticket to success, because up close that big ball or bullet can be placed accurately, and when it is, the result is going to be a clean kill. Another factor looms clear on the horizon of black powder ballistics—caliber is of paramount importance. Where the differences among .27, .28, and .30 calibers seemed often to make but little difference among various smokeless cartridges, the differences among .50s, .54s, and .58s do count for something in black powder, especially if ball is used.

The so-called round ball is still the most popular missile among black powder fans, including the hunters. The reason lies partly in tradition, partly in the fact that the round ball can produce excellent results with good hits on big game. The old mountain men used ball to hunt everything from rabbits to the formidable grizzly bear, but they learned rapidly the value of mass in a hunting projectile, calling for bigger and bigger calibers when they could lay hands on them. How does the ball kill? Asked this question, a game warden replied: "If you drive a half-inch hole through a deer's chest, you've got a deer."

Simplistic as the statement is, there is more truth than fiction in it. A ball of a large caliber makes a hole that causes the loss of vital body fluids, and can break bone, too, if the bones are not too large. Of course, the really large ball, in calibers such as the .58, will break even huge bone when given a reasonable velocity.

Because of the nature of a sphere, mass increases out of proportion with diameter. A sphere of caliber .36 is going to weigh in at about 71 grains, quite small when one considers that high velocity is not the major factor in black powder ballistics. Going up to .40 caliber, the ball now weighs about 92 grains. A .45 ball will go around 133 grains (.445 ball). Going up to caliber .50, the ball (.495 size) weighs 177 grains. Already, it can be

An example of ball and elongated projectile in the same caliber. Here a .45 ball, 135 grains, is shown with a .45 Minie, 290 grains. The use of ball or bullet is dictated by many factors. Ball loses velocity rapidly and is considered safer in areas of human density. Ball is an extremely accurate and deadly projectile and will take game cleanly with decent powder charges propelling it. Most rifles today are made in a twist to compromise between ball and bullet, which is unfortunate, as ball shoots better in 1-66, 1-72, and even slower twists, while conical performs better with faster twists. The choice, as always, is up to the individual, but he must remember that if you can't hit it, you can't get it into the bag. Accuracy simply has to be a major factor in consideration, and so does the game being hunted. On a grizzly bear the big calibers in conical would be better, on deer it is up to the accuracy of the rifle to dictate the choice.

clearly seen that from caliber .36 to .50 the ball has grown in mass appreciably, but wait for the real heavyweights to show up. A .54 (.535 size) weighs 220 grains. Now we are getting somewhere. But going a few calibers more, to .58, such as the swaged Hornady .58 ball, the weight jumps all the way to 280 grains.

Famous as the ball is, and effective as it can be, the sphere is still a very poor projectile, ballistically speaking. It seems to have a good energy level when KE is used as a descriptive formula for power, but the shape of the ball means tremendous energy loss, due to velocity loss. The .50 can throw a 177 ball out at about 2,400 feet per second at the muzzle. This gives a KE figure of 2,264 foot pounds of energy. However, this figure at a mere 100 yards drops off to the neighborhood of 665 foot pounds because so much of the initial velocity is lost, from 2,400 at the muzzle, down to about 1,300.

In spite of these facts, the ball remains deadly in the hands of a cool shot. A friend took an antelope buck recently at a measured range of 100 yards. The ball struck where head joins neck, nearly separating one from the other, and this force from a .40 caliber. More than that, the ball is accurate. Patched round ball, from rifles of slow twist, have made groups at 100 yards that are more than satisfactory. While many of the elongated bullet-type projectiles are lucky to stay inside of a five-inch group at the same range, the ball may be drilling 'em in under two inches, often better. Part of this is because few black powder rifles are given a twist designed for long projectiles. These rifles will shoot Minies and Maxies, but only with lighter loads. Of course, some black powder rifles will shoot that first Minie right on the money, but due to shallow riflings that fill with soot rapidly, consequent shots are far less accurate.

The old-timers conquered all manner of big game with ball, but they also knew that an elongated bullet would be more efficient ballistically if they could get one to shoot. Many designs were tried. Many were rejected. Around 1840 a bullet that worked was introduced. Captain C. E. Minie of the French Army, at that time, designed the hollow-based bullet that would carry his name. The design came on the heels of many other models, but it was Minie who put the final touches on it. He reasoned that a bullet could be made about a caliber under size, so that it would easily slide down the barrel of the rifle during loading. Of course, such a bullet would be highly inaccurate

Caliber in black powder is very important, for the mass of the ball increases as the density of the sphere increases. Here is the .45 ball, far left, which weighs in at 135 grains. Next to the .45 is the .50. By going up .05 inches, the weight increases from 135 to 177, and next to the .50 is the .58 ball, which goes from 177 to about 280 grains, all by adding .08 of an inch. On the right is the .30-caliber 150 modern bullet for comparison.

because it would allow gas to escape all around it, and more than that, it would lack power, not make proper contact with the riflings, thus flying through the air like a sock with its toe filled with sand.

The hollow base, however, allowed for the terrific gas pressure in the bore to flare the sides of the Minie bullet out, thereby engaging the riflings for accuracy, while sealing the bore for power. It worked. That the Minie is not accurate is totally false. In fact, in one test a Minie in caliber .50 out of a Navy Arms Hurricane Hawken grouped consistently into two inches at 100 yards, but the powder charge was low, around 53 grains of FFFg. Still, this showed that the bullet itself was capable of accuracy. The main problem with the Minie is moulding one that has skirt thickness of exactly the proper dimensions. The thin skirts flare out too much from heavy powder charges, thus destroying accuracy. In fact, sometimes the skirts blow altogether and the Minie whistles downrange in disarray.

On the other hand, if the Minie skirt is made too thick, it will not flare out enough to engage the riflings and the result will be inaccuracy and loss of power. Therefore, the best choice is a Minie with a skirt thickness that is just right, and the only way to gain full accuracy from this Minie will be to try various powder charges until the best group is arrived at. Charges lower than this will have failed to force the skirt out properly. Charges over this optimum load will have failed for the opposite reason, blowing the skirt out so much as to destroy accuracy. The perfect load will be found by trial and error.

There are other kinds of bullets for black powder guns. These are solid base and actually are engraved by the riflings upon their ramming. Thompson has its Maxi, a very fine projectile; Lee has its REAL, another good one; and Shiloh has its solid conical. Under the pressure of the chase, it is more difficult to ram these solids home than to ram a Minie home; but the solids are accurate and shoot very well in guns designed to shoot them.

These last forms are based upon the older sabots (sah-bows) which were also solid conicals and had to be engraved upon forcing them down-barrel. The real advantage, then, of the conicals, which are, simply stated, bullets instead of balls, is their retention of velocity and energy, and their ability to penetrate well. Oversimplified, the reason for the higher retention of energy/velocity for the bullet over the ball is its better sectional density, hence ballistic coefficient properties. The sectional density, crudely, is a proportion in terms of a bullet's mass in caliber, and the ballistic coefficient is a number used to express the sectional density in a larger sense, including shape. Bullets have a lot of ballistic coefficient compared to balls. While the ball is losing a total of about 50 per cent of its initial velocity over the course of 100 yards, the Minie or Maxi types are losing only 7 per cent.

Appropriateness is the answer to the bullet versus ball question. The patched ball is highly accurate in barrels of slow twist, and at modest ranges is very effective even on large game with well-placed shots. It flattens out well on impact, yet drives deeply into tissues. If the caliber is large it leaves a hole that looks like a tunnel through a mountain. The ball is cheaper to shoot because it requires less lead to make it. As a small game load for the hunter, the ball is normally a wise choice, even though rifles which shoot ball with optimum accuracy rarely shoot bullets with the same top accuracy. Still, a patched ball will normally do quite well out of almost any black powder rifle when the powder charges are kept at a reasonable level, decided upon by careful experimentation.

When maximum power is required, the bullet type projectiles come into their own, be they the Minie types or the solid conicals. Still comparatively short range in their effectiveness, mainly due to rainbow trajectory, and not because of a real lack in retained energy, the bullets are best used on large beasts. Val Forgett, president of the Navy Arms black powder company, has tackled Africa twice with black powder arms. His choice for the really ponderous beasts has been the large bore rifles shooting Minies, especially the Navy Hunter in caliber .58 firing a 610-grain Shiloh-moulded bullet of hollow-base design, and backed by an incredible charge of 175 grains of FFFg powder. In one instance, this charge resulted in the 610-grain bullet travelling through 18 inches of an elephant's cellular bone. The same bullet drove the length of a water buffalo, certainly one of the most fearsome of wild animals weighing in at over two tons.

Black powder power is a reality. At the same time, the challenging aspects of black powder hunting remain in effect. It is still a game of getting close, and of having only one shot, usually, when the moment of truth does arrive. Also, it is rewarding to gain competence in the sport, being able, at times, to get a second shot loaded down the muzzle of the old smokepole. Loaded properly, which is the topic of the next chapter, the black powder firearm generates the kind of force required of clean, quick kills on all game, which is the demand of every hunter.

CHAPTER 6

How to Make and Gauge Custom Loads

The old-timer held fast to many superstitions connected with building optimum loads for his muzzle-loading guns. Some of these rules of thumb survived the onslaught of time and remain in practice today. Unfortunately, only part of them hold any practical, tested value. Generally, when a mountain man wanted to load up for grizzly he poured a double handful of black powder down the muzzle of his favorite rifle and topped it with a round ball and tight patch, feeling satisfied that this would do the trick. It did, usually. If the resulting load kicked like a runaway mule, and belched fire and smoke like the halls of Hades, the old trapper was satisfied. Unfortunately, these attributes did not always spell out maximum power since a lot of the kick and blast was because the charge had to propel not only the ball and patch out of the barrel, but also the resulting soot and residue built up by the supercharge of black powder, along with, in some cases, unburned portions of powder.

As the frontiersmen caught onto the idea that maybe their loading methods needed improvement, they began to compile and advertise a whole series of rules of thumb other than "the more smoke, flame, and kick, the more power." Some of these rules were sensible. Others were poppycock. One of the relatively sensible breed was shooting over clean snow to see if unburned granules would show up. This wasn't a bad idea, really, and the practice is seen today, with some shooters using butcher paper when none of the cold white stuff is on hand.

The idea is to start low in powder charge, increasing until flecks of unburned propellent are discovered. Then the charge is cut back to the point where, by observation, at least, all the powder is being consumed in the barrel behind the bullet or ball. This would be all right, except that black powder rifles are individuals unto themselves, and owing to a curious phenomenon we will call the "velocity curve," the chronographed speed of a bullet or ball may steadily rise with the powder charge, then, strangely, fall off—and then, by adding further powder, pick up again! For example, at 80 grains the velocity might be 1,300. Suddenly at 90 grains this speed levels out. At 100 it has been known to go *down,* perhaps to 1,275 or so. The shooter would reason that his best load would be 80 grains. However, it is conceivable that at 100 grains the velocity may again *rise,* perhaps to 1,400. This wavy curve in the velocity does not seem to present itself in every situation, but it has occurred enough times to be considered an element of the black powder load-making process.

Another notion derived from common sense that fails under the scrutiny of modern science is that once a rifle of a particular bore has its optimum load, that load will become universally wonderful for all rifles of that bore size. Again, even with the same powder charge and brand, same ball and same patching, this is not true. To repeat: the black powder rifle is an individual. This is not to suggest that smokeless rifles are standard in nature, for a registered velocity difference of a full 200 feet per second has been found in many modern rifles using identical loads. The point is, each rifle must be tested for itself in order to arrive at its own optimum load. But that is all right; it's part of the fun of black powder shooting and hunting.

A notion handed down from yesteryear that has survived a close look by the modern technician is that of rifle twist and powder charge ratios. When shooting ball, it has been shown that the slow twists, beginning with the 1-60, and the 1-72, and even slower, will successfully handle greater charges of black powder behind a patched ball. If a person is going to shoot ball exclusively in his rifle, a slow twist should be selected. Unfortunately, this rule of thumb is not foolproof because bore diameter is a factor of consideration. Because the ball is a sphere, and due to a sphere's peculiar traits, it is best advised to try various charges with various patching material and thicknesses in different barrel lengths and diameters of different rates of twist. While this sounds very simplistic, it is the best way of assuring the ultimate accuracy/power load for the specific arm in question.

Fouling is a very important factor in black powder accuracy. The old-timer did hand us down a good rule here: swab between shots, especially when working up a first load. After all, we, as hunters, are interested in that first shot out of the barrel far more than consequent volleys. Yes, that second and third round is important and can come in handy; but if that first one out of the barrel will go into the black every time, the hunter should be happy and secure. Ball seems to do better with deep rifling, so the rule of thumb says. Conicals shine with shallow grooves and fewer riflings, three or four as compared with four to eight for the round ball barrel. Deep riflings foul faster. But shallow riflings tend to offer less stabilization, even though they may be cleaner. Unfortunately, many of these notions remain surmises to this day, and a lot more testing is in order before a maxim can be set down.

We have learned that a Minie may flare its skirt out way too far due to heavy charges of powder, thereby destroying accuracy. If a skirt is blown totally, with gasses cutting away part of the lead, that Minie will whistle off course. But modest flaring out seems to have but little actual effect on hunting accuracy. This is a testable situation, and since part of this chapter is designed for testing the load, it is fair to mention here that recovered Minies tell a story. By firing at long range into a clay bank the Minies can be recovered intact. Three hundred yards may be required, for shooting at shorter ranges will mean an adequate velocity retention to completely deform the bullet.

Recovered Minies can show whether or not the skirt has flared beyond its limitations. Supposing such a Minie is found? We know, then, that the powder charge is high enough to flare the skirt out. So, we take that same Minie style, use the same heavy charge of powder, and try for accuracy. This test has shown that the Minie with a modestly flared skirt will stay fairly accurate.

Why, then, does the Minie fail in terms of acceptable hunting accuracy? Probably twist. Rifles need to be made with faster twists for shooting the long conical bullets. Experimentation is underway to produce rifles with barrels of much faster twists designed for conicals only, and not ball.

"Load with the sprue up, facing the direction of the target for best accuracy." We have heard that one since the rebirth of black powder shooting. It is quite true that the rear of a projectile has much to do with steering from muzzle to target. Proof of this rests with modern bullets and a very simple test anyone can try. Taking five identical rounds with spitzer soft-point bullets, two of the cartridges are slammed nose first on a flat surface until they are perfectly blunt. These two rounds will land on the target right with the other three, no difference in accuracy being discernible.

However, before handloading, if two of the bullets are nicked appreciably at the *base*, these will fly out of the group, showing (we hope) that the base of the bullet does have a lot to do with guidance. Provided that the sprue of the ball is a bit crooked or bent, it might, and that word is carefully chosen, make a difference in accuracy. If the sprue is bent, it is perhaps best to have the uneven part of the missile aiming nose-first to the target, with the more uniform portion being the rear part. But most sprues are not bent or broken. In an actual test, loading the sprue as carefully as possible *toward the powder charge*, accuracy did not suffer one jot.

So, sprue should be loaded facing the powder then, and the old-timers were all wet, right? No. If the sprue is loaded haphazardly, accuracy does suffer, and it is more difficult to get the sprue portion dead center if loaded out of sight. Therefore, the old maxim holds true, though not for the reasons originally handed down: load the sprue out, facing the muzzle, even though a smooth, well-proportioned sprue will shoot accurately if pointed toward the powder charge, serving as the base of the missile.

Starter loads also had attending rules of thumb, and more than that, these old wive's tales have survived and are told and retold to this day. The first one is to place the round ball in the palm of the hand, covering it with powder. The result will be a perfect proportion of black powder to the ball. Probably, the old-timer meant this as advice for a starter load, something to work with, and no more than that, but forever we are being told this is the simple, but proper way to build up that perfect load.

Trying this method, I arrived at a charge of 62 grains (by weight) average with a 177-grain .490 ball for a .50 rifle. My hand is somewhat large, and the ball was fairly lost in the palm, resulting in a smaller charge than delivered by other hands. As a further test, members of my family tried the ball in the hand bit, each arriving at vastly different powder charges. My 62 grains of powder behind the ball would result in a pip-squeak popgun load that would be a disgrace to use against any game animal of size. The best thing to do with such advice is to erase it from the mind totally.

If one must select a romantic notion out of the ages to arrive at a good load for his black powder soot belcher, another old-time axiom, this one quite useful, is the suggestion that "a black powder rifle will handle a proportionate amount of powder and ball." In other words, if a rifle of .50 caliber shoots a 177-grain ball, then it will burn 177 grains of powder with maximum efficiency. Tested, this theorem has proved quite successful. But, alas, it seems that with calibers around .50 and under, the ball/powder ratio works well. Over that size, it leaves a lot to be desired, and the shooter can only imagine the results of practicing it with a .58, which would take roughly 260 to 280 grains of powder, since the ball weighs that much!

The problem, perhaps, lies with barrel length. Theoretically, it could be true that even the ponderous .58 bore will indeed ingest 260-280 grains of black powder with admirable results; but the barrel might have to be quite long, and the rate of twist very, very slow for this proportion to work. And the recoil? Even a stout plains rifle of 10 to 12 pounds heft would come back with a vengeance using such an amount of propellent if indeed that load of powder would be totally consumed without a barrel longer than an elephant's trunk.

While it may seem that yet another of the old-timer's commandments has been rendered defunct, in actual testing a ball of 177 grains backed by 177 grains of FFg black powder was chronographed in the 2,400 feet-per-second category, which is premium performance out of a .50 caliber rifle with a 30-inch barrel. Of further interest, a .58 was also tested with the ball-weight/powder-weight system. The 260-grain, heavily and tightly patched ball was earning about 1,800 feet per second and the velocity spiral was still climbing upward, but barrel length and common sense dictated a cessation of the test at 200 grains of FFg powder.

Another notion that can be quickly dispelled and placed in the book of superstitious folly is that of listening for the crack of the rifle to tell when an optimum load has been reached. All the shooter is hearing when the rifle goes from a boom to a crack is the speed of sound being reached, and even that statement could be open to argument because such a sound could also be made by the environmental surroundings, such as canyons or embankments. Still, supposing that the crack does mean that the sound barrier has been broken, so what? The speed of sound is about 1,120 feet per second, hardly maximum. Black powder rifles are capable of much more than that, safely.

Loading two balls down the bore, one right after the other, on top of heavy powder charges is to be discouraged. Although this method works for some, it cannot be recommended. Pressures will be high, usually, with this combination; moreover, the first ball will end up with a badly flattened base, and as we have discussed, the base of a projectile can be very important to guidance and accuracy. In other words, making a good clean kill at the longer ranges could be quite a problem if the two-ball method is used, since at least one of the balls may well be off target. At the same time, it must be admitted that a few top black powder hunters in the country use the two-ball method. However, they are careful and concerned outdoorsmen, and they get close. One such fellow took a beautiful Dall ram in Alaska with two-ball, but he worked until he closed the range to 30 yards before firing.

Arriving at that peak load for the personal hunting rifle, using more modern means and methods, is both rewarding and just plain fun. Bullet selection is going to depend upon the rifle, of course. If the hunter has selected a gun with a 1-72 twist, he better be content shooting ball. Even in caliber .58 such a slow twist would dictate round ammunition. However, in the larger calibers the twist can be fairly slow and we can still get away with *acceptable* hunting accuracy using a conical missile. The 1-60, for example, in .58, will produce a five-inch group using a big Minie and heavy charges of powder. Using the heavy bullet for hunting is a good practice for reasons stated in Chapter Five—power. The heavy bullet offers a great deal of resistance to the powder charge, too, and a lot of propellent can be burned behind it, giving reasonable velocity.

As for powder, the modern hunter has, mainly, four choices: two of them granulation, two of them powder types. Of granulations, there are two that perform in the muzzle-loading rifle quite well, FFg and FFFg. The former, of course, is of larger granulation size. Of these, there are two main brands readily available to the average shooter, Gearhart-Owens, made in Moosic, Pennsylvania, and Curtis-Harvey, Nobel's powder out of Ayreshire, Scotland. Both are good. But first, which granulation to use in the particular bore size of the rifle?

Turning, once again, to the old-timer's logic, the suggestion is usually made that FFFg be used in rifles of the sub-bore sizes up to caliber .45. Over .45 caliber, on up to the .58s, .60s, and so forth, FFg takes over. Fg, the most coarse granulation, is reserved for the super-big bores and the 10-gauge shotguns. Further suggestions, which bear more testing, state that FFg will result in less recoil and often greater accuracy in the large-bore muzzle loaders. Many old shooters still attest to this. At the same time, makers of well-constructed hunting frontloaders of the day are recommending FFFg in their arms, because they claim this finer granulation burns cleaner, being more totally consumed in the bore and giving higher velocity per volume than FFg.

A compromise situation actually results, with FFFg being used more and more in arms that go from squirrel gun size to .54, and FFg used after that. Probably, this rule we can live with. Also, it is important to turn to the suggestions made by the manufacturer. Every gunmaker or importer has done tests on his arms and he will be able to suggest which granulation to use. For example, one company making a .58 feels that about 100 grains of FFg is all it is willing to recommend for its arm, while another rifle maker says up to 175 grains of FFFg is all right for his .58, both using heavy Minie bullets.

After the shooter has consulted with his manufacturer, he will have selected either FFg or FFFg for his rifle. If the maker of the arm feels that either granulation is all right, then personal testing is in order, in a manner prescribed below. Of the two brands of black powder, G-O has shown itself to be "hotter" in tests, and usually results in higher velocity using like charges. This does not mean that C&H is a poor propellent. It is good black powder. But using exact amounts of both G-O and C&H

normally results in the former gaining from 7 to 10 per cent increases in velocity. Naturally, these results will vary with different arms.

The fourth choice is Pyrodex, the replica black powder sold through Hodgon's Company. This is a modern invention, developed to act much the same as black powder, but to be an improvement. It is an improvement on all but one count. First, it burns cleaner than black powder. In fact, no bore-swabbing is required between shots for fine accuracy. Second, on the average, it can develop as much as 100 feet per second gain over the same *volume* of black powder in many rifles. Pyro seems to have a lubricating quality all its own. There is consistency in pressure, which is not always the case with black powder unless the latter is uniformly compressed. Pyro has a built-in rust inhibitor. Another plus of Pyro is that it can be used in exactly the same *volume* as black powder.

Black powder loading is very unlike smokeless when it comes to throwing powder charges. In one testing session black powder loads were weighed to within one-tenth grain accuracy, and the result was no result at all. There was no improvement in accuracy, nor any discernible effect on velocity uniformity by carefully weighing each charge on a scale. Pyrodex fits right into this mold. The best way to load it is to use a charger, or all-brass adjustable measure. The charge, by weight, will be less than black powder gives. However, this turns out to be just right, for by using around 20 per cent less Pyro, the velocity levels with black powder remain about the same, with Pyro often gaining about 100 feet per second over black in many rifles. A powder measure set at 100 grains will toss, of course, 100 grains of FFFg, for which it was designed. Using the same measure set again at 100 grains about 83 grains of Pyro will be thrown as an average.

Pyro, then, is quite an invention. Using it need not hurt the sensitivity of the old purist, either, for original black powder is no longer available, and current offerings of black powder are not the same as the black powder of the mountain man days. But we said Pyro was wonderful except for one quality. That one quality is ignition. It is definitely harder to ignite Pyro. In fact, in the flintlock Pyro gives particular trouble. Thankfully, there are ways to overcome this problem in percussion guns. The most sure-fire way, pun intended, is to use the Flam-N-Go device, the replacement nipple that allows for modern primers to be used rather than percussion caps. This will bring ignition right back to snuff. Another way that will aid the ignition problem of Pyro is to use the musket cap, the large tophat percussion size. Navy Arms imports a noncorrosive RWS tophat cap that is very hot, and will usually fire Pyro with no trouble.

In the romantic past there were other uses for black powder that might interest the reader. Thankfully, these have gone the way of the dodo, but in the olden days a little black powder was burned in a man's quarters before retiring, in order to purify the air. Also, black powder was salted over meat as a condiment. And some hearty souls used to mix black powder and rum for a drink that would brace anyone against the chill of night. Finally, black powder was sometimes poured into a nasty wound, and then ignited as a cauterizing and sterilizing measure. Our use of black powder today seems tame compared with these, but a lot more fun.

Step one, then, in arriving at that sought-after perfect hunting load for the black powder muzzle loader is to consult the manufacturer as to maximum charges, and which powder granulation to use. Pyrodex can be substituted for that granulation at will. Also, if G-O is elected, it must be remembered that it is somewhat stouter than C&H, though the latter can be used with excellent power in its own recommended portions. The maximum recommended by the maker of the rifle is never exceeded. He should know what his product is capable of. Often, it is thought that black powder is as harmless as soot. This is terribly wrong. Black powder is potent and any manufacturer's suggestions as to its use in specific arms should be adhered to.

A chronograph is the best single tool in the world for the black powder hunter to build up that special optimum load. Not so very long ago this statement would have bordered on foolishness because chronographs were in the hands of the wealthy or large testing labs only. Ken Oehler, and others of his engineering ability, have changed all that, and now accurate models are for sale under $100, a modest investment that will end the guessing on *all* loads forever. Furthermore, the cost can be shared with friends. A club can buy a really fancy chronograph, one that will give instant readouts, for about $300, a pittance when shared by many. Maintenance on these models is very low, and no screens are required on these types.

Starting with about half the top charge that was recommended by the maker of the firearm, the shooter fires his first round through the chronograph for a reading. This is done from about three feet out so that the shock wave that is in front of the ball or bullet will not start the machine counting, since we want the projectile to do that. Very simply, the shooter reloads, going up five grains (in weight) at a time. This is quickly accomplished by using an adjustable powder measure. The velocity reading is recorded. The hunter may wish to swab the bore between shots. This is quickly and easily accomplished with a wiping stick, which is usually a long wooden rod with a tip on its end that will accept a cleaning jag, worm, or screw. With the jag in place, a patch is dipped in "moose milk," a homemade barrel cleaner and conditioner explained in Chapter Sixteen. The crud is loosened and removed with the damp patches, and the bore is dried completely before the next load is sent home. By keeping a careful record, the hunter will soon know *exactly* what powder charge, of what type and granulation, gives him optimum results. In some cases, the optimum will be reached before the maximum charge.

An example of this was experienced recently with a .50 Hawken type percussion rifle. The max load was to be 140 grains of FFFg, G-O brand, behind a 367-grain Maxi ball. At 120 grains the velocity of the Maxi was 1,545. In the 130-grain level it remained about the same average, using three-shot averages. At a full 140 grains, manufacturer's suggested max, the velocity was up to 1,615. In that particular rifle it would seem fruitless to burn the extra powder. At 120 grains the velocity was so close to the 140-grain charge as to be the same for practical use.

Turning to Pyro, the max charge by volume did result in more velocity, however. Set at 140 grains by weight, this volume of Pyro turned out to be 115 grains by weight and the velocity was an even 1,700 feet per second at the muzzle. Without a chronograph this sort of precision would have been impossible. As good as the loading manuals are, and they are good, they cannot tell a shooter exactly what he will derive from a rifle, because, as we have belabored now, that rifle is an individual and must be tested individually.

Reviewing the loading procedure, it is possible to insert some information by way of *tips* that can improve black powder hunting ballistics a great deal. Beginning with step number one, we already know that a volume of powder is the best way to go with black or Pyro. So, a measure can be used effectively. The pet charge is tossed down the barrel. Of course, the nipple is clear of any cap.

If round ball is going to be used, there will be a patch, naturally. This patch should be tight. Tight patches give a better seal, hence better velocity and accuracy. The patch is lubed, naturally, and excess material is cut off with a sharp knive. A pre-cut patch may be opted for, and this eliminates cutting off. The lube must do several things—first, and obviously, it must lubricate. But it must also act as a black powder solvent, swabbing the bore, in effect. This helps cut fouling. And the lube must not be absorbed by the powder charge, or attracted to the powder chemically. Saliva will get the job done for the plinker, even the target shooter, but it is not the answer for hunting.

The modern chemical preparations whip the natural method all hollow. Saliva can dry out, and there goes the lube quality. Saliva can encourage rust, which is surely not desirable. The modern chemical preparations are superior in every way, except, perhaps, that saliva is handier, and cheaper.

We have said that the patch has to be tight. It does. After all, the patch engages the riflings. The ball does not, being .005 to .010 smaller than the bore. Trial and error will reveal the best patching material, resulting in a combination of accuracy and velocity, the latter tested with the chronograph. However, some hunters use lighter patching while in the field, because the tight stuff can be very stubborn about ramming home.

Three basic cloths are excellent patching material. These are pillow ticking, denim, and canvas duck. All must be washed thoroughly before use to get rid of any sizing and to soften. Other cloth may work, but it should be plain, not a wash-and-wear, or anything that has been chemically treated.

Ramming a ball home means just that—ramming. This does not suggest that a ball or bullet should be deformed, but it does mean that a lot of pressure should be put on the powder charge. *Black powder works best when it is compressed.* Velocity losses up to 200 feet per second and more have been recorded due to sloppy loads where the powder charge was left in a loose state. Also, this condition can be dangerous, for the ball must be smack against the charge. If there is room for the powder and its bullet or ball to be separated, a bulged barrel can result.

Ramming the ball or bullet down on the powder charge is

A plastic sabot (sah-bow) in caliber .50 eliminates the patch; however, for long hunts the older cloth patch, lubed and rammed in tightly, is still excellent, while the plastic "patch" is ideal for repeated shooting, and will work perfectly in the field as long as the ball pinches the plastic tip of the sabot against the barrel for a tight hold.

best accomplished with a good ramrod, hickory of straight grain, well oiled and carefully made, or a substitute of fiberglass or metal, with the last two fitted carefully so that they don't fall out of the guides in field use. A flimsy rod can break, leaving the hunter stranded for a ramming device, and possibly injuring him if a piece of the rod has entered his hand or arm. Some of the modern hunting frontloaders now have metal ramrods, solid and tapered, such as found on the Navy Hawken series. There is only one thing wrong with these: the small tapered ends hurt the palm of the hand during hard ramming.

Back when the bullet or ball (except a Minie) was being pushed into the muzzle, every shooter will either be familiar with, or employ, a tool that aids that process. This is the short starter, the ball of wood with the little ramrod on it and metal tip that gets things started. This is the key to stopping all injury to the hand. A hole is drilled in the ball of the short starter opposite the ram. This hole is just large enough to accept the end of the

Here is a very simple modification that makes sense. A hole is drilled in the base of the short starter. Now the starter can be used for final ramming of the Minie or ball so that a good pressure can be applied. Remember, compressed powder means surer ignition and more uniform velocity, as well as a bit higher velocity. The slim ramrod, as shown here, would be rough on the hand, and it would be nearly impossible to apply the kind of pressure that will make for a compressed powder charge, but the hole in the short starter solves the problem.

metal ramrod. Now, instead of the shooter jabbing his hand with the metal ramrod, it is snuggly fitted into the ball, and the hand rests on the wood of that ball. More pressure can be applied this way. It is a good trick.

Cap and shoot. This is about all there is to it. Using good patching, being sure to put plenty of pressure on the load, lubricating with a quality product, all of these enhance the hunting load. If the Minie or Maxi is used, a good quality lube is just as essential, though the former will ram home much easier than either ball or Maxi. In fact, the Minie should be checked throughout the hunting day to insure that it is still in place, remembering tht a gap between powder and projectile can cause a ruined barrel. This goes for the Maxi and ball, too, though these two stay in place better than the undersize Minie.

Eventually, the black powder hunter arrives at his own pet ways of doing things, including working up his own loads, and that is part of the personal aspect of the sport. Trial and error play an important role here. For example, some will snap a cap or two on the nipple before loading the arm, and some of us consider this a wasted motion. The object is to clear out any oil, grease or whatever from the nipple. In effect, I have seen debris *deposited* in the nipple by this procedure. Firing caps on the empty nipple means there will be no blowback from the powder, and the detonating material from the cap, as well as some tiny metal particles, too, may lodge in the nipple. Then when the moment of truth arrives, the spark won't get to the powder at all and there is a fttt! for a reward of the stalk.

A trick that works well is to use a tapered pipe cleaner to get the nipple clean. The pipe cleaner will fit, using the small end for No. 11 size, and the large for musket. Its fuzzy cloth will soak up any excess oils and the wire section will push out any lodged debris. It beats the heck out of firing caps on an empty nipple.

Once a fine load is worked out, it is a particular joy to watch it cleanly harvest game, big or small. The load will serve time and again, and should not be changed because, after all, it is optimum. The chronograph will still get plenty of use because there are always new rifles to work on, and shotguns, too, as well as handguns. And the chronograph will also see time testing smokeless loads. Sighting-in and grouping are all that is left after that maximum load is worked up.

Sighting the black powder rifle is not difficult, for it is the same process used on any iron-sighted firearm. But there are a few tricks that will enhance the task. First, bullets, especially, should be swiftly weighed out on a scale before any serious shooting, and certainly before sighting-in or hunting. Making bullets with pure lead and a mould is fascinating and very successful, but on occasion an air pocket can occur, especially in the large projectiles. This air pocket could cause the bullet to stray off target, meaning a miss and that is no way to end a stalk. By quickly weighing the bullets that will go into the field, any chance of a poor one being fired on game, or in the sighting-in process, will be avoided.

The sighting-in methods always used, the solid rest, good sight picture, and careful squeezing of the trigger are the same in black powder sighting. A handy rule of thumb, however, does apply. Since most of the Minie and Maxi loads are under the 2,000 feet-per-second level, and since the round ball loses its velocity rapidly, either can be sighted initially at 13 yards. The magic figure works because the ball or bullet will cross the line of sight twice, one time out around 100 yards, just about right for a black powder sighting, and the other time up close, just around 13 yards, so convenient. When the bullets are printing on the money at 13 yards, then the hunter can move out to 100 for final sighting.

This may seem quite short to the hunter used to sighting at 200 yards, or sighting to hit three inches high at 100, which, for many modern arms puts the bullet back on at as much as 285 to 300 yards. But black powder is a short-range proposition. It always has been, in spite of the tall tales we sometimes hear to the contrary. Yes, the old-timer, using his firearm as a daily tool, learned it well, and probably strained every ounce of ability and range from it. Still, he tried to get close whenever he could. In the first place, even the huge Minies will stray off target in a stiff wind. This is because a slower bullet allows for more *time* for wind to react on it. And the rainbow trajectory is ever present, too.

The story of Joe Rose, a mountain man of the Old West, points up some truth about how far a far shot was in the days of the pioneers. Joe was at rendezvous, where the mountain men had come to sell furs and trade. A bunch of the boys were standing around camp near the Wyoming sage flats when a curious antelope buck wandered by. A group of Indians was standing by Joe and the mountain man could see that all eyes had turned to the buck antelope. Joe wanted to impress the Indians and his friends. He took his best aim and sent a ball whistling out over the flatlands. The buck went down. The throng responded with a universal war whoop at the wonderful marksmanship of Rose. Some said they wanted to pace the shot off so they could tell their grandchildren about it, and they did so. It was a full 125 paces at long stride, about 125 yards. It seems that at least some of the old-timers considered a shot over 100 yards a pretty good feat.

Accuracy in terms of a black powder muzzle loader is an often controversial subject. Yes, some special arms do indeed match their modern counterparts. But most of the off-the-shelf muzzle loaders do not, though they certainly shoot groups capable of the field. Partly due to the fact that a rifle of faster twist cannot be easily found, the Minie normally does well to stay within four inches. I have gotten a two-inch group, but only with very mild loads under perfect conditions. More often, four or five inches is average. At the same time, this does not fully tell the story about black powder accuracy because swabbing between shots can produce tighter groups. That first shot, after all, is the one we are after. Again, if the hunter can lay that first one in the black at 100 yards every time, he should be happy.

The ball is usually more accurate, but not always. Patched ball out of rifles with modest to slow twist often shoot into a couple inches at 100 yards, provided the rifle is a good one, of course. The fact is ever present, however; black powder hunting, by modern standards, is short-range work, and a constant group of four inches at 100 yards will put a lot of meat in the freezer. Stalking is the key to success. Hunting. Getting close. Firing that one good shot. That is black powder hunting.

Pre-testing hunting loads, especially with the accuracy of the chronograph, is more than working up a good round. The process results in a learning of the firearm and its function. The hunter gets used to a successful routine, and when he is in the field that routine takes over under stress or excitement. Some rifles are finicky. Best to discover this on the range, and learn how to load food for her that she likes to digest. Confidence is often built on the range, too, before going into the hunting grounds.

After several shooting sessions the hunter will be familiar with his rifle and its idiosyncrasies, and he will know how to repeat his successes. Another trick to aid in this is marking the ramrod after a favorite load has been discovered. When the load is rammed down fully and properly, a mark is placed on the ramrod where it meets the muzzle of the rifle. This is important because in consequent loadings the ramrod should drop down into the bore the same distance for the same load. If the mark is riding high, then the load is not properly compressed, which could cause the trouble already alluded to earlier, barrel bulging.

The black powder rifle has been the topic of the discussion so far. What about the handguns and front-feeding shotguns? Fortunately, these do not have all of the ins and outs found in getting a good load worked up for the rifle. The single-shot pistol, in essence, follows much of the pattern of the rifle, but on a smaller scale. The six-shooter loads quite differently, and can use ball or bullet, but it, too, is somewhat easy to work with. Proper fuel for handguns is normally FFFg or Pyrodex. The latter works especially well in six-guns because of the limiting factor of the chambers. Since only so much powder can be held by the chambers, and since Pyro, in effect, takes up less space than normal black powder, for all practical purposes more propellent power is allowed with Pyro. Also, the ignition problems encountered with rifles are not as apparent in the revolver, partly due to the straighter line of fire from the cap to the charge. In fact, in a .44 Army that was tested, out of 100 attempts to fire, there were 99 successes, and there was strong suspicion that a faulty cap caused the one failure.

This wooden ramrod reveals a grain pattern that suggests breakage in the field. One can almost see where it will fracture when pressure is applied, and we know that black powder ignites better and functions better under pressure. A snapped rod in the field can ruin a trip. The best thing to do with this ramrod is replace it with a good one, be it wood in proper grain, straight and strong, or a metal or fiberglass rod.

The handguns seem to fire most accurately with very light charges of powder, whether using bullets or ball. Of course, loads are dependent upon the use that the handgun will be put to. Since some states allow small game and varmint hunting with black powder handguns, accuracy may have to be sacrificed for power. And the handguns in black powder configuration have plenty of snort to them. In fact, guns such as the Ruger Old Army and the .44 Remington styles hold enough powder to propel bullets in the 200-grain category at excellent speeds, often over the 1,000 foot per second mark. Handgun hunting with a black powder model is quite rewarding. Of course, all the safety measures must be adhered to, including a generous coating of grease over the mouth of each cylinder on top of the loaded bullet. This prevents chain firing, which can occur, meaning that four of the cylinders, usually, go off simultaneously. Those kinds of thrills nobody needs.

The revolver limits itself on powder by means of its chamber dimensions. The big Walker, for example, can hold nearly 60 grains of black powder when loaded with ball. A very well-made revolver, such as the Ruger Army, can withstand all the Pyro or black powder that can be put in the cylinders, thus making the loading process an easy one to arrive at. A little scoop can be made from a cartridge case, filing or cutting the case until it holds just the amount of powder that will fit in the gun's chamber and still take a ball or bullet.

Since black powder revolvers and single-shot pistols are normally limited to small game and varmint, if allowed in the hunting field at all, discussion of their ballistics and ability has been, understandably, limited here. However, a handgun can be used effectively where allowed, and these sidearms saved many a frontiersmen from disaster in days gone by. Sighted at 25 yards, a black powder handgun in the hands of a practiced shot will do its work right along with most modern arms.

A final word on handguns—for those who are going to hunt game that "shoots back," such as the grizzly bear, or brown of Alaska, it should not be considered unsportsmanlike to tote some firepower of more modern vintage, such as the .44 Magnum. Handloaded with a hard bullet, such as Hornady's 265-grain .44 soft point, the modern .44 has the ability to penetrate deeply and even break bones. Should the first, and probably only, shot from the black powder smokepole miss the vitals, it would be comforting to have a repeating jacketed bullet shooting six-gun close by, not that a booming old Walker loaded up would fail—but let's call it added life insurance.

At last, perhaps the most pleasant of all black powder arms, the scattergun. Placed at the end of this discussion, it takes up the rear not because of its intricacy or finicky nature, but for reasons quite the opposite. The black powder shotgun gives the joy of an obedient and wonderful child, always ready to please, and never requiring anything more than a deserving type of care. The first maxim, and it arrives to us today as words out of the distant past, is to load the shotgun with equal *volumes* of shot and powder. Here is a rule of thumb that works.

Loaded in this manner, one scoop is sufficient to throw both charges. If that scoop holds one ounce of shot, then it will hold the correct volume of powder, and here is another blessing— almost always FFg works just fine, and Pyrodex takes over for it admirably. Some say that Fg will produce slightly better patterns, but so far I have discovered no black powder shotgunner who was unhappy with the patterns he was obtaining out of his smokepole. Out in the field, it is practical to carry along some prethrown charges of both shot and powder. Again, if the charge of shot is 1¼ ounces, then the same volume of powder will be used. With the healthy 1½-ounce charge of shot, this turns out to be about 100 grains of FFg powder by weight. Velocity will be about 1,200 feet per second, plenty for wingshooting, not too much for the pattern.

The loading procedure is simple, too. With the hammers up the powder charges are dropped home—please, one in each barrel only. I have found plain .135 card wads to serve just fine as over-the-powder devices. Here, a little experiment may be in order, for some prefer to use only one over the powder, and others of us suggest two. The shot is poured home, and another .135 is seated on top as an over the shot wad. Again, the idea is to seat firmly, with pressure. Lack of pressure leads to poor velocity and can also mean an unfired load becoming dislodged in the barrel. Naturally, other types of wadding may be employed, but the above seems to produce well.

As for lube, there is now a shotgun sealer on the market, a chemical compound that acts to aid bore-sealing itself, and cut fouling. The old-timers simply puckered up and spat down each barrel. Generally using number 11 or 12 percussion caps, the shotgun has a good record of instant ignition because of the relatively straight line that the cap fire takes to the powder charge. Leaving the hammers up is a good practice because a tight-fitting wad will almost "poosh!" right back out of the barrel if air cannot escape through the powder charge and past the nipple exit. Powder will not be lost due to the very small hole in the nipple.

Many variations to this load may be tried, and a very good one is the use of the one-piece plastic wad. Yes, these are somewhat undersize for they are made to go *inside* a 20- or 12-gauge hull, not a 20- or 12-gauge barrel. Some velocity loss will be experienced with most one-piece plastic wads, around 100 feet per second. The birds won't know the difference, and loading in the field is much faster. The Herter one-piece plastic wad is an especially good one for black powder shooting because it seems to fit the bores a little more snugly than some of the other brands. Groups about 10 per cent tighter are realized with this type of one-piece plastic wad, with its characteristics of closed sides and its ability to hold about the amount of shot that the wad is said to hold. In short, the Herter wad that is for a 1½-ounce loading holds about 1½ ounces. This is not true of some brands, which say 1½ ounces, but a good part of the shot column is actually *above* the wad in the barrel.

A chronograph that does not have screens and screen holders, such as the Oehler Model 31 with Skyscreens, can be used to test the velocity of the black powder shotgun load. One will find that the velocity will increase with the shot charge's decrease. That is, the 1½-ounce proportion of shot/powder will go about 1,200 feet per second; the 1¼-ounce will deliver about 1,300; and the 1⅛ can go up to 1,400. If one wishes to open up his load, he can go about it two different ways. Since some black powder shotguns are now being offered in full/full, such a need may arise.

A spreader load can be made easily by placing a thin wad in between the shot charge. Half the shot is dumped; a wad is rammed home, and then the rest of the shot is loaded on top of the wad. This will spread the shot. Also, a shot pattern may be opened up some by increasing the powder charge by one-half dram, and decreasing the shot charge by ⅛ ounce. This sort of "blows" the pattern (a half dram would amount to about 13.5 grains of powder by weight).

Tightening a pattern, aside from going to a closed one-piece plastic wad, can also be achieved by changing the shot size, up or down—this will have to be determined by testing because

A friend of the author tries his own black powder rifle and loads through the screens of the chronograph. Here, a very simple machine is being used, with screens that must be replaced for every shot. The cost is under $100, and the results are highly accurate. The machine used for the velocity figures mentioned in this book were computed with a more sophisticated Skyscreen model, which does not use screens at all, and gives instant readouts on a lighted grid at a rate of about a shot per minute. The Skyscreen model sells for about $300. (Photo by Kenn Oberrecht)

shotguns do vary here according to the choke—and by using less powder, about a half dram again, and more shot, about ⅛ ounce.

While little has been said about the *testing* of our loads after we have decided that we have arrived at exactly what we want, this part of making an optimum charge is easy and rewarding. It is interesting to see just what our loads will do by way of performance, and there are many ways to check them. Since the shotgun is fresh in mind, it will be well to discuss her first. Aside from testing with a chronograph to determine velocity, the checking of a pattern is most vital. In effect, the shotgun pattern is worth more than its speed. A pattern free of holes, and able to deliver more pellets to the target, will take more birds than a faster shot charge with a lot of holes in it.

Testing for the pattern is simple. Two long sticks are placed in the ground and a large sheet of paper is attached to them. Butcher or meat wrapping paper works fine. Then, from various yardage, though 40 yards is the normal distance, the shotgun is fired at an X on the paper. A steady hold on the gun is useful. Some people count the number of pellets that land inside of a 30-inch circle at 40 yards in order to determine the action of the choke, with about 70 per cent of the shot landing inside the 30-inch circle representing full choke.

It is simpler to shoot from the ranges at which most of the field work will be done, varying the shot size until the best pattern is obtained. Sure, small shot makes denser patterns, but sometimes going up one size in shot will produce a better pattern, in which case, that larger shot should be used, even on smallish game and birds.

Testing big game loads is even more interesting because a bullet is recovered and each load may be kept on record with samples. There is an elaborate homemade testing device that amounts to a wooden box with partitions in it. In each partition a different medium is placed. One such box contains a heavy catalogue in the first partition, followed by a huge hunk of modeling clay, followed by a balloon filled with water in the next partition, with the last section holding another catalogue. Some of the real brutes in .50 on up will drive all the way through this arrangement at up to 150 yards and a backup, such as a clay bank, is necessary to catch the bullet. Such a clay bank, in fact, is useful in itself as a bullet corral.

The object of such testing is to measure the upset of the lead

bullet or ball, and to see how deeply it penetrated. Some of the
600-610 grain .58s with heavy charges of FFg or Pyrodex will
penetrate 18 inches of loamy clay at a full 125 yards, smashing
the bullets back into mushrooms that go over one and one-
quarter inches in diameter. Somehow, a look at these radiates
confidence in the modern black powder hunter when he plans to
go up against just about any soft-skinned game.

After being lured by the magical call of the black powder
sirens, many men try to improve on black powder ballistics.
Essentially, this is an attempt to turn the old-time guns into
modern arms, a mistake on at least two counts. First, it can't be
done, and even if it could the effect would be deleterious to the
whole concept of black powder hunting and shooting, something
akin to taking a beautiful antique oak chair and painting it
dazzling white with the latest latex paint. In time most of us
come to recognize black powder shooting and hunting for what
it is, a horse of a very different hue, and we appreciate the sport
as a remarkably rewarding interest.

One more aspect of the personal and individual nature of
modern day black powder hunting is the uniqueness of each
arm, and its ability to perform with its own special load. Working up that load ourselves we learn more about black powder
shooting. Testing those loads we gain more confidence in our
frontloaders. When Old Smoke 'n Thunder is shooting right on,
we take it hunting, the pinnacle on the mountain of black powder shooting. Black powder puts the hunt back in hunting. A
man finds his game and must stalk close, which is the topic of
our next chapter in which the hunter finds out just how close he
can get. Because he has built and tested his own loads, the
modern black powder hunter knows that with the proper load
his smokepole is equal to any animal on the continent.

CHAPTER 7

Methods for Closing in on Game

The hunter moved like a phantom through the large pines that bordered the canyon wall. Below, in the valley, ran the river, and among the trees and in the meadows he had located his quarry on a prescouting trip. At the end of the pines, at the very edge of the abrupt canyon, the hunter found a shelter in a cut that ran downhill to the valley. Here, he sat out of the breeze, where he could study the scene below. The sun was up. The day was already warming. A thick white fog that followed every winding bend of the river, as if to camouflage the water, was rising and thinning.

The hunter held his walking stick out into the breeze, watching the thin leather tassels as they danced on its end, telling him not only where the wind was coming from, for he could feel that, cool on the side of his face, but also how the eddying currents were playing. The tassels stood outward, then bent back slightly, not enough to carry his scent if he worked with the wind in his face steadily. Satisfied that he could make a successful stalk into the lowlands, the man leaned back against

a smooth white boulder, pressed the tip of his walking stick
firmly into the earth in front of him, and rested the 9 x 35 binoculars on the other end of the stick, where the tanned leather
padding held the glass solidly.

Now he could detect every detail below. He was rested, out
of any disconcerting wind, warm, comfortable, able to stay still
for a long time while searching for his game. This game would
be easy to see, once it left the shadows and thick grasses that
grew along the river, feeding out into the open spaces. Had he
been looking for the deer, which blended its gray form with the
habitat, he would have concentrated on every suspicious object,
slowly moving the focusing wheel of the glass in and out to fuzz
up, then resharpen the picture, a good way of separating the
game from its surrounding, of locating that feeding, even bedded buck out of the tangle of look-alike growth. But this quarry
would simply feed out into the open, a group of them, pecking
and picking among the grasses for food.

The sun appeared as an electric globe now above the horizon, its rays burning off the dew in steamy patterns that danced
in the damp lowlands. The hunter looked especially hard in
those places first struck by the morning's heat. Here, his game
would enjoy soaking the warm rays, and small insects might be
stirring, too. The view in the glasses was clear and bright and
the man knew he was doing a good job of searching, for he had
already located five deer as the animals fed. And he had seen
many birds as they flitted in and out in the underbrush.

Appearing like an image popping out of a paint-with-water
coloring book, there was suddenly a flock of birds feeding beyond a small rise in the ground that had previously hidden them
from the hunter's view. Now the wild turkeys, about 15 of them,
skipped and scratched along looking for food. There were no big
toms, but any bird was legal, and time was a limiting factor. The
man decided to slip in amongst the birds and harvest from the
flock what he could.

From above he had formulated his hunting strategy, to stay
in the cut as he descended the slope, following a white trail into
the woods, a soft path made by the river when it overran its
banks in spring, depositing a bed of smooth small pebbles. The
damp trail would muffle the sound of his boots, and it led to a
marker that the man had discovered from above, a defunct
monarch of a cottonwood tree, its bony arms outstretched to
serve now as roosts for birds.

Time was on the hunter's side. The flock would feed for a couple of hours in the turkey restaurant of the forest floor along the river. Before leaving his sentinel post on the high ridge, each detail of the land below was recorded in the hunter's mind and he had no trouble locating the wild birds as they fed among a large patch of deadfalls on the ground. A wild turkey is not brilliant, but he is wary, equipped with a radar of hearing and sight, the latter in color, as a human, rather than in the black and white shades most of its mammal cousins are limited to.

The hunter closed ground on his game, remaining under cover, lest the birds detect a movement or sight a glimpse of a red shirt. He moved slowly, trying not to break a single twig that would be detected by the acute, though almost invisible, ears of

The author poses with a wild turkey taken from the river bottoms. The bird was approached to about 20 yards for the shot, which was taken with a .50 Hurricane and the 367-grain Maxi slug, backed by a reduced load of 60 grains of FFFg G-O black powder.

the wild bird. Looking through his binoculars into the deadfall, there was nothing; then a neck craned up out of the branches like a snake's head waving to and fro testing the air. The flock moved now into a gulley that was lined with interesting plant life, and probably a host of insects. The scene appeared as a nature film in the clear picture of the glasses. The birds were stripping seeds from grass blades, bending their heads sideways, locking a beak on the stalk of grass, then swiftly moving the head upward, cleaning off all the tiny seeds.

The flock moved through the gulley. The wind was right, from bird to man, and the hunter carefully stationed himself by a lone tree so he could intercept the flock as it fed past. At the tree he waited, muzzle pointing at the gulley. In a tangle of dry fallen branches the flock began to appear. At last, a head rose at only 20 yards, poking straight up like a snake once again, curious. The sights of the .50 lined up carefully. The trigger was squeezed. Boom! Even the underload of 60 grains of FFFg burst forth with a large cloud of smoke that hung on the damp still air. The flock exited with its strange rolling gait and disappeared directly into the thick foliage alongside the river.

The hunter walked through the fog of his own creation that hung on the quiet air. He could all but taste the sulphur. On the ground lay his prize, a mature hen turkey shot right through the neck. Had he missed with shot number one, chances are there would not have been a shot number two with the slow-loading sootbelcher.

Success had come on the heels of planning. First, the hunter knew his game and the habitat of that game. Next, he had prescouted to learn the exact whereabouts of his quarry. He carried with him the tools that aided his success, and he also knew a few tricks that helped him. Getting close and placing that one good shot were a total of all of these. The modern black powder hunter can experience these kinds of rewards by acquiring and practicing new skills.

As modern hunters, we have come to chase game by strolling the hillsides and woods in hopes of jumping something out and getting a shot at it. With a scope-sighted long-range rifle, this tactic works for thousands of hunters every season. It can work for the black powder hunter, too, sometimes. And it is not a method to be totally ignored. But is is a method to be improved upon and often replaced with more stealth, more planning.

There are special rewards in getting close, a joy in spotting

Getting close is possible even in open terrain, as shown here. The record-class antelope has just spotted the hunter, but the does are still confused. The hunter moved in on the animals with the aid of camouflage clothing and by using every swell in the ground for concealment. Patience is a mainstay of the modern black powder hunter.

the quarry in his domain and under his rules, before it spots the hunter, then working our clumsy biped bodies to within only yards of those big ears, sharp eyes, and keen instincts. The first step in getting close is attitude. We have gotten used to shooting across canyons and now we have to conjure in our minds another picture of the hunter, more patient, persistent, and observant. Slower-moving, he stays to look longer and harder, and he is willing to *work* harder, too.

And we have to discard the nonsense, and improve the sound basics that will get us close to our quarry. Advice such as "you have to think like a deer to get close to one" is supersitious nonsense. We don't even know how man thinks, let alone how the furry beasts carry on in thought. But we can learn our game by studying its habits and habitat. Knowing what a deer eats, for example, can be invaluable in finding his feeding grounds and being there early in the morning, and even more, late in the afternoon when he is at supper.

There are numerous books on the subject, and even courses

in schools that reveal much about the biological nature of our game animals. Best of all, there is experience personally gained in the field, not only during the season, but before and after as well. A picnic can be a game-learning trip that the whole family will enjoy. This type of nature study can be coupled with another factor in learning how to get close to game: the prescouting method. Prescouting means going hunting before the season opens, without any firearms, of course. This differs from scouting only in terms of semantics, with scouting being performed during the few days a party arrives early on the hunting grounds, prescouting taking place at any time, and not in close association with the seasons.

Of the tricks, or types of hunting tactics that get us close to game, we must employ those that best fit our personalities and idiosyncrasies. Using the stand, for example, is a good way of getting close, actually allowing the game to work in on us, instead of the other way around. However, a man who gets nervous sitting still is going to gain little pleasure from posting him-

The wary Coues deer, or Arizona whitetail, is often found resting where he can maintain a good view of the country surrounding him. From any distance at all it will take a superior set of optics to detect this gray animal in the neutralness of his environment, even though he is, in effect, out in a fairly open spot. (Nick Fadala photo)

self on a stump or up in a tree waiting for something to walk by, even though these tactics bring results when stands are intelligently located in feding areas or on game trails.

A combination of methods often helps. Knowing the quarry and its home grounds, a man can seek a high spot in the terrain for field position, searching for animals that will feed out into open spaces. After the game is discovered, by keeping the wind right and using methods of stealth, the hunter closes in. A few tricks can help, such as covering boots with large heavy socks during the final part of the stalk. This is much quieter than clacking over the rocks with hard-soled shoes.

Knowing the habitat means knowing the specific hunt area. A waterhole can be a valuable piece of strategy in the hunt if signs show that game is frequenting it. But knowing the nature of the game itself will dictate the hunting method. For example, the well-used waterhole would be of value to an antelope hunter, for they water by day. But a whitetail is rarely going to come in to drink until after dark, doing the hunter no good.

There are many means of getting close to game, and they work with varying success dependent upon many factors, including the time of the year and the skill of the hunter. Calling game is an example. There are duck and geese hunters who know the language, convincing the birds to drop in on them. And there are others who send the birds fleeing for cover when they toot on the same calls. A varmint call can work wonders in an area where the animals have not been called too much. But it can be hopeless on educated varmints. A deer call is useful one time, and worthless another. One spring day a friend called in 25 mule deer, all does. Back in the same area in the fall not a single deer came to the same hunter, same call, although fresh signs indicated that the animals were still there. Rattling antlers is another method that works for some sometimes, but not for everyone all the time.

There are olfactory decoys, too. The bear bait is one. The bear finds the decoy with its nose most of the time. By placing a white scarf on a bush, antelope have come up to look at it, which is a visual attraction but by adding a few drops of "deer scent," the pronghorns have remained for many minutes sniffing the cloth, enough time for a very careful and unhurried shot. Other olfactory tricks include scents that man puts on himself. We have all sorts of "deer lures" for sale now, meant to cover man's odor. Whether they work or not depends upon the conditions, wind, humidity, and disposition of the animal. There is supposed to be a chlorophyll tablet that destroys man's odor "from the inside out."

Camouflage is another excellent ruse, but it must be used properly. Now we have the blaze orange camouflage outfit, which allows hunter to see hunter, but which aids in hiding man from most game, all but the birds. In a duck blind, when conditions are safe, camouflage works wonders, especially if the hunter goes the whole route, including a mask for his face. Ducks and geese see in color and see well. The face and eyes are dead giveaways from the sky, as anyone who has flown in light aircraft low to the ground will attest. Ducks and geese have come right into hunters who were wearing the meticulously patterned Royal suits of camouflage. One time on a totally private ranch which had no other hunters on it, in Sonora, Old Mexico, two hunters had the thrill of deer walking right up to them on a game trail as they sat in the brush camouflaged.

Safety is number one in hunting, and camouflage should not be employed where many hunters roam the woods. The law is becoming quite specific about this, in fact, and state after state is now demanding the wearing of blaze orange apparel. What defeats camouflage are mainly two things. First, the hunter does not cover *all* his body. The idea of camouflage is to break up the outline. When a bare head sticks out of the grass, game spots it. Second, we often are not truly hidden. Just because we cannot see out does not mean the game can't see in, but often, like a child with his hands over his eyes, we half hide behind a stump saying "Bet you can't see me" to game. Motion, finally, will destroy any kind of camouflage. Whatever the pattern, whatever the extent, camo cannot work when the hunter moves. Game sees motion better than anything else.

There are interesting tools that help us get close to game. Modern black powder hunting is a personal sport and a person should do it his way, of course, but there are some tools that really work in the total picture of hunter getting up close to the quarry. One of these tools is the binocular. The number of hunters who misuse this tool is staggering. They employ the glass for locating the pickup truck at the end of the day, or for looking at something they have already seen. These are just fine uses, but the glass is for *finding,* too. It takes a little practice and style.

First, a glass has to be optically good. This may sound all too obvious, but hunters continually try to locate game with cheapie

An array of excellent binoculars for the black powder hunter. All of these models will perform superbly because all of them have good definition, possibly the most important single aspect of a good glass. Also, they are full-sized optics meant for serious work.

binoculars that have poor definition. Definition is just that— optical excellence in terms of defining things in the distance. Using two pairs of binoculars one dusky afternoon, it was soon obvious which one defined the most. Looking at a distant tree, one glass defined the limbs, but the leaves were just blobs. The other, a tool of the same power, allowed its user to see the very serrated edges of the leaves.

In the latter part of the day, when much game comes out to feed, the man with good glasses can rest in that part of the habitat that has food, and just look. He does not gaze through the glass. He picks out a place and studies it faithfully. It is thrilling to see a deer materialize where once stood a rock. And it is rewarding to have the nonbeliever along when game is found bedded or feeding in thick foliage. Many hunters simply do not believe in the glass as a tool. They do after being shown first hand its value.

The binocular can do a lot of walking for the hunter, covering terrain that is at a great distance. However, it must be kept steady during use. This is important because a blurry picture is not conducive to picking out camouflaged animals. One means of getting that steady picture is to sit down with elbows rested on knees. Another is to use the device known as the Moses Stick. This tool is better explained in Chapter Sixteen where its manufacture is discussed. Basically, it is a light stick about the height of the hunter, with one end fixed with a crutch bumper for use against the ground, the other with a tanned soft leather "handle," used to protect the hand from splinters, but also to rest the binocular on. There is no heartbeat in the stick to blur the picture in the glass.

Excellent optics aid the modern downwind shooter in his quest for big game. Here are a pair of wide-angle binoculars with a special feature—The Insta-Focus modification. One good way of discerning camouflaged game from their environment is by slowly focusing and refocusing the glass. The Insta-Focus aids this handily by allowing a rapid, yet accurate, focusing change. Also important to the black powder fan are shooting glasses. Here, a yellow pair is shown; however, there is also a gray-lens model that is easy on the eye while hunting. Yellow is better for the range than the field.

The Moses stick, or walking staff, is being used here as a binocular rest to steady the glass in searching for game. There is no heartbeat in the stick to make the picture shaky. The stick has many other advantages, including the obvious walking aid that it was originally designed to be back in biblical times.

The Moses stick is also used for shooting. It steadies the rifle both from the sitting and standing positions. It is a fine tool for the black powder hunter, and sort of fits in with his free-spirited style, aiding him in covering a lot of ground when he wants to, or in staying put and looking at a patch of country with the binocular resting steady.

Game that is spotted before it sees the hunter is oftentimes freezer-bound. Carrying a short-range single-shot black powder rifle, seeing that game first has great effect on the outcome of the stalk. If the game is located in the distance, a plan of stalking may be figured out. Naturally, this is not always possible, and a snapshot in the brush with a black powder boomer can be just as rewarding both aesthetically and materially as a shot fired with a modern rifle. Getting close to small game is important, too. Sometimes just sitting still is the best way, such as on a squirrel hunt. And sometimes the hunter has to walk in close, stalking up on his game big or small. Clothing is as much a tool,

By spotting this mule deer doe before she spotted him, the author was able to get up close, keeping the wind in his face and moving slowly. Black powder hunting means getting close because of the rainbow trajectory of the firearms. The doe has just detected a presence, as witnessed by the movement of her ears. Now is the time to remain perfectly still until she returns to her feeding.

then, as anything else. It was a main factor in glassing, where the hunter who was comfortable was able to sit for a long while using his optical support system. Being cold and shaky, he would probably not have found his wild turkey. But scratchy noisy clothes can also spell defeat when trying to get near a game animal.

So can boots. Many modern black powder hunters are opting for the clothes of the old-timers. These buckskins and leather moccasins are wonderful for both camouflage and stalking, but they can be dangerous in hunting country where the hunter, in effect, ends up looking like a deer. Also, romantic as it is, the moccasin is not for everyone in all terrain unless its sole is heavy enough to carry the tenderfoot over the sharp rocks. Keeping the spirit of the black powder hunt is not at all difficult, even though the outdoorsman is dressed in a modern way. However, most of us will go along with something that sets us aside from the standardly bedecked hunter, be it a somewhat strange hat, or maybe buckskin pants, though coupled with a blaze orange top. As for boots, a pair of Browning Waterproofs may keep a man much happier than the romantic moccasin when the land is wet and cold.

Hunting has always consisted of three parts, finding the game, stalking it, and then putting it into possession. Man, being a creature of strategy and tools, has put together various combinations of all three that work for him individually. In finding the game, tools such as the "eye of the hunter," as binoculars are sometimes called, aid the search. Finding the game also means strategy, knowing the animal and his home.

Stalking, an all but forgotten art, becomes, again, a matter of style and tools. The hunter wears clothing that fits his needs, tools, as it were, and he fixes his mind on getting close. He plans the chase, rather than having it merely happen by chance. He uses tricks and cunning. He studies the movements of his game, both big and small, and learns where to wait and when, or when to move and how fast, how far.

Finally, there is the climax of any stalk, and here is where the personally selected, modified, and loaded black powder firearm comes into its own, getting the job done with real dispatch the hunter can be proud of. The trio, finding, stalking, and shooting, weds itself in time to a personal and individual excellence, and there is a sense of inner pride, not bravado, not bragging, that attends the clean harvest of a game animal big or small taken with the old smokebelchers.

CHAPTER 8

Big Game with Frontloaders

The ultimate black powder experience for many is the big game hunt with frontloaders. Elk, moose, bear, deer—all can be taken cleanly with muzzle-loading arms. The object of the chase is exactly what it was in smokeless powder hunting: find, stalk, and bring to bag. But black powder hunting differs in philosophy. After all, the black powder hunter came to the sport because he wanted to put more of the hunt back in hunting, purposely handicapping himself on the one hand, while improving his chances for overall success on the other. He is handicapped, obviously, by the short-range single-shot slow-loader he carries. But he stands an excellent chance of improving his success because of the deep rewards gained from the experience of black powder big game hunting, even when the freezer is not filled.

The road to big game success has been partially traveled at this point, because the basics have been discussed. The hunter has selected his rifle, that which best suits him, and he probably has modified it to fit him personally with a good sling, sights, and other additions and deletions. He knows that black powder

Author with an exceptional black bear taken in Colorado with the Navy Arms Hawken Hurricane .50-caliber percussion frontloader. The bear was hit with two 367-grain Maxis, both of which exited because of the close range.

ballistics are strong medicine, and this knowledge gives him confidence in his smoke belcher. He has also worked up that special load that delivers accuracy and power, and he has tested it, at least on cans filled with water, or clay banks, if not on more sophisticated devices. He may have chronographed the load, too, and he knows what it will do in terms of lethality and range.

Finally, he has the will and dedication to locate his game, stalk close, and place that one shot for a clean kill. He may have developed a new opinion of what hunting is all about, and a new definition of success. As the hunter learns his sport, the tools, and the methods, his chances of bringing home the game, big and small, increase, while he enjoys the unique experiences embodied in the black powder type of hunt itself.

The black powder big game hunter may elect to hunt trophy heads, trying to find the big ones, or he may choose to be a meat hunter, harvesting to table the world's best meat with his primitive weapon. But, primarily, the modern black powder hunter is a combination of these things, trophy hunter sometimes, meat hunter always, enjoying the fruits of his labor on the dinner table, shared with family and friends. There is room for both of these pursuits in the sport. The idea is to decide upon a hunting style, and employ all guns and gear with alacrity and skill. Black powder hunting success leans heavily upon proper use of the tools, as well as learning the many tricks of the trade—and there are many.

Mastering the muzzle loader means practice, of course, on the range, or just plinking at tin cans in a safe area. Better yet, the hunter will use his big game piece on small game and varmints, where the transfer of skills is very high. On the small game/varmint field the hunter can decide how he wants to carry his loads and he gains mastery of loading as well as shooting techniques. He knows the trajectory of his frontstuffer, just how far it will shoot, and how far he can shoot it. He may experiment with new projectiles as they appear on the market, but basically he sticks with what he knows, both in bullets and powder type and charge.

In carrying powder and ball, or bullet, the old powder horn is not only romantic, but also practical. A tip of horn may be cut off at the proper length to act as a charger, holding just the right *volume* of black powder to match up with the missile. Or, the horn can be used in combination with a brass adjustable powder measure. Either way is excellent, fast, and accurate. Even though I always carry what I call "readyloads" on my big game hunts, the horn still occupies its place tucked under my arm, its strap slung over a shoulder. The horn comes in handy because the big game rifle, sighted properly for about the century mark, will be right-on with light load and ball at close range, in the 20- to 50-yard category, just right for small game, which is often welcome fare on a big game hunt.

Finding habitat stocked with rabbit, squirrel, grouse, or other tasty in-season morsels may cause the hunter to shoot away his big load into a safe backstop. Now he can reload with the short-range, small-meat getter, putting edibles in the pot.

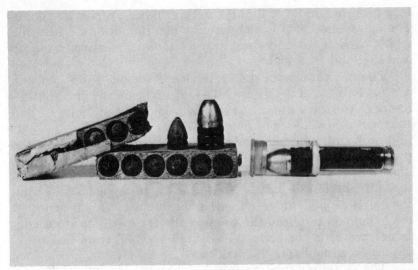

The wooden box on the left is an original container for bullets and powder charges as used by the frontiersmen. On the right is the reliable "readyload" as referred to in the text. This particular .58 caliber Minie has been lubed with a beeswax base so that it remains clean to handle, but any kind of lube will also work beautifully contained in the plastic medicine vial. The vial on the right contains the powder charge. Note that it is narrow, so that it can fit right into the muzzle of the rifle, avoiding any spillage. (Photo by Kenn Oberrecht)

Aside from this plus, another reason for carrying the powder horn is simply having on hand about a half pound of powder, sometimes much more with the larger (though more cumbersome) horns.

The "readyloads" are also very worthwhile. First, how they are made, and then their advantages. The best type I have found is that made of plastic vials, or medicine bottles, those used for filling prescriptions. Two sizes are glued end to end. One bottle is narrow, smaller than the inside of the rifle bore, and long enough to hold whopper charges of black powder, since many of our better black powder hunting rifles are capable of handling such loads. The second bottle is fatter and shorter, big enough to hold the bullet or the ball.

The premeasured powder charge is poured into the long vial and a bullet or ball is placed in the fatter plastic vial. A cap is taped on the side of either bottle, preferably the fatter one because it is easier to remove. Heavy wrapping tape is good, as is masking tape. The cap is taped firmly in place, but the end of the tape is curled under so that it can be grabbed up, just like a tab. The cap will stick to the tape and when the latter is lifted, the cap is there, staring the shooter in the face, easily plucked up and stuck on the nipple.

The advantages of the "readyload" for big game hunting are fairly easy to see. First, they are fast for second-shot attempts. And they are accurate, too, holding the bullet or ball that was pre-weighed at home to insure absence of air pockets and uniformity of lead, and a proper powder charge. Also, the prelubed bullet retains its lube because the plastic does not absorb it. If ball is used, a pre-cut and lubed patch is placed on top of the ball in the bottle. When the top is popped off the vial, the ball is tapped into the hand, and since the patch is on top, it too is popped free into the hand ready for use. The stout container prevents the soft all-lead bullet or ball from becoming deformed while being carried, too.

The system of loading in the field with "readyloads" is an easy one to learn. The top is popped off the powder vial, and the narrow little bottle is thrust right into the muzzle of the gun. Not a granule of powder is spilled this way. The top is flipped off the other vial on the opposite end of the glued together arrangement. The lubed bullet or ball and patch is laid into the palm of the hand. With one swift motion the bullet is seated. Be sure to put pressure on it since pressure is necessary for full power development. The ball is treated the same way, but may have to be prestarted with a short starter, as will a Maxi type of bullet that needs to be engraved. The Minie is very fast here because it readily slides down the barrel. After a fast job of capping, the shooter is ready for round number two.

The "readyloads" are easy to carry, fitting well into the possibles bag. If they are glued properly, using hot melt cement or the new miracle speed glues, the "readyload" becomes one unit. They may be toted into the field inside of old Army .30 M1 Carbine clip holders, canvas pouches that slip onto a belt. But the possibles bag is just as handy, and looks more "black powder like." The small possibles that attaches to the belt is perhaps best for carrying the plastic vials because they could be lost in the slung bag. Both of these types of possibles are discussed in Chapter Fourteen. If the hunter must negotiate rugged terrain, the former bag is better, hanging onto the belt and never swinging around, which could allow the little Readyloads to fly out on the ground.

With rifle and loads ready for action, the hunter turns to his own person for outfitting. Again, the choices are wide and open. He can go with primitive dress, even making his own, from tanning the leather to cutting out and sewing the patterns. Or he can simply use the hunting clothes he has always worn. And, naturally, a combination is perfectly sensible. If the old leather style is chosen, the man has to be careful about looking too much like the game he is after, and the often mandatory blaze orange will have to cover a good part of his person. Of course, back in camp he can enjoy the full nostalgic powers of his leather clothing around the campfire. Chapter Twenty-One lists manufacturers and distributors, along with addresses. The black powder hunter can look into the catalogues and decide for himself how he would like to appear when he takes his smokepole on the trail of big game.

Selection of the tools that accompany the black powder hunter is also a labor of love that can take up many enjoyable hours of browsing the wish books. Knives are of special interest, as are tomahawks and other tools. In most cases these items are as useful as they are decorative. The essential knife is discussed in its own chapter because it bears a large part of the necessary hunting chore after the game is down. The knife may be the extremely useful Green River type carried by the mountain man, or a modern style of cutlery. And they may vary according to the style of the hunt, from a close-to-home foray, to a real backwoods experience. Their use will vary with the job, too, all to be discussed in Chapter Fifteen.

Many are the aids and tips that will enhance the black powder hunting trip, and the modifications of these tricks are often personalized and enhanced by the hunter himself as he uses them. On a recent antelope hunt one major tip concerning the proper weatherizing of the big game rifle spelled out success, where failure was imminent without the trick. The original buck hunt had changed its complexion before the opening day of the season. Two days of scouting proved that the area held few if any trophy bucks. The bucks were smallish youngsters. However, the ranchers pointed out that many of the antelope roaming the prairies thereabouts were very old and barren.

The more sensible harvest would be one of the old does, rather than the immature bucks. And this is what we went for, leaving the horned "teenagers" alone. Actually, as the hunt progressed, it was obvious that the old does were going to be

twice the sport anyway. They beat it out of the country whenever we showed up, but the spindly horned bucks stood around
foolishly studying us.

Not only was the hunt atypical. So was the weather. Rain
had turned the area into mud, and we had to walk everywhere
we wanted to go, not being able to penetrate the country at all
otherwise. In fact, rain came down on us most of the hunt. Steps
had to be taken to insure that the rifle would go off when she
was called upon. Normally, a cap is placed on the nipple by first
squeezing it so that it must be forced in place. This holds the
cap, be it a number 11 or a tophat, on the nipple discouraging it
from falling off while the rifle is being carried in the field. However, this was not enough for the wet conditions.

After the cap was squeezed, a tiny dab of primer sealer was
applied to the end of the nipple. Primer sealer is the usually red
substance that is painted on the primer area of metallic cartridges. Nail polish works about the same and can be used. The
sealer dries and forms a barrier against the moisture, while
helping to hold the cap in place on the nipple at the same time.
At the other end, a small penny balloon was placed over the
muzzle of the rifle. This waterproofed the piece stem to stern.
Accuracy is not disturbed by the balloon, for it blows free from
the pressure in the barrel before the ball or bullet ever reach it. If
no balloon is available, a bit of plastic wrap taped in place works
as well.

Under these soggy conditions the precautions of waterproof-
ing were imperative, of course, but they pay off during good
weather, too. A bit of wax can be melted around the cap, sealing
it on the nipple, if no nail polish or sealer is available. The wax
will not harm anything, and in fact, can be used on the six-
shooter with equally excellent results. If the rifle or pistol, or
shotgun for that matter, is weatherized, the load can be left
intact for a full weekend. However, most of us elect to shoot or
pull our loads at the end of the day for reasons of safety, loading
with fresh powder and ball the next morning.

On the hunt for old doe antelope it ended up being a combination of black powder hunting strategy and tricks that brought
the game to bag. One nice herd of 22 animals was spotted in the
distance. By using the natural breaks of the land, the range was
finally closed to about 75 yards, but the group bolted up a hill.
Trailing behind were two gray animals, no youngsters near
them, the barren type of doe, free of kids and probably quite old

An old doe antelope is harvested for the freezer with a .50 Hurricane. Note that the ramrod is part way out of its guides due to the recoil of the rifle. The pack frame was used to carry the meat back to camp because the country was soggy and would not permit off-the-road vehicle travel, which would produce ruts and injure the landscape.

for their kind. By the time the .50 belched its terrible cloud of smoke into the wet air the animals were 125 yards off, but moving at little more than a walking pace. I held right on. When shooting *either* uphill or downhill under normal black powder ranges, it is wise to hold a tad under the target. Since I was sighted for 100 yards, holding right on at 125 yards was, in effect, like holding low.

The Maxi caught the doe in the chest area as she turned a bit sideways, and the old animal went down without a quiver. The black powder wound channel was typical—long and wide, but without bloodshot meat. Had the rifle not been fitted out for foul weather the result of this hunt quite probably would have been "Ftttt!" instead of "Boomm!"

In spite of a long history of success on big game, the modern hunter still expresses doubt when considering the authority of black powder guns on big game. This notion is often dispelled with the first kill, but for those who might be hesitant, the results of a black powder safari should be related. Anyone who doubted the effectiveness of the old smoke throwers on American big game can lay aside his fears, for Val Forgett knocked off all types of big and mean African animals with his muzzle guns. Val is president of Navy Arms Company, and he wanted to try out two of his own favorite products on the animals of the Dark Continent. He chose two .58 caliber rifles, the smaller Buffalo Hunter, a shorter rifle patterned on a musket lock, and the

Val Forgett, president of the Navy Arms Company, poses with the elephant that he got in Africa with a Navy .58 Hunter, proving that black powder can get the job done. The bullet was the .58 Shiloh 610 grain.

American-made Hunter .58, a superbly crafted firearm capable of digesting tremendous powder charges behind big bullets.

Val wanted sectional density for penetration; therefore he eschewed the ball and chose the Minie type bullet instead. The bullet turned out to be a wadcutter design, flat-nosed and long, weighing a full 610 grains out of a Shiloh mould. The skirt was heavy, because Val wanted to stuff a lot of gas pressure behind it without blowouts. Starting out easy, the hunter went up to a full 175 grains of FFFg as optimum behind the long .58 Minie. Due to the resistance of the heavy lead bullet, all of the powder burned in the barrel. Because of the 1-60 twist, which is probably too slow for such a long bullet, accuracy was in the 4½- to 5-inch group at 100 yards, but most shooting would be done at 50 yards, and never over 100, so this was acceptable.

Hippo was first to be hit with the 610-grain Minies out of the Hunter with its 26-inch barrel. One bullet drove 18 inches into the tough animal, and another opened up a channel that a man could insert a closed fist into. The Minies reacted in a normal fashion, expanding well, but losing almost no mass whatever, weighing when they were recovered about what they weighed before they were fired.

The Buffalo Hunter was used on lion with its maximum charge of 125 grains of FFFg and the same 610-grain lead bullet. Simba was struck low in the shoulder from about 40 yards out. The bullet passed completely through the nearly nine-foot lion and whined off in a ricochet with apparent power remaining. Later, again with the .58 Hunter, an elephant was hit. The bullet went through 18 inches of boney head, but missed the brain. The elephant had to be finished off, but with better placement, the .58 would have been up to the task at hand.

Finally, there was the cape buffalo. Val fired upon this animal of reportedly two to two and a half tons, 4,000 to 5,000 pounds, again with the Hunter, and one bullet drove the *length* of the animal. The animal was not knocked flat, nor is it often boomed over with modern African rifles, being as tenacious as it is. But the bull did not go far. A second Minie finished it off. Val and company also collected a good many beautiful plains antelope and other trophies on the African trip, proving that his guns were up to it.

As part of the big game hunt, there is glassware for the black powder hunter. These fall into the category of rifle scopes, spotting scopes, binoculars and shooting glasses.

Val Forgett, Navy Arms president, poses with an African antelope that he got with his .58 Hunter rifle using a Shiloh 610-grain Stakebuster Minie bullet.

Rifle scopes are a matter of personal choice. Most of us elect to keep these on modern cartridge guns, staying with peep and open sights on the muzzle loaders. Peep sights work well, and are in tune with the old-time spirit of the hunt, as are open sights, of course. This is not to say that scopes on rifles are new. They are not. In the Civil War cannon crews were annihilated from tremendous range by snipers equipped with black powder rifles and target scopes. Still, the modern black powder big game hunter will have to make up his mind on the issue of scopes on frontstuffers.

As for spotting scopes, Lewis and Clark had such a device on their famous expedition and used it throughout the trip. The sheep hunter, antelope hunter, the trophy hunter, any of these can feel justified in carrying this tool, as it only serves to better identify, sometimes find, game. It does not directly enhance the kill.

Binoculars have been discussed elsewhere, and are destined to be mentioned again. They are an aid to the hunter in finding game, as well as identifying it. They make for a safer hunt, and a more successful one. Given hunting seasons of several months and an empty woods, these might be dispensed with, leaving the finding of game to more basic strategy. But they are not to be considered unsporting for the modern black powder hunter. On one occasion a companion was prepared to shoot at a small mule deer buck that was feeding in a thicket of oaks, when I stopped him. "Can you tell for sure which way to sight for a clean kill?," I asked. He said he could, but as I watched the small deer and tried to imagine a line from my friend's muzzle to the deer, that line seemed way off course. "Wait," I suggested. "Take a look through these." I handed him the binoculars. He looked.

Through the binoculars he could tell that he was not aiming at the small buck that we had seen, but rather at a doe in the brush next to it. Doe was open season, but still, the hunter wanted the buck. The glass cleared up any doubt about the target. It is a fine tool to carry on a hunt.

At last there are shooting glasses. Although we do not always follow our own good advice, the shooting spectacles should be worn out hunting. While the blowback of debris and soot can be directed away from the shooter by carefully deepening the hammer nose, still, it is conceivable that some foreign matter could enter the eye. In fact, so could a twig or tree branch. Bushnell now offers, aside from the yellow shooting glass that we have come to appreciate so much on the range, a gray-lensed glass that makes its wearing out hunting very comfortable. The optics are clear and the light through the gray lenses is easy on the eye. Plus, there is the protection of the high-impact shields in front of the eyes.

In speaking of black powder big game hunting there has been no mention of two weapons well suited for the task, the shotgun and the handgun. This is not to insult either, but rather it is due to the fact that the rifle has been the mainstay of the black powder hunter. A properly loaded shotgun in black powder style will do as well as its modern brother. Enough said. It will handle heavy charges of powder and either single balls or buckshot.

The handgun is still in limbo as a black powder hunting weapon. Some states allow its use, many do not. If a man were to take to the field with one, as a few have, including the extremely fine handgun hunter, the late Al Georg, he would have proper weapons available to him. The big Walker would be one of these. Designed by Sam Colt and Sam Walker in about 1847, it was made to shoot a ball that went 50 to the pound, or about 140 grains each. The huge cylinder of this nearly five-pound six-shooter holds 56 grains of powder and is supposed to drive the 140 ball at a maximum of 1,500 feet per second at the muzzle. Not having chronographed this load myself, I will not vouch for it, but even if it were less, it would be lethal in the hands of an expert shot. A .454 ball from close range will open a large wound channel.

Aside from ball, bullets can be used. They usually are not as accurate, but then, getting close, very close, is surely the object of hunting with any pistol, especially a black powder model with standard sights. By the way, scopes have been fitted to the black powder handgun with great success. Again, the hunter must decide upon the protocol of this move for himself, but it seems that a man toting a black powder pistol for big game might be entitled to a sighting advantage.

Other good handguns for hunting would be the super powerful Harper's Ferry, alluded to several times before, shooting not a ball, perhaps, though it can do so, but rather a 525-grain Minie bullet. And there is also the .44 Army model, an 1858 Remington that will shoot well. Another fine hunting handgun would be the more modern Ruger Old Army, a very accurate six-shooter capable of heavy charges because of its excellent design and construction. In the hands of that practiced cool shot the black powder pistol or six-gun would be, and has proved to be, effective. Where allowed, its use would constitute a real challenge.

The world of modern black powder big game hunting is panoramic in scope, wide open, awaiting the hunter to enter at his own pace, his own style, using arms of his choice loaded properly and fully capable of clean harvest. Hunters soon find which is right for them, and often they become crusty about their choices and will argue at the drop of a lead ball over which caliber is best, how to load for it, what to wear on the trail, what to leave at home, which way is an honorable approach to the hunt, and which is sacrilege. But one thing they all agree upon: taking that deer, bear, elk, or any big game home after it has been hunted with a single-shot black powder frontloader is one of the finest experiences of all outdoor activities.

CHAPTER 9

Small Game and the Smokepole

The black powder hunting story would be incomplete without mention of small game and frontstuffers. Small game hunting in general is immensely popular for many reasons. The hunt normally takes place close to home, conserving in time and gasoline, and is inexpensive. Little planning is necessary, and a modest amount of hunting gear is required. Game is normally abundant, meaning action for the shooter. The game is good to eat, easy to care for, dress out, carry home, package, and prepare. There is a great deal of transfer in skills from small to big game hunting. Learning how to pop a running rabbit at 25 yards can mean a lot when the hunter meets a quick whitetail buck in the brush later. While small game hunting, new equipment and methods can be tested before going after the bigger stuff.

Small game can mean anything that isn't classified as big game, but for our purposes the term applies to the little edibles, such as rabbits and squirrels. Sometimes we hunt them as a side dish to the big game main course. Sometimes we hunt the littler animals as the main attraction. Either way, black powder

119

pursuit puts back in the small game hunt what may have been lost for many of us along with our youth. The rabbit remains number one over the continent in terms of abundance, and more hunters go after him than any other game. This "whole earth game animal" is universal in distribution, and is a starter for most beginners.

The young hunter is most likely to have his first hunting encounter with a rabbit in one form or another, and that meeting will be as worthwhile on the plains as in the desert, in the mountains or the badlands, in snow or among the fall leaves. He may be hunted by innumerable methods, from chasing with dogs to glassing for him like big game. We try to kick him out of bushes along the farmlands, or cactus patches on the desert. In the northwest he makes trails through the snow that resemble elk runs, and the hunter is often bedecked like an arctic explorer as he chases the snowshoe through drifts and snowbanks.

The mundane rabbit is often teacher of the beginning hunter, not only in the area of mastered skills, but also in ethics. As a boy I chased the long-eared jackrabbits of my Arizona desert. One old jack became a memory for us; he was an adversary with two split ears that flopped over his forehead like limp leaves on a cornstalk. He lived near the Yuma Canal in a protective stand of thick grasses, and though we saw him many times, the hare had escaped each encounter unscathed. We planned and schemed, but we never got the rabbit. Not that he was so smart, or we so stupid. He was at home in his environment, and the outdoors was still an unknown for us. Many young hunters have rabbits for teachers.

The squirrel is another widespread small game animal that gives many hours of pleasure and good eating to hunters. With such names as tassle-eared, gray, Kaibab, red, fox, Abert and others, he comes in many variations on the theme. But he usually inhabits some form of forest where the hunter can scout for his favorite big game from whitetail to elk while putting bushytails in his game coat.

Hunting methods vary only a little from smokeless small game hunting to black powder, with the main difference being pace. The black powder hunt is usually a bit slower because the frontloaders have to be attended to between shots. This is not a drawback. In fact, the black powder style tends to be more relaxing, and the hunter seems to gain more of what he went out for, relaxation and communication with the outdoors. If there is one

Here, in the midst of the smoke thrown by a soot belcher, is a rabbit that became dinner that night. Knowing how to down a running cottontail at 25 yards takes considerable skill and plenty of time in the field.

caution the black powder small game hunter may want to take, it is hunting with his cartridge and shotshell firing friends. Often, they can dash ahead after that hare while the black powder man is reloading, and by the time he rejoins the chase the whole tenor of the hunt is changed. Frankly, the outing can be ruined when this mix of smokeless and smoke belcher join hands, unless there is an understanding of the goals of the hunt beforehand.

There are, basically, four types of black powder firearms used on the small game hunt. First, there is the standard rifle, the big game piece. Loaded with patch 'n ball, and petite charges of black powder, these big game getters work well on small animals because low velocity round ball does not tend to destroy much meat. Still, .50s and .58s are an awful lot for hares and squirrels, even if the latter are "barked" off the tree limb instead of hit directly. If no other gun is available, however, the big boomers can be tamed with mild loads and brought into the small game field.

Next is the shotgun, preferably the same 12-gauge double-gun that will be used on upland birds and waterfowl, as well as deer where suitable. There is no performance difference on small game between the modern or front-loading shotgun. The difference rests in the loading manner alone. In fact, the versatile black powder scattergun allows for instant switching of charges in the field to meet the circumstances. Normally, if we were to measure the distance that rabbits and squirrels, and like game, are taken, a range of only 10 to 30 yards would result. For this close-up work, the black powder shotgun can be loaded very effectively with equal *volumes* of shot and powder in a 2½-dram measure. By weight, this would be about 68 to 70 grains of FFg and ⅞ ounce of shot.

The plastic wad comes in very handy for rabbit hunting when the action is hot, for it speeds up loading greatly. Losing the approximate 100-feet-per-second muzzle velocity is of no consequence. The load with the all-plastic one-piece wad will still be traveling over 900 feet per second from the muzzle, and that is quite ample for the short-range shots on small animals, rolling a rabbit, or flipping a squirrel off its perch with no trouble at all. Shot size varies with the wishes of the hunter, but the old standby, Number 6, is hard to beat, with 5s working well on either rabbit or squirrel, too. Should the tempo pick up, and the rabbits start jumping farther out, or the squirrels take to the taller tree branches, the black powder scattergun can be quickly converted into a magnum with the 4-dram load and 1½ ounces of shot. Of course, tight fitting wadding will up the pressure and the velocity, too.

The third weapon choice is the handgun, where it is allowed by law for small game hunting. For this type of hunting the handgun is no longer a backup tool, but comes into its own as a mainline weapon, and it should be fitted with sights to match the occasion. These can be added by a gunsmith, or the sidearm can be purchased with good adjustable sights in the first place.

Carrying loads and loading for the handgun have been tertiary issues because of the ancillary use of the firearm when big game hunting, except, of course, when the pistol was carried as a main force by the big game hunter. Because the sidearm was used as a trail companion, it was carefully loaded in camp with heavy charges of powder and possibly the big conical slug. The mouths of the cylinders were sealed, sometimes with a thin ring of molten wax to start with, followed by a good grade of lube.

Now the six-shooter is the main actor on the stage, and it should be loaded with ball preferably. If the ball fits properly, a small ring of lead will be shaved off by the mouth of the cylinder when the ball is rammed home. The powder charge should be light. The combination of round ball and light powder charges usually spells fine accuracy, which is needed more than big power on the thin-skinned small game animal.

A good means of fast reloading is the use of a powder flask set for the small charge of black powder that is required. The flask is accurate enough in its dumped charge to produce good groups, and it is fast and handy to use, carried in the possibles bag usually. Ball can be carried loose in the possibles bag if the leather is clean, but the soft lead can be injured by mishandling, and it can pick up bits of dirt which will harm the bore of the six-gun. So, a ball bag can be used to good advantage. This is a small tanned leather pouch, sometimes with drawstrings, something like the tobacco containers used by the old cowpunchers who rolled cigarettes.

Some use a capper to facilitate the loading process. This device holds a quantity of caps, usually Number 11 size, and it deposits the caps one at a time on the nipple of the handgun. Some of us find loading the capper more trouble than carrying the caps in a small pouch similar to the bullet bag. They are extracted from the bag one at a time and pinched onto the nipple. When it is quite cold, however, the capper can be a welcomed accessory. A trained monkey can outshoot me with a sidearm, but many men produce small clusters with their guns at small game ranges. The secret to top accuracy in the handgun is the aforementioned round ball and light load, but it is also consistency of the loading process, being certain to put fairly equal pressure on the rammer, for example. Compressed powder, as we know, raises pressure, gives better ignition, higher velocity, and more uniform results. The handgunner must also carry along a tiny bit of thin wire, such as "piano," or a fine tapered pipe cleaner to keep the nipples clear of debris and fouling, insuring that his piece will fire on time, every time.

Weapon number four in the lineup is the very special breed of small caliber longarm designed specifically for small game black powder hunting. What a wonderful excuse to add a graceful Kentucky/Pennsylvania type to the gun cabinet. "But dear, you know how we love to eat those rabbits and squirrels. I don't want to blow them up with my big ole .50. This small-bore rifle is a necessity!" In a way, it is a necessity, like a special hunting hat or golf club.

Arbitrarily, the caliber range for this rifle would be .32 to .40, not that smaller or larger would fail, but .32 gives enough thrust for a clean quick kill, and .40 is not so large that it will rip tender game to pieces with mild loads. The best of these rifles are handmade beauties we call customs. But an awful lot of pleasure can be gained from the sound and functional under-hammers in .36 caliber, which sell for under 100 dollars, as well as many kits that can be put together for modest cash outlays, these in small calibers.

Good sights are a must on this piece, especially if the hunter intends to "bark" that squirrel from its branch, or make head shots only on rabbits. A small ivory bead is best for a front sight, especially for squirrel where the forest can be dark. The ivory stands out well in poor light. The rear sight must be adjustable, of course, and it should have a flat top with a notch wide enough so that a bit of light can be seen on both sides of the bead when it is centered. Although it would seem to the contrary, the notch-to-bead fit with light showing on both sides of the bead allows for most precise aim. The eye centers the bead almost automatically when it can see light on both sides of it, whereas the bead that fully fills the notch may be held slightly to one side or the other without detection by the shooter.

In caliber .32 the ball weighs under 50 grains. An optimum load would be 50 grains of FFFg, according to our workable rule of thumb. However, in this case, where squirrel and rabbit hunting is accomplished at close range, a charge of only 25 to 30 grains is perfect. The little rifle goes "crack!" and the game comes tumbling down fast, not mutilated, just dead. The .36 ball goes about 71 grains, and again, 71 grains of FFFg would be optimum. But 30 to 40 grains is best for small game. Velocities of the above two will fall between 1,300 and 1,700. But full charges will render speeds in excess of 2,200 for both, more than is needed for little animals up close. Of course, if the hunter encounters large varmints on his small game grounds, he may want to load full charges or go to the upper end of the special small game rifle scale, the .40, which can also serve, with top loads, on deer-sized game.

The .40 will fire a ball of about 92 grains, and with the same volume of FFFg powder it will drive that ball at over 2,200 feet per second from the muzzle, enough for fox and coyote, and deer when a good shooter is doing the job. The .40 can be loaded down with about 40 grains of black powder to give a velocity range of about 1,400, ample for small game.

Naturally, the individualistic black powder hunter is going to modify his guns and methods to suit himself, which is half the fun. But small game hunting with black powder puts back into the hunt something that has been, perhaps, missing for a long time—the thrill of a challenge. Strangely, the feeling seems to last, and men who have hunted with smokepoles for years, even on the smaller animals, still express a great deal of satisfaction in the sport. Part of the modification process comes not only in molding the firearms and loads to suit the occasion, but also in the different attitude that attends the hunt. A bag full of bushytails is a pleasure to carry home any day, taken with any weapon. But that same bag of squirrels seems elevated to an exotic station when harvested with a black powder frontloader.

In fact, some hunters prefer the small game foray to the involvement of the big game hunt. Often, these men own several long rifles and the groups they attain from them make the rest of us jealous. They have experimented with different patching materials, arriving at the perfect thickness for their particular arms. They use lubes that have proved themselves. Balls are moulded as carefully as if they were precious stones, and guarded from dents and digs the same. They have written down the results of various tests and can return to their notes for best powder/ball combinations.

Most of us will do both big and small game. But we still like to keep the two separated at least to the extent of having different possibles bags for each firearm, or a different loading technique that we rely on for best results. The stout small caliber rifles are no-kick pleasures to shoot, and they sharpen the eye of the hunter both for his small and large game hunting. The light loads for the big game rifle also allow the black powder man to become more familiar with his standard hunting caliber in a most pleasurable way.

All of the virtues of the small game hunt, from practicality to pleasure, are increased by the addition of black powder smoke to the scene. The low cost small ball shooting black powder rifle is as economical as it is effective. The shotgun in frontloader form gives all the versatility that could be demanded of any arm. The handgun is a special challenge, and a treat for those who master its use. The reward, aside from the good meat in the pot and the recreation, is embodied also in the spirit of the hunt, and in the revival of a pleasure that many of us thought we had outgrown. The acrid odor of black powder, however, turns out to be a smelling salt that snaps that pleasure back to life.

CHAPTER 10

Upland Birds the Old Way

The coastal waters of Old Mexico, near Libertad, Baja, offer vivid contrast to the surrounding landscape, one of the world's driest and most forbidding wastelands, home of the desert bighorn sheep and the scorpion. Along the sandy beaches the *cardons* and boojums are within earshot of the migrating whale, speaking their foreign language among the whitecaps. A strange place to have a first encounter with black powder upland gunning, but this is where it happened to me.

I had tired of surf casting for sea trout and *sardinaras* and had climbed a rugged coastal hill of cactus and decomposed soil so that I could watch the whales frolic below in the ocean. The cliff jutted out by the sea and I was perched atop the most stable rock I could find. As I took in the view, a "chi-qui-ta!" sound came to my ear. I looked for quail, but instead found a man I had not previously seen.

He was poised in some thick brush, dressed in khaki and sneakers. In his mouth was a call and from it came the "chi-qui-ta" that I had heard. I did not want to disturb his work; so I watched silently. Before long he got an answer, "chi-qui-ta!" And a lone bird walked in at a Sunday pace and perched himself on a dry lump of earth at the edge of the sea. I had seen these quail before, apparently a Gambel's type, and enjoyed their feeding tactics along the beach, where they rushed up to the receding waters, pecking things washed up on the beach, then fluttered madly for shore, the returning waters chasing behind.

The lone bird continued its whistle. The man stopped his. The cockbird's assembly call worked, for several other birds began to gather around the top-notched male. Almost on cue, as the last bird took its station in the covey, there was a "boom!" and a jet of blue smoke boiled into the air from the bush that secreted the Mexican hunter. Several birds toppled over.

The tennis-shoed man hopped lively over the ground and gathered up his family's supper. I scrambled down from the cliff after the strange scene and approached him. "Que tal?" (How goes it?) The hunter smiled and proudly displayed his caplock single-shot of a caliber or gauge indiscernible, vintage questionable, too, and a barrel that looked like a mast on a ship. In my poor Spanish we discussed the smokepole. I did not understand, then, what the man meant by cutting his own shot, but later found out about cubed shot, cut from sheets of lead into tiny squares.

The smoke that clung to the air that morning remained an olfactory lure, I suppose, for years later I found myself sending clouds of smoke into the air in pursuit of upland birds with black powder.

Anyone who already hunts the upland bird with modern hull-shuckers is not going to experience terrible difficulty making the switch to black powder. The essentials of the sport are the same. For those not initiated to the upland life, there are many books on the subject which can offer beginning advice on how to fill the game coat. At the same time, there are some hints and tricks that lead to more enjoyment and success using the smokey type of scattergun.

As suggested earlier, if a man is going to hunt with friends who are carrying modern guns, he had best stay on the other side of the field, or have an understanding beforehand about the pace of black powder bird shooting. If the group rushes ahead to bust another covey while the old-style hunter is pouring new powder and lead, the black powder shooter is going to be on the tail end of things all day, enduring more frustration than ful-fillment.

If a full bag is the one and only requirement of the shooter, black powder style for upland birds is best forgotten. This does not mean that the smokepole shooter can't gather in his limits. He can. But it does often take more time and patience. Hunting with an over/under 20 gauge in good quail country I have taken limits of 15 birds in a few hours. In the same terrain under the same conditions using the scattergun of black powder persua-sion I have still gotten 15 birds, but it took all day.

One of the major differences between modern and old-time shotgunning for the fast birds is lead distance and shotgun swing. I originally, and wrongfully, thought that the old gun was simply slower ballistically, thus requiring more lead. But this is not true. Later chronographing of shot loads from black powder guns proved that. Still, it became more and more appar-ent that I had to lead farther ahead of the fast bird, and swing my shotgun with more alacrity, if I wanted to put a bird in the bag. The reason for this is lock time. In other words, there is a greater delay between the pulling of the trigger and the shot leaving the barrel, due to a slower ignition as well as hammer fall. When I learned to swing a little faster on the bird and get a bit more out in front, more game was dropped. Lead style differs among shotgunners and for the bird being hunted, of course. On those upland birds which normally rise in front of the shooter from cover, such as quail, partridge, and pheasant, a good way to lead is swiftly mounting the shotgun, blotting the bird out with the silhouette of the barrels, and pulling the trigger *while the gun is still in motion.* If the swing of the gun is smooth and in the same direction of the bird's flight, a hit will be scored.

On the crossing shots, the secret to knocking them out of the air with the black powder gun is, again, plenty of lead and a fast swing, with the gun going off *during* that swing. Taking high-speed photos of good shotgunners, it has been learned that many things happen when a hit is scored. One of these is follow-through. The barrel will have continued to swing *beyond* that point where the shot was turned loose. Another thing learned from studying high-speed photos of shotgunners in action is that most men score best when their knees are relaxed, rather than locked. And most do better when the forearm of the gun is gripped quite loosely, rather than held tightly.

The shotgun, be it modern or ancient, sends out a string of shot, not a cloud of shot. Picturing this string in the mind, it is easy to see that too much lead is hard to have. After all, if the first part of the string misses the bird, there is more shot on the way to connect. But too little lead spells certain failure, for if the first part of the shot string is too far behind the bird obviously *all* the shot is too far behind. In short, the idea is to put the beginning of the shot string in front of the bird's flight path.

Aside from a bit slower lock time, there will be few other major disadvantages in black powder upland hunting, as the slow-loading technique will soon be considered an addition to the sport. The hunter will learn what loads work best on which birds. And it is no trick to develop personal loads that take the birds cleanly and efficiently. V.M. Starr of Eden, South Dakota, has used a black powder shotgun longer than most of us have been alive, and his advice for loading is simple, but tested by time and many experiments. Mr. Starr often uses a heavy cardboard $3/32$ of an inch thick for his wadding, two over the powder and one over the shot. "You can put in more wads on the powder if you wish," says Starr, "or if you enjoy cutting them, but my experience tells me that you are just wasting your time. . . ."

I have tried Starr's way and it works, producing fine loads. A variation can be laying in the two cardboard wads followed by one plastic one-piece modern wad. The seal of the barrel is accomplished by the first wads, and the plastic produces a pattern roughly 10 per cent tighter, if a tighter pattern is needed. On fast rising, close birds, such as the quail family, the plastic is best left out. Sometimes on pheasants and the plains birds, such as sage and sharptail grouse, it pays off to have a tighter pattern of shot for longer range work. The plastic has a tendency to leave more debris in the barrel, and it is wise to swab the bore out after a few shots to insure a clean barrel.

A rule of thumb is that the less choke a shotgun has the better it will handle larger shot. Naturally, shotguns can be finicky and particular, as can rifles, and it is best to pattern a load that is going to be used on game. But it is true that in some cylinder and improved-cylinder bores the bigger shot works better. A case in point was an improved-cylinder barrel that made beautiful patterns with No. 6 shot, but fairly lousy patterns with 8s. Even on the small dove and quail No. 6 was the choice for that barrel.

As for powder choice, Mr. Starr says that small granulations blow patterns. His tests have revealed many patterns with Fg powder that were better than FFg patterns. It's worth a try in any shotgun, but especially in the 12 gauges. Also, we must remember that modern black powder seems to be of a finer granule than the old stuff. Today's Fg is much like yesterday's FFg in granulation, and FFg is like the old FFFg. It's best to test each shotgun by testing the patterns on large sheets of paper, as described earlier.

On upland game the smaller gauges come into play. The 16 gauge with three drams of powder and 1⅛ ounces of shot is excellent for birds, and also works well keeping the three drams of powder and dropping to only one ounce of shot, which opens the pattern a bit. The 20 gauge is also good, with 2¼ drams of powder and ⅞ ounce of shot. A very light 20-gauge load is two drams of powder and ¾ ounce of shot for quail and dove at close range. In all of the above FFg is the smallest granulation of powder suggested, and Fg works better in some guns.

Carrying the components for the shotgun must be an organized and practiced method or birds will be leaving the county as the hunter fumbles in trying to load his gun. Starr's methods are simple and practical. He uses a shot flask and a powder flask with adjustable spouts. After setting the flask for the powder/ shot charge he wants, that operation is done for the day. Wads, the heavy cardboard type, are all kept in one pocket since they are all the same size and thickness. In another large pocket, caps are carried. In reloading, a charge from the powder flask is dropped directly down both barrels, followed by two wads in each barrel. Then the shot flask is tipped into action, throwing its measured dose in, and a wad is rammed home over each charge. A cap is placed on the nipple, or nipples, and the job is done.

I have two beautiful matched horns that I carry when hunting birds. Each horn has a spout that can be unscrewed and replaced with other spouts of longer or shorter length to vary the amount of shot or powder. This set was made by the black powder arms maker, Dale Storey. The horns are carried slung crossed over the chest, where they ride one under each arm. For reloading, the lever on the powder horn is tripped and the thumb is held over the mouth of the spout. Then the lever is released. The powder is caught in the tube and then transferred to the barrel, followed by over-powder wads. The same action renders a shot charge, and it is topped by a wad. Then the caps are fitted on the nipples and the hunt continues.

This arrangement works very well for the smaller birds, where many shots may be fired. Generally, the littler birds have greater limits and a man may fire 40 or more times a day. The shot horn is heavy when loaded, but this problem is overshadowed by the large number of loads the horn will hold. Also, the shot horn works best with smaller shot, large pellets having a harder time flowing through the cutoff bar.

When going to the larger game, such as the sage grouse, where limits are two or three birds, a simple method of carrying loads is used. In the possibles or coat pocket 35mm plastic film containers are carried, half of them holding the shot charge that was premeasured commensurate with the bird being hunted, and the other half loaded with an equal *volume* of powder. After shooting, the powder container is extracted from the pocket, the top flipped off, and the charge poured home. The wads are inserted, followed by the same pouring of the shot from the plastic film container, and the over-shot wad is rammed down. Cap and shoot.

Two important tricks in the loading process are blowing down the barrel after shooting and nipple priming. The first rule, blowing down the barrel, does not apply so stringently to the rifle because it is normally not fired in rapid succession. The shotgun, of course, can be, especially out upland bird hunting. Blowing down the barrel gives an oxygen supply to any sparks remaining, causing them to burn out before the next powder charge is poured down. However, blowing a little bit, and then immediately sending powder downbarrel can be worse than not blowing at all, because the draft has actually ignited the lingering spark and now the charge hits it. Blow, wait a few seconds, blow, then load, is the byword. Another mistake is priming nipples on the shotgun. While in a rare few cases there will be a rifle that fires better for priming the nipples, the practice is almost always negative. Priming the nipple loads the powder charge right up to the face of the cap. Now the cap ignites that powder, which must burn before the main charge is reached. Anyone can see that this is actually adding to the lock time and a mighty poor practice, the opposite of what we want, which is the fastest possible lock time. Ideally, the nipple itself will be clear. The spark will dart down into the nipple, through its hole, and strike the main powder charge—the more directly, the better. When

Sage hens are extremely interesting upland game for the black powder shot-gun. Here, a limit of three birds was taken with a 12-gauge Navy Magnum muzzle-loading shotgun. The load was a full charge of powder behind 1½ ounces of #5 shot using over-powder wads as well as one-piece plastic wads.

the cap's spark has to ignite the primary charge before it can light the main charge, this is known as a "cook-off."

As already stated, the styles of hunting upland game with black powder are much the same as with smokeless. Good dog work is still a joy to behold, whether the bird is smoked down with an old "meat in the pot" double caplock or a modern repeater. And working the fields to jump birds is again the same. The major differences lie in the black powder methods of loading and carrying loads and in the philosophy of the hunt. The modern soot shooter has to be content with a slower pace, usually, and this almost always turns out to be a plus. The rewards are supreme when the man masters his loading technique and shooting style and can bring home the birds with the old smokepole.

The challenge is somewhat greater with black powder, of course. On dove, so small, so fast, and so difficult, there is a real thrill in being able to bag a limit as the birds cross fields or desert expanses. If they are flying high, the black powder man can quickly change his load column, going to more shot or powder, depending upon what he is after, tighter patterns or more speed. Often the tighter patterns are best, because usually those birds are not nearly as high as they appear to be. Dove are small and seem very far away when they are flying up over the head of the shooter. A good way to prove this to oneself is to watch pigeons as they fly over tall buildings in the city. A pigeon flying near the top of a 10-story building, which is about 100 to 120 feet up, looks like a fly speck on a window. Actually, it is only about 35 yards away, which is a deadly range for a well-loaded smokepole.

The truly successful black powder upland hunter has adjusted his philosophy so that he gains great rewards from whatever he experiences in the field. He may have but one bird, but he appreciates that bird. And as his expertise widens, he usually catches up with his old smokeless shotgun record anyway, especially if he uses his imagination. Our quail caller at the opening of this chapter had his way of feeding the family, a plan which we don't use because we want much more than the meat of the birds we hunt, and because we honor the game by keeping the odds balanced. However, there is nothing wrong with using the call to locate birds in the first place, thereafter hunting them on foot and shooting them on the rise.

Often, I have employed my binoculars while dove and quail

This nipple is shown in the upright position, as well as lying on its side to indicate the small hole in the bottom portion. The reason for the small exit for the flame is to avoid a cook-off, where the spark from the cap ignites the powder up into the nipple itself and then has to smolder down into the main powder charge. With the small hole, the spark flashes right into the charge and ignition (lock time) is faster.

hunting in the Southwest, where we spend our Christmas holidays black powdering three kinds of quail—Gambel's, scaled, and Mearns—as well as other game. The glass often locates that flight across the desert, where the dove are traveling from water to feed, or vice versa. This fast bird is open season in parts of the Southwest during the winter months, and he is a rewarding target. The man who takes home one dove for three shots is doing well on them. An attitude can change, and when a man is bragging about his hunting ability, that is, getting close and taking his game cleanly, he is doing much more than when he speaks of long-range shooting in which some of the birds are hit hard, but others crippled.

Aside from the loading tricks and maneuvers, the black powder hunter tends to pick up other information about his upland birds that help him fill the bag. He learns about natural camouflage, that he is better off nestling into the brush facing incoming birds, rather than getting behind the brush, this actually concealing him better through more blending. He finds out the nature of his birds, and switches loads as the day progresses and the quail are growing wilder as hunters scurry over their territory.

All the upland birds can be successfully harvested with black powder guns. Mr. Color, the Chinese ringneck, looks even more beautiful when seen through the blue haze of black powder smoke. The Hun, sharptail, huge sage hen, prairie chicken, dove, chukar, wild pigeon, snipe, ptarmigan, and all the quail—the Valley, Mountain, Gambel's, scaled, bobwhite, and Mearns—are fine fare for the old smoke-belching shotgun. Sometimes the wild turkey, too, is considered on the upland list, especially when we hunt him in close cover, or with a call, getting our shots up close. A heavy charge of a full 4½ drams of black powder and 1½ ounces of shot works well on this big bird, as it does on geese, especially with a plastic one-piece wad to help hold the shot string close together and as short as possible.

Often, the black powder uplander picks out a favorite bird after a few years, and mine has been the Mearns quail. He lives in some of the most fortunate country in the world, the southern terrain of Arizona and on the Mexican border, a rare quail as far as range goes, but quite plentiful in his own domain. This is a country of deep grasses, hilly, working its way up into the blue mountain ranges that normally surround it. On the horizons, purple rimrocks rise up like castles and small white washes crisscross the land like roads on a map. All over, the small oak, referred to as the "live oak" in that area, dominates. The Mearns, also called harlequin, lives in coveys of up to 10, sometimes 15, birds, and hunting him means walking a lot behind a good dog. Although it is not as pretty as we might like, a sling on the shotgun is very welcome as the day wears on, especially since most of the birds will be shot at over the dog. These quail hold tight and will let the hunter walk right by. The all white meat of the almost round bird is plump and tender, a special flavor imparted, perhaps, by its diet of tubers and bulbs that it digs for, leaving tiny craters in the earth where it has worked. The only thing that makes this prince of birds taste even better is a liberal dousing of black powder smoke before cooking.

Is there really any difference, then, between shotgunning for upland game with a modern weapon and going after the same game with a frontloader? The answer to that question is best experienced in the field, but for most men who would pick up a book of this nature, the response is going to be a definite yes. There is something new to master, the loading and shooting of the old-style gun. Sensitivity to the sport is heightened. Something like the safecracker who files his fingertips to gain a better feel of the wheels he turns, the black powder hunter seems to gain a greater sense of the hunt with the smell of soot and smoke on the wind. Sometimes his bag is not as heavy, at least not at first, but each individual bird is appreciated more because the hunter stuffed the load that took the bird himself, with his own hands, powder, shot, and wads. It's like getting a little closer to your work, and at the end of the day each bird taken remains a picture on the mind, from the cover it broke out of, to the boom of the gun and that perfect shot that brought the game cleanly to bag.

CHAPTER 11

Waterfowling with the Black Powder Shotgun

One cold day two youths snuck along the bottomlands of Montana in quest of trophies. One of the sixteen-year-olds, the normal fellow, carried a standard single-shot break-open shotgun. The other toted, with pride, an odd-gauged "flinchlock," of questionable ancestry and sporting a 52-inch barrel. It looked like a flagpole without the flag. On approaching a small pond, a flock of bluewing teal whistled overhead. The boy with the smokepole thrust the preposterous barrel into the air with plenty of lead and touched off. Three things happened.

First, a lone duck wheeled out of the sky like a stricken fighter plane, splashing down into the water with a resounding smack! Second, the boy with the contemporary gun was also down. In a curious desire to see what was going to happen, he had rushed up beside the flintlock, his face right next to the spark tosser when it went off. Fortunately, he was not harmed, but the flash of light and deluge of smoke literally shocked him off his feet. Third, the shooter of the strange gun was himself all but decked, tilted off balance by the gun's recoil when he fired.

A fourth thing happened that day. His first duck with black powder in hand, the lad was stricken with an incurable case of black powder fever from which he never recovered. Of all birds taken with the old-style guns, it is perhaps waterfowl that render the biggest thrills. Big ducks are trophies when a bag limit is realized with black powder guns, and geese are absolute prizes. A waterfowler already knows the thrill of taking ducks and geese from the sky, but the addition of black powder smoke to the scene paints a truly aesthetic picture, and a rewarding one.

Loading "Ole Meat in the Pot" is a familiar process to the reader by now, but waterfowling does have a few additional wrinkles. Mr. Starr had a special load that he liked on ducks, 4½ drams of powder with 1½ ounces of shot, number 4, 5, or 6, with the latter his preference because of the good patterns from his shotgun. Starr preferred Fg powder for this load. Amending it slightly, I have tried the heavy 4½-dram charge with FFg black powder and the same shot sizes in the same 1½-ounce load. It's a performer. Over decoys, where the range is short, the 6s are swapped for 7½ shot, an even deadlier combination, with a veritable cloud of pellets hitting the air.

Normally, shot and charge are balanced for best patterns, and with the heavy powder charge of a full 4½ drams, the velocity of the load is up, but so is the chance for more blown patterns. There is a reason for gaining the ultimate velocity in the case of ducks, and there is a way to cure the pattern problem. The reason for high velocity on ducks is two-fold. First, ducks and geese can be tough to bring down, especially if the shot strikes the bird when its feathers are aligned to meet the oncoming pellets. By increasing the velocity of the charge, energy and penetration are also increased. When pass-shooting is the order of the day, with shots in the 40- to 45-yard class, the larger shot sizes come into their own. On ducks, 4s and 5s are good. On geese, No. 2 shot is good. These sizes retain more energy than the smaller numbers, hence penetrate better and kill with more authority. Up close, that aforementioned cloud of smaller shot is terribly effective, for it means more pellets in the bird with the same hit, and a greater chance for a head/neck shot.

The second reason for desiring higher velocity for waterfowl is the speed of the duck or goose itself. Waterfowl have two general speeds, one being the migration, or standard-flight, rate, which is used to cover large expanses of territory, and for short flights from feed to water, water to roosting, or for scouting a place to put down. Then there is escape speed, and the Canvas-back has been clocked at 72 miles per hour for short bursts when in "overdrive." Because of these birds' ability to turn on the gas, they must be led by a good margin, and higher velocity takes some of the guesswork out of that lead. In spite of the increased velocity, the fast-flying birds still require a good lead, swing, and follow-through when they are using escape speeds.

Remembering the slower "lock time" of the black powder shotgun, the extra speed of shot is even more important. But we have admitted that the pattern can be somewhat less uniform by the addition of powder to the load. And we know that pattern is most important to good shotgun effectiveness. A way to put back some of the pattern capability of the gun while using the off-balanced powder to shot load is the use of the one-piece plastic wads mentioned earlier, especially the Herter type, which are pinned together at the slit, preventing the charge from scattering immediately upon leaving the muzzle. Also, the Herter type has capacity commensurate with its declared cup size. In other words, a 1½-ounce wad holds about 1½ ounces of shot, whereas other brands allow some of the shot charge to ride up above the mouth of the plastic wad. The shot string hangs together a bit longer when confined in the longer unit, giving a denser pattern at the longer waterfowl ranges.

Another aspect of the loading method for waterfowl is that good black powder 12-gauge double duck guns can be bought today that have full and full barrels. These offer tight patterns so useful for longer range shooting, but they are also harder to load, and though ducks and geese do not necessarily require the loadability that some upland birds call for, it is still nice to be ready when that second flock bursts in, seemingly from out of nowhere. A partial cure for the full-choke loading problem is the use of the plastic one-piece wad, again. A good trick here, how-ever, is gluing a felt wad on the base of the plastic tube itself. This helps to seal the bore, something that is needed when using the usually undersized plastic wads. And it means more speed in loading, too, for the one unit can be rammed downbarrel ready to go, felt always in place. A quick-dry cement is good here, such as the new touch-dry glues.

Another plus factor of the plastic wad is its safeguarding of the bore and choke should a nonlead shot be used, such as the new steel type becoming prominent today. Steel shot can be rough on the barrel, and the plastic offers some protection

Loading up for the big stuff, such as large ducks and geese, a tight pattern can be obtained by using a very carefully constructed load. First, the cushion wad is pressed down firmly on the powder charge–cushion wad shown on the far left–and then a one-piece plastic wad is pushed down on the cushion wad. The selection of wads is great and varied. Here are a few. On the left is a cushioned wad and next to that is the same wad cut off with a knife. The wad in this column is for restraining the shot, and the cushion effect is not necessary. Next to that is a wad which is slit, and will contain 1¼ ounce of shot, but can be used with 1½ ounce of shot. The wad on the right is slit, but the slits are not open at the top. This wad holds a full 1½ ounces and will offer a very tight pattern. Over the shot wads are .135 cards cut in half, as shown on far right.

against scoring. Original black powder shotguns can have thin barrels, which could be ruined by steel shot. Again, the tall plastic wads offer the most protection. The use of steel shot, incidentally, is a conservation measure based upon findings that date back to at least 1919, when it was learned that as few as six No. 6 pellets ingested by a duck could spell death to the bird in less than two weeks' time. Ducks love to pick up the shot, partly as a digestive aid, since the pellets act as small stones do in the gizzard, grinding foodstuffs. The duck has no instinct that tells him of lead poisoning.

While we have discussed the waterfowl gun as a full and full weapon, it must be recognized that the upland game-getter with modified and improved cylinder chokes is also very effective, even for geese. Remembering that large shot patterns well in guns of more open bore, the shooter will understand that a heavy dose of big pellets can be a deadly blow at modest to medium-long ranges. Getting close, already discussed in an earlier chapter, is quite possible in waterfowling, and not only by using the duck blind or the goose pit. There are other ways, to be described here in mild detail. Of course, the gun has to be mastered first, not only shooting it, but loading properly and with facility. And there is another point about the modern black powder double barrel. Even in the full and full waterfowl version it is a very light piece, often under seven pounds. The big 4- and 4½-dram charges with 1½ ounces of shot can be kickers. The hunter will welcome the cool "duck" weather, for it means a padded coat that takes almost all the sting out of the recoil.

Getting close is important, not only for the sake of clean harvest, but also because the black powder shotgunner is going to be limited to two shots. He has to make them count. Two shots per pass are it. But this is hardly bad. It only means that the shooter must be patient and careful, waiting for the good opportunity and passing up the doubtful ones. The sporting level is raised. The hunter knows that his hits will be deadlier at the closer ranges and he is conserving his game. The overall reward using the old-style guns is apparent when the gunner gets close and takes home a good ratio of birds per shots fired.

One way to get close, alluded to earlier in the book, is camouflage. Here, duck and goose hunting, camouflage is generally acceptable and safe. Naturally, the bright orange patterns are of no use, since the birds see in color. But recently we have been given extremely effective colors and patterns, such as the Flexnet suits that Royal has introduced. With a face mask in place, ducks and geese will work right in on the hunter. The hunter blends well into the vegetation. Naturally, decoys will help put the birds even closer. And blinds need no introduction as to their effectiveness when built properly.

I recall hunting a series of small ponds that were fed by warm water springs. In the dead of winter, toward the end of the season, these ponds were still open and frequented by ducks, but the land was flat and there was little to hide behind. Duck hunting, in spite of good flights, was very spotty until a camouflage method was put into effect. When I was decked out from head to foot, including the face mask, ducks came right into the ponds, usually flying overhead at a good speed, but sometimes actually dropping to the water near me, making for two good bursts of smoke, soot, and shot into the air.

While I huddled in the cattails in a Flexnet suit patterned for that background, there was a lot of exciting action. Often, the ducks could not be seen until they were almost on top of the ponds, but I learned to listen for the whistling of their wings, and after locating them by ear, I would be ready as the fast birds winged by. Using a sustained lead, and shooting with the barrel still in motion, with lots of follow-through, I compiled a good score on the ducks and took home many limits of seven birds a day from the warm water lowlands.

Puddle-jumping for ducks may have the connotation of shooting fish in a barrel, but this need not be the case at all, and in some areas it is about the only reasonable hunting method. The virtues of puddle-jumping for ducks are many, and hours of hunting have been enjoyed in the desert regions, where small ponds called "tanks" dot the countryside. Ducks come into these and the method of stalking is almost like big game hunting. Often, the birds are spotted from a very long distance, sometimes with the aid of binoculars. And then the hunter must approach the waterhole without being seen or heard, not easy when the keen senses of the duck are at work. If the hunter can approach the pond at the right point, where the ducks were last seen, and if the ducks are still there, he usually must make a mad dash from the last piece of sparse desert cover to the edge of the tank, shooting at the birds as they rise to flight. Usually, the shots will be relatively close, but they can be fast and very misleading. Plenty of ducks have been missed as they curve out over the water heading for gray skies.

The hunter should not try to get more than two ducks as they depart the pond. Flock shooting is unproductive and unsporting. A few stray pellets may hit a bird, only to wound it when a whole group is fired upon. It is far better to pick out one bird, lead it properly, and shoot only at that bird for hit or for miss. I cock only one barrel at a time; the barrel is fired, and then I cock and shoot my second barrel. I find that this pattern is safer and more conducive to good shooting. Also, it offers a stride, a kind of rhythm. The gun rises up to position, the shooter moves forward to meet it, the hammer is cocked during the motion. The gun is shouldered and the swing and lead is put into play. After that barrel is discharged, the same motion recurs and barrel number two is used up.

One of my favorite haunts for puddle-jumping is the Northwest's high country, where beautiful blue ponds dot the landscape among pine and oak trees at elevations in excess of 9,000 feet above sea level. The colorful ducks amidst this splendor all but take away the breath. Sometimes we go into the woods with camping in mind, living out of a tent and walking a series of high country ponds each morning and afternoon. Other times we have hunted from a cabin high in the mountains, where we ride out on horseback, hunting and enjoying the outdoors all day, then returning to the cozy cabin at dusk where a rousing fire greets us. These hunts are great with any type of legal shotgun, but black powder is a pungent spice added to the hunt for flavor and appreciation.

On one such hunt I took a full limit of beautiful mallards by riding the mountain trails to vantage points where a stalk could be made after ducks were located. And I got a triple, the only one of my life. Admittedly, it was a confused duck that made up number three, but as the birds circled I was able to ram home a one-piece cushioned wad and stick an over-the-shot cardboard in place before the duck made one full circle of the pond. The low IQ bird came over me just as I finished stuffing one barrel and capping it, and the haste of the moment actually made for a smooth flow of movement that is often impossible when you "consciously" try to lead right.

Back at the cabin, we stoked up the wood burning stove and put the cleaned ducks in a dutch oven filled with water. We added two diced onions, paprika, pepper, salt, and soy sauce to the water. After the birds cooked tender on the even heat of the wood stove, cooked barley was tossed in along with cut carrots and celery. The mixture bubbled until dusk, and we ate steaming bowls of duck soup by the firelight of the open hearth. They seemed to taste better for being taken with the old frontloader that day. That evening an October chill clamped down on the mountain cabin, and we sipped a hot drink and re-shot every bird of the day.

Getting close on waterfowl, such as geese, can often mean

letting the birds move in on the hunters instead of the other way around. With geese this can mean many things, from a well-constructed blind to pits and sheets in snowy fields. A pit can be very comfortable, except in subground country—land that allows water to seep in from below. In dry terrain the pit is especially fine to hunt from. This is a waiting game, and in the Midwest I have lain in cedar-lined pits in wait for the beautiful wild birds. A welcome addition to the pit when really cold weather creeps in is a heater. The new propane types are spoilers indeed. A small tank is used, and these propane or butane heaters fit well into the blind and make it a warm wait. Decoys lure the big birds in, and the hunter springs into action when the best shot presents itself.

When snow covers the fields, a white sheet over the hunter is fine camouflage. Again, decoys help, especially oversize models. Geese and ducks cannot seem to determine dimensions and will light among huge decoys that would weigh 50 pounds if they were alive. Three dozen decoys make a good spread. Two dozen are all right. A dozen is better than no decoys, but offers much less luring power. Very large decoys are useful for hiding under, too. In a field the hunter covers most of himself with dry weeds or stalks, with the upper torso, especially the head, resting underneath the decoy itself. This works.

An interesting thing has happened to those of us seeking a hunting spot for geese, or other game for that matter. When asking the farmer for permission, we have made it a point to tell the man that we were hunting with black powder weapons only, and we have shown our guns and gear as if we were putting on an exhibition. First, this has created interest in what we were doing, but more than that, the farmer has had a chance to see that we are serious hunters, using slow-loading guns that require a lot of attention. Sure, accidents can still happen with black powder guns. But many farmers have stated that they were glad to see us come back with our "funny shotguns" to hunt more geese, or other game.

Of course, geese can be very destructive to crops, and this fact has also allowed many hunters access to private property. Sometimes whole grain fields have been stripped by both ducks and geese, and the trampling that these birds do in the fields destroys as much as four to five times more grain than the eating. In Canada so much damage was suffered that a compensation program for the farmer had to be enacted. The man was reimbursed for at least part of, if not all of the damage done by game.

As far as stalking geese is concerned, with black powder shotgun or contemporary shell shuckers, I have never had the least success. And I know of no man who has repeatedly stalked these keen-eyed birds in open fields. The goose can be called in, lured in with decoys, outwaited sometimes, outwitted some-times, but seldom stalked.

There are many other fine birds of the waterfowl breed, but most of them are of less wide range than the ducks and geese and far less known. In a few locales the huge sandhill crane is open to hunting. I have never taken one of these big birds, but I have stalked them with a camera and they seem to be much easier to get close to than geese. Their song is wild and melodi-ous and one of the finest sounds in all of nature, surpassed only, in my mind, by the loon of the far north. The little brown crane is another open season species, again limited in range when com-pared with the duck and goose.

Black powder waterfowling is the addition of another di-mension to already superior sport. The extra care necessary for success, the loading drawbacks, the clean-up required after-wards, these and more add to the thrill of taking the duck and the goose in fair chase. Black powder smoke in the waterfowl field is like adding color to a black and white picture.

CHAPTER 12

Varmints and Black Powder

From the beginning man has insisted upon control of his environment and dominion over the wild things of the land. His controls have not always brought positive results, but man would still be hunting like a caveman without his attempts at management. Hunting varmints has been considered a part of the control system, although sporting use of arms has had little effect on either game or nongame populations. Drought, foul weather, disease, habitat loss, as well as programs which do not use arms, have had much greater effect.

So it is with varmint hunting. Once the situation is out of hand, when the rodents are devouring Farmer Jones's field, and when the coyote is eating sheep like hungry kids down popcorn at the movies, the hunter will gain small inroads on the ballooned population. Adding black powder to the scene, with its handicaps, proves to be an even more fruitless situation in terms of keeping check on varmints. However, there is another side to the picture. The hunter is usually very welcome in a varmint management situation, and the black powder man is often invited with open arms. The key is management. By keeping a steady pressure on the predator population, at least a modicum of control is in effect.

Historically, the black powder hunter, with his methodical approach and slow-loading system is considered a careful person. His one and only shot is consciously aimed, for he cannot employ rapid fire. He must be cautious. He must be careful. He is noted as being responsible. If he will introduce himself to the landowner and explain his hunting style and desires, more than likely he can gain access to private property. And he is, of course, equally welcomed on public land. While he may not be able to curb an out of control predator population, he can help in terms of management. That is one reason the modern black powder hunter takes up his arms and possibles from time to time and sets forth to nab himself a varmint or two. But there are many, many reasons, good ones, for pursuing nongame animals.

Usually, the season for vermin runs long and limits are nonexistent. In terms of practice, a black powder hunter can upgrade his style and ability by leaps and bounds. As with small game hunting, only more so, he can try out new methods and equipment before the game seasons open, thereby eliminating that which does not work for him, while adopting that which does. Treated as big game hunting, the pursuit of varmints becomes an interesting endeavor; its greatest advantage is a transfer of skills and knowledge. Further, the hunter often gets a chance to scout new territory before the open season for large game while hunting varmints.

Aside from the obvious transfer of learning from the varmint hunting trip to the big game field, another very positive aspect of collecting nongame animals has been the use of their furs. Of course, with prices of furs going up, and since round ball black powder rifles do not normally tear great holes, there is the possible financial gain, but the fur is equally valuable to the black powder hunter for personal reasons. The coonskin cap or special possibles bag made from furs and skins taken by the hunter himself, tanned himself, and cut into useful products is especially pleasing and rewarding.

Black powder varmint hunting methods must differ from smokeless ways. Range and rapidity of fire, naturally, dictate a different hunting system. And this is why the black powder man is best off treating varmints as if they were big game. Once, in a field where prairie dogs were totally destroying the crop, several of us were invited to thin the rodents down. A friend and I used our black powder rifles. After a full day of hunting we had taken 15 dogs each. Another party of two used .22-250 rifles with target scopes. They had almost 100 dogs down by noon alone, after which they left. We had to stalk our prey, just as if it were big game. The long range men could shoot from great distances. The farmer may have appreciated the work of the modern rifle-man most in this case, but nonetheless he warmly invited the men with their curious smokepoles to return any time. He en-joyed watching the stalks and found the guns interesting.

Among the methods of varmint hunting with black powder are the bait-and-wait hunt, the use of blinds and trails, still-hunting in thick cover, calling, and using the vantage point with optics, as described earlier. All are effective. All can teach the hunter a great deal.

The bait-and-wait method can be accomplished in two ways. The natural bait is that which is normally located, a sheep or cow that has died on the range, or the offal left behind by elk and deer hunters. On the other hand, a dead animal can be brought to a location and laid out. Either way the hunter secretes himself and waits for vermin to show up. The method works well, but requires patience. In fact, its greatest asset is the teaching of patience. A camouflage outfit is useful here, and the hunter may also wish to employ scents to see what value they may have. A bit of lure can be splashed near the bait and the hunter can watch the varmint's reaction to it. Then, later on, this bait may prove effective by using it near a campsite and checking it daily for fresh tracks. It is well to brush the immedi-ate area with a natural broom of some sort so that the tracks of visitors will show up readily. The bait and wait can be very exciting since with black powder there will usually be only one shot to bring the animal down.

Blinds can be set up along trails or in natural feeding places. Of course, a blind can be used in conjunction with bait, too. On a trail, the hunter waits in his blind to see what will come along. The method works well in the tangle of forest and in the desert places. Late evening and early morning are the best waiting times, when the varmints will be moving out into the fields to seek their fortunes.

Still-hunting through the forest to see if varmints can be approached is a very interesting form of varminting, and is most rewarding when scouting is desired. The hunter can see a lot of new terrain while enjoying himself in pursuit of some predator or other. He will carry along with him those weapons and tools he finds most desirable for the big game hunt, thereby learning them more and more as he uses them. Sometimes very tricky shots are required when a fox or jackrabbit is suddenly encountered. Here is where shooting at running targets is learned. Naturally, this method works well in fields frequented by rodents that may be in large numbers, such as rockchucks or woodchucks. This is still-hunting and stalking at its best, except perhaps the stalk that follows the finding of vermin from vantage points.

The optics approach teaches the hunter to locate his quarry and then to stalk it to within shooting distance for that one good shot. Anyone who thinks that getting close to a coyote or other wise varmint after locating it in the distance is easy has a surprise in store. Hunting varmints in this way is a fair chase, and the man who learns to locate predators, or rodents, for that matter, and then close in for the shot, is going to find that he is much better later in the season when he must find bigger specimens and get close to them.

Naturally, many varmint hunting methods can be combined. Building a blind next to bait is one example; and adding a call to that is a further combination of black powder methods on nongame. The call is especially exciting to use because its results can be very explosive. I remember a bobcat that refused to leave after being called in. He wanted a scrap, and it didn't matter that the man who had called him was not interested in collecting his skinny hide. Head tucked low, and not daring to rise from my cover, I was squalling away on a varmint call, all decked out in camouflage and hidden in a clump of oak brush. Being well hidden, it was as difficult for me to see out as it was for the approaching animal to see in.

I wailed away for maybe 10 minutes, then decided to move on. If I get no results within 10 to 15 minutes, I usually try another spot. Normally, if nothing happens fairly soon, chances are there are no animals close enough to hear the call, or the ones who can hear it are educated and won't come in. This scrappy cat came right in, and he would not leave. I didn't want him. His fur was a tangle, and he looked like he had not had a square meal in a month. I rattled the brush around me and said, "Scat!" The fool cat let out a scream of his own and walked right into the brush with me. I guess that was enough for him, because when he caught my scent he turned tail and literally scraped claw marks in the ground beating a retreat. I had taken my Saturday bath, but apparently it had done no good as far as the cat's nose was concerned.

Calling game is nothing new, but it is just as exciting as it must have been for the first Americans who practiced the skill. Men such as the Burnhams, famous for their Texas calls, have made a science of studying calling methods and equipment. A recent development from the Burnham company is a new philosophy of calling, not the imitation of a food source, which is what the rabbit squeal is, but an attempt to mimic the call of a distressed predator. We don't know why, but often an animal giving out with a distress cry will be attacked by its own kind. The Burnhams have tried to prove their theory with a fox yelp, and so far the results are convincing. By squealing a distress cry

A coyote comes running in to answer a call. Varmints are most responsive to calling techniques in areas where calls have not been overused. In an area where call use is high, this coyote might well have run away from the sound that was meant to attract him.

of a fox, others of the same ilk have come right in ready for a fight. Calls work best, of course, where they have not been over-used. Varmints stay in high numbers because they are adaptable, not only to changes in their habitat, but also to the methods of hunting employed against them. They learn to detect the call for what it is when many hunters use a given area. I have watched coyotes actually run in the other direction from callers who are proven experts and who have a lot of success in less invaded locales.

The varmint gun to the modern hunter is usually a small caliber, .22 to .24, firing jacketed bullets at high velocity. Of course, when precious furs are being hunted, other guns are often chosen. One hunter, for example, uses a .280 Remington with heavy-jacketed target bullets so that the fur will not be badly torn. For the black powder man, however, the varmint arm takes on very different dimensions. Usually, it will be a rifle, and most often it will be the favorite arm used for big game hunting. This is wise because of transfer value. In other words, the learning takes place with the very arm that will later be used to harvest that deer or elk. In close cover, a shotgun can be employed. A 12-gauge black powder scattergun loaded hot with 1½ ounces of heavy shot and a full 4½ drams of black powder is a powerhouse. Handguns are usually quite legal on varmints, or other nongame animals. Of course, in this context, nongame means those animals listed by game departments as open season and does not at all imply that any wildlife can be taken just because it is not listed as game.

If there is an arm that might be considered a varmint black powder gun, it could well appear in two types. First, there is the small-caliber rifle such as the .36, which, in the Numrich Buggy version is a joy to handle and carry, fitting into tight places easily and going along on the informal hunt with a minimum of effort. The small caliber is nondestructive in round ball use, and can also be loaded with a conical for heavier varmint work. Some employ the little .36 on their traplines because it can be loaded way down with its small bullet doing minimal damage to hides.

On the other side of this coin is the long-barreled rifle of larger caliber designed to burn heavy charges of powder. One such rifle I know of is a custom. It is a highly accurate piece, fitted with a precision peep sight, and its stout barrel will handle strong charges. The man who learns this type of rifle might well stretch the normal range of black powder by using intelligent holdover. The larger ball or conical will have plenty of energy remaining at 150 plus yards because the varmint is going to be, on the average, smaller than any big game normally encountered. This highly accurate black powder firearm may well be considered a varminter's special for the modern smokepole user.

Perhaps the main reason for black powder varmint hunting is the outdoor experience itself. The hunter need not always fire a shot in order to be fulfilled on his expedition. In the far north one time I had two wolves walk right up to me. I had not seen wolves in that country before. They were surely not plentiful there. But here were two strolling right by me as I rested comfortably in a snowbank doing some binocular scouting work. They were no more than 50 yards away. I watched, enjoyed, and let them pass. Had I been even further north, where an excess of wolves had been decimating caribou herds, I may have fired on the predators. I may have shot if the taking of a wolf would have been a good hunting experience for me. As it was, these travelers trod their solitary way south. The hunter must decide for himself when to shoot and when not to.

There are many philosophies concerning varminting, with black powder arms or otherwise. A sensible approach is a management system. The numbers of varmints are managed, best as possible, through whatever measures are safe and sound. The key is the word "manage," which does not mean annihilation. The theory that predators cause all that is ill among wildlife and livestock valuable to man is wrong. The removal of predators would not necessarily mean more game or livestock coast to coast. The opposite view, as often promoted these days, showing the coyote and his kind as eaters of watermelons and peanut butter and jelly sandwiches, is even more ludicrous.

The black powder varmint hunter can support his claim to varmint hunting in light of many recent studies. The state of Wyoming released figures after exhaustive studies showing that sheep losses to predators of that state were $3,586,200 for one year. Even more weighty is the study by the U.S. Fish and Wildlife Service which revealed that the greatest single loss to sheep herds was again the predator. Farmers can show figures that reveal great losses to crops due to rodents. In Idaho it was clearly revealed that the coyote was a major cause of death among antelope infants. New Mexico arrived at a similar conclusion.

Each state game department determines its varmint list based upon its own studies and conditions. The larger cats, as well as some of the smaller felines, are becoming "game animals" in some states, with regular set seasons and limits, while other animals, some designated as pests, such as skunks and rodents, continue to have a year long open season with no limits enforced. In some states and provinces a nonresident, as well as resident, may hunt without a license if his targets are varmints only. A simple review of the game laws of any given state will tell the modern black powder hunter just what he can pursue, when and how, in terms of varmints.

A lot of learning attends the black powder varmint chase, and good relations can be built with farmer or rancher. The hunter can go into the field when conditions are right for him, when he has the time off, or when the weather best suits his fancy; in short, when he wants to. He can practice and develop his hunting style from finding game to shooting, and he will learn a lot about himself as well as his guns and gear as he looks for wily varmints, or waits patiently for them to find him. Later, he is better prepared for the big game challenge if he has seriously hunted for the smaller, and sometimes very slippery, creatures.

But most of all, varmint hunting with black powder is another chance to get outdoors carrying the fascinating tools of yesteryear. While 100 rodents may be gratifying to the scope-sighted cartridge hunter trying to help his farmer or rancher friend who is overrun with the destructive animals, the black powder man may have to settle for only 10 per cent of that number as his success level. But he will have earned what he has taken, having to stalk close and put that one shot just right before a wary animal dives for its hideout. The larger predators often take on the qualities of big game, too, when they have to be stalked by the man with a front-feeding sootbelcher.

CHAPTER 13

Backpacking into the Outback

If big game hunting is the highest mountain on the black powder outdoor horizon, then the "primitive arms" backcountry safari is the peak on that mountain. Hunting game in the outback with muzzle loader gives an atavistic sensation of returning to days gone by, quiet days, fulfilling times that leave lasting memories. Hunting the outback is already a fine sport. Black powder puts the icing on the cake, uplifts the experience to a new dimension. The old-style weapons bring a different thrill and sense of satisfaction. Large game, small game, even varmints, take on a heightened importance when the combination of lonesome terrain and the guns of the pioneers is blended. The big game increases in trophy dimensions. The smaller animals provide food and further hunting experience.

The backcountry can be any haunt that is away from the road. Even that first range of hills beyond the highway takes on pristine qualities when the hum of traffic is out of earshot and the skyline is free from wires and poles. Rewarding as the hunt is, however, a greater amount of planning and preparation is required when the trek gets away from civilization. Equipment forgotten at the truck is out of use the whole trip, and there are no hot dog stands to appease a voracious appetite. Ingredients of a successful black powder backcountry hunt include, aside from the planning phase, good gear and the knowledge to use it properly.

There are many styles of outback hunting. Among these are the fully guided trip, where a professional takes the hunter into prescouted terrain, staying with him until the sought-for game is bagged. The men may still backpack after reaching a main camp, or they may remain camped-in, hunting out daily and returning by evening. Naturally, this is a first-class ticket, with plentiful food and shelter provided. The guided hunt is expensive, but sometimes a man has limited time and prefers to have an expert lead him directly to good game country.

Related to the guided hunt is the outfitted safari. Here, a knowledgeable outdoorsman guides the hunter back in, often leaving him to his own resources for a predetermined amount of time, and then picking him up. Gear and supplies are packed in on horses or mules. Everything but the kitchen sink—even that sometimes—can be brought in for comfort and convenience. The outfitter knows the country and the game, and will position a man where he can do best at the given time of the hunt. Less expensive than the fully guided operation, the outfitted hunt can be a fine experience. Another close cousin to this type of hunt is the drop-off camp. Here, a guide or outfitter sets up a camp ahead of the season, sometimes providing wood and shelter. The hunter is usually driven to the camp and left there, again for a predetermined time. This is often the cheapest assisted hunt and is becoming very popular.

Another way to hunt the far reaches is with a pack mule. The animal carries the gear, of course, freeing the hunter from the burdensome task of playing pack animal himself. The man can walk leading the mule, or he can be horseback, much as the old mountain man covered the country. The surefooted animal totes the possibles in, and the game out. Some of these animals are quite wise, too, and can lead a hunter back to the ranch headquarters or the horse trailer. The mountain man often relied upon his mule as an early warning sounder as well as a pathfinder.

Still another way to enjoy the out of the way black powder hunt is by using waterways as routes of travel. A canoe or other small boat is loaded with gear and grub for the in-going trip, and game meat coming back out. A small motor can be fitted to a square stern canoe, making the upstream travel a pure pleasure. The system of boating to lonesome hunting is an excellent one, with enhancements in the way of fishing, as well as enjoying the water scenes, recommending it. In parts of southeastern Alaska even the mighty brown bear is often hunted by the waterway method.

Then there is the backpack hunt, perhaps the loftiest style of all. Here, the man is close to nature and trods into the wild places carrying on his back the essentials for the hunt. He is free, free to roam at will, sleep where he chooses, and hunt those far-off canyons, rather than returning to a base camp at the close of each day. Late in the evening, when game is roaming the woods, feeding and moving about, the backpacker is there, rather than making for the home trail. When he gets his quarry, or when he decides to bed down for the night, he stops where providence has taken him, unloads his gear and sets up camp. Sometimes the backpacker will go cross-country, being left out along a road and then striking out overland to intersect another road where he can be picked up at a prearranged time and place. Or, a man can pack into a lake or other landmark and simply stay put, setting up a small base and returning to it by evening. But he should make sure that his camp is situated in good game food country. There is little point being right out in the field while game is showing itself, and then retiring to a locale where animals are less likely to be spotted.

Gear plays a major role in the black powder backcountry hunt. Roughly, there are two categories, which we will call the software and the hardware. The software is normally considered clothing, or wearable objects of one type or another. The hardware is the tool line itself, from gun to walking staff. A man who continually works at upgrading his gear and his mastery of using that equipment, such as trying it out on small game and varmint hunts, will be much better prepared for the outback adventure. Testing tools and methods has no place on the hunt itself. Finding out that a piece of equipment is faulty or incompatible with the shooter's style, should occur long before the actual hunt.

Clothing for the primitive hunter can range all the way from copies of original leathers to the everyday hunting dress of the moment. The main consideration is the spirit of the hunt. If the spirit of the hunt is violated for the individual by dressing up in contemporary hunting garb, then he should opt for the old-style clothes. They worked fine a hundred years ago, and still fill the bill today. These are the greatcoats of hide, the fur caps, heavy moccasins, and leather shirts and pants. Looking back into Chapter Two, where the mountain man's dress was discussed, the hunter can see which clothes he likes the best, trying them out prior to the actual hunt. They are comfortable clothing, when made carefully by hand, or purchased from a reputable tailor—but they are not for everyone. A man who has tender feet, for example, will not appreciate a moccasin, unless it is custom-made with a super heavy sole of thick leather. And in rocky terrain a good solid modern boot with tough soles of synthetic material can prevent foot bruises that may occur when wearing the soft moccasin. But these points are more detailed in Chapter Fourteen.

Let it suffice to say that it is up to the individual to decide for himself what he wants to wear into the backcountry, and all the way from original to modern is fine if it does not bruise his own spirit and the flavor of the hunt to dress as his contemporaries dress. One point must be brought home sharply, however. The wilderness is no place to take chances. While the aloneness is wonderful, so is the sharing, and a party of two or four is advised over the single hunter going in on his own. Also, just to hammer in the point another notch, the gear must be tested before striking out. Clothing is for more than comfort when the truck is a brisk two day walk away. Hikers and backpackers have suffered from a type of stress that we now have a label for—hypothermia. This means, roughly, the abnormal lowering of body temperature. The human body does a superior job of maintaining its temperature, throwing off heat when it is working hard, and conserving heat when it is at rest. But prolonged activity of an exertion level that can bring exhaustion, coupled with a lack of proper food and harsh weather, can bring on hypothermia. And it does not have to be severely foul weather for this to occur. In fact, most serious cases of hypothermia have been associated with mild weather conditions.

Shelter comes not only in the form of clothing, but also in a totable house, in other words, a tent. Since the body is hard pressed to remain comfortable and healthy at more or less than 72 degrees (F), the tent becomes an essential part of the black powder man's backwoods gear. We might still classify this unit as software because it is soft and because it is carried along, usually tied onto the packframe. Tents are certainly nothing new to man; they have been around for centuries, and the Indian teepee is no more than a tent, albeit a wonderfully designed shelter that will ward off high winds and offer great protection from the cold. Tents were well known among the mountain men, too. They often preferred the Indian design, but when staying for a long period of time, they used the wall tent. A visitor to the Far West in 1842 noted that wall tents were quite popular. These are essentially the same types of tents that can be purchased today.

Some of the wall tents are of custom design, and a man does not have to travel to Omar the Tentmaker back in Baghdad to get one sewn up for him. There are a surprising number of modern tent builders around, who will take a floor plan, improve on it, and arrive at a fine shelter for the most wicked weather. These often have no floors, but are comfortably set up with straw to walk on or sleep on. The ceiling has a hole, sometimes two, cut in and lined with fireproofing so that stove pipes can be run out. With a supply of wood, these are comfortable motels in the backcountry. Naturally, they are big and heavy, and they must be brought in on horseback or by vehicle.

Then there are the modern backpack tents, remarkably light and roomy. A host of styles are available from numerous dealers. The most expensive are well worth the money, for they are homes away from home on a cold night, and can ward off a deluge of rain. An economical approach to procuring a backpack tent is to buy a kit and sew it up. These are, for the most part, the same design and material as the expensive ready-made outfits. Usually, the tent for backpacking is made of nylon with a floor. A good addition to these tents is a fly, in other words, a tent that goes over the tent. It does not add much weight, but it serves an important function. In order to remain comfortable, the main tent body has to "breathe." If it does not, body moisture will collect inside, rusting gear as well as causing discomfort. But a good breathable tent may also leak in a heavy rain. So, the fly collects body moisture on its underside, while its rainproof upper side repels water.

Another piece of personal software that acts as a shelter is the sleeping bag. I have used both the old and new styles and both work fine. The old type I had—it happened to be in Alaska—was a caribou hide for a base, which is extremely warm because the hollow hair traps insulating air. Then there was a very thick horsehide blanket on top of the hide. A softer wool blanket was next, and a terrifically heavy hair-on moose hide was over that. Sleeping with long underwear in that oldtime "bag" was a warm experience. But it was also terribly heavy, bulky, and unwieldy.

This is why the modern sleeping bag has come to the fore. There are many texts on backpacking and the gear that goes with it; this is not the place to belabor the issue. However, the discussion is important because the backcountry hunt is a rather serious undertaking and improper equipment can render the trip dangerous. A sleeping bag can be a lifesaver. The big argument today is down versus Dacron. Down usually wins because it is warmer per weight. Down bags are very light, easy to carry, and warm. But the newest Dacrons are excellent. The synthetic does not absorb moisture as readily as down, does not pack as easily, and dries faster should it get wet.

Carrying all the software, plus food, some hardware, and accoutrements requires a backpack if a mule or other conveyance is not a part of the trip. Many fine models are available in both frame and bag, with the better ones being light, tubular designs contoured for the back and fitted with padded hip belts to help distribute the weight. The bags themselves are rip-stop nylon, strong and capacious. Modified backpacks are also wise. The major modification is by way of adding little projections from the frame. One projection can be used as a sling support; so the heavy black powder rifle need not be carried by hand nor slung directly on the shoulder. Also, the metal projections can be used to hang other gear on. They are handy and easily fitted by drilling a hole through the tube of the frame and using bolts and nuts. The metal piece itself is simply a cut-off strip with a hole in it.

All kinds of things go into the bag, from food to extra black powder and parts for the rifle. Capacity for just about any hunt should be about 3,000 or more cubic inches for the bag in order to carry all this load. Again, there are many guides to consult concerning what to take on a backpack trip or hunt. But the black powder man is going to have to work up his own list by first looking at a basic list, and then trying his own modification of it. He must have his possibles along, which in this case will mean his field care and repair kit as described in Chapter Seventeen. Extra powder can be carried in a small tea tin. These have two lids, actually, an inner and outer covering, and will not leak powder, nor admit moisture.

A sheath should be carried. At night the unloaded rifle can be encased so that it will not attract body moisture in the tent. The sheath of tanned hide is excellent, and can be made by the hunter, as shown in Chapter Sixteen. As part of the hardware, a small backpack stove may be included. In country where wood is hard to find, this little item is especially welcomed, but where there is ample natural fuel a "mountain rock stove" can be built. There is a lot of comfort in this stove, for it is constructed of natural materials and then dismantled on leaving the spot so that all will be natural once again. The mountain rock stove is simply an arrangement of rocks. A feeder fire is built, and coals from this are transferred into a shallow two-foot-by-two-foot pit. A long rock at the front of the pit serves to keep frying pan handles cool. Little rocks around the fire are used as food warmers. Rocks around the fire serve as windbreakers. On a more permanent camp, the rock stove is expanded and can even have a chimney.

A central part of the hardware, of course, is the hunting tool. Forever we are pinned down as to what caliber suffices when the game can range all the way from edible tidbits such as squirrels and rabbits, all the way to elk or moose. If an answer simply had to be formulated, the .54 caliber would probably gain a first position on the list of calibers. The .54 is well balanced. It will toss a ball of decent proportion, and it will also, of course, shoot a ball at small game velocities. And then it will propel a big bullet at very good velocities.

But another arm must be considered for backcountry hunting and that is the handgun. The big .44 Ruger, for example, or the .44s, such as the Remington, Walker, and Colt types—even smaller calibers. Sometimes rapid fire is important. On one lonesome trail a fellow hunter encountered a big grizzly. He certainly did not want to harm the animal, but he did not like the idea of becoming a meal, either. By firing his six-shooter into the air several times the bear was frightened off. Our man did not want to expel his only big round from his rifle, leaving himself unarmed; so the handgun was ideal in this rare situation. Should a man become lost or injured, the handgun can again come into play because of the universal three-shot signal system. Firing three shots close enough in succession with a single-shot frontloader can be a feat.

Another fine arm for the backcountry hunt is the shotgun. Broken down, even the full-size double guns can fit into the bag or on the frame somewhere. These shotguns are light, some not much over six pounds. They will serve not only for small game edibles, but also for waterfowl that are occasionally encountered on ponds or lakes in the backcountry in season. Forest grouse may also be available.

A piece of equipment mentioned before, and deserving of mention again, is the walking stick, or Moses stick, as we have named it. This chunk of hardware is a must, not only for its shooting and glassing aid, but also for its original purpose, as a hiking staff. A twisted ankle way back in the woods is more than a twisted ankle—it is a serious handicap and can even be dangerous. And a fall is even worse. The hiking staff can very often prevent these potential hazards.

Of course there is the game-finding binocular, another piece of hardware. And there is cutlery, which includes knives, possibly a meat saw, and for farback work, some sort of hatchet or tomahawk. The hawk is better aesthetically; but only if it is a working model, and not an all-brass show piece. Chapter Fifteen discusses knives and hawks for the black powder hunter, and the essential method of using the cutlery set in the boning process. Taking the meat out of the woods is not only a matter of law in most places, but also a matter of ethics. If a man can't get it out for use, he had best hold fire. By using boning methods, the meat can be packed out of the woods, leaving the skeleton behind.

Food is a matter of personal taste, even prejudice, and no one can dictate a diet for the backwoods black powder hunter. Some enjoy carrying the freeze-dried foods; others prefer to eat off the trail in part, supplementing what meat they can get with rice, beans, and other staples out of the backpack. Of course, the man in the big backcountry camp who has been packed-in has no problem. He can cook up what he wishes right on a stove that works about as well, sometimes better, than the one he has at home.

I prefer to carry the staples and trust in my luck to come upon in-season meat. Hunting with two black powder friends one season, night fell upon us and we were backpacked into a

The amazing Moses stick, a homemade device with dozens of uses for the modern black powder hunter, is employed here as a signalling device in heavy brush so that hunters can keep track of each other's locations.

thickly wooded zone at least three miles from the nearest road. "Supper time," one of the men announced, and he sat down by our campfire and began opening packages. "Space Age food," he said, and his partner got busy and tossed in a couple more Space Age delights. I figured I would give it a try.

The men had been riding me hard all day about my clothes, and a little gremlin inside of me was craving revenge. I was going to take one bite of their dinner offering, for I was an invitee for the supersonic treat coming up, howl like a wolf with a belly full of strychnine, roll on the ground, and shout that I had been poisoned. The chiding had not ceased. One of the fellows, who, admittedly, had a buckskin outfit that I envied, laughed about my faded denims and old cowboy hat. The other man, also decked out in homemade garb fashioned from buckskin, put an exclamation point at the end of each goading sentence the first one levelled at me.

Then it was my turn. "Oohh," I began, "that's poison." But it wasn't funny, because I wasn't kidding. I recognize that some brands are better than others, and perhaps my amigos had picked a particularly bad batch of trail food, but after honestly trying a couple of main courses—one was supposed to be meat and potatoes—I gave up. The meat and potatoes looked like, and tasted like, a few chunks of heavy cardboard soaked with grease surrounded by plaster of paris. I reached into my coat and took forth a large forest grouse, clean as the air I was breathing in the pines. A tad of lard was placed in my small fry pan, and in went the meat. I had some premixed pancake batter, and I whipped that up, too.

The pancakes were not store bought. They were stoneground flour that my wife milled at home, with baking soda, powdered buttermilk, and eggs, salt, and sugar. Water added, they turned out pretty fine, though not as good as they are at home with all fresh ingredients. I like my friends. They shared my food with me. They continued to tease me about my nonprimitive clothes, but they never brought up the topic of trail food again. True, my grub weighed a bit more than theirs, but packing the extra weight was worth it to me, and seldom do I go a whole day without running across at least a rabbit or squirrel that can be bagged for supper.

Food, then, can be anything the backpacker desires. The man in the big camp has limitless options, too. Going too far in any direction can be a problem, however. Carrying 40 pounds of eats on a three-day trip is not using common sense. On the other side of the coin, an Alaskan guide friend who is a black powder hunter goes out for weeks at a time living on only what he can carry on his back and bring down with his rifle. What he carries for food is oatmeal, and a few raisins. He boils the oats, throws in the raisins, and chows down. Meatless nights are pretty ho-hum in his camp.

Employing all of the tricks of black powder hunting is especially important in backcountry black powder work. Following the rules of caring for and repairing guns and gear is essential. Having that rifle personalized is also important. Carrying an unslung black powder nine- or 10-pounder can make one arm longer than the other in only three days. And after working for a few days to find that game spot, then getting a good chance and muffing it because of a hasty load or a rifle not sighted properly is defeating. All of the house has to be put together, brick by brick, for outback success. Failing to seal a gun with wax and balloon is an oversight on a weekend hunt, but could be a real frustration on a long backpack hunt. The practiced hunter is rewarded when he whips out his "readyloads" for that second shot and makes the grade.

You must also stay "found" while on the backpack hunt. Most men are not natural born pathfinders, nor do we get a lot of practice in finding our way in the wild places, unless one considers the morning rush traffic a challenge. Those of us who have a natural sense of direction have little trouble. We are always lost. "I'm sure the main camp is this way," I have said to myself, as I trod off 90 degrees opposite from the right trail. Fortunately, there are some ways to keep from "getting turned around," which is the euphemism that saves face for those of us who get lost.

First consideration is reading a map. A hunter's cartography is a fascinating subject, and using a topographic map is not difficult, especially if it is simply to take note of the major landmarks with a compass to stay in the right direction of travel. An even simpler means of staying found is to start out with compass in hand and hunt in only one direction from a known landmark, staying in that direction all day, and reversing the direction at the close of the day. Of course, on longer hunts this still works, though the hunter may be in the woods for a week. He knows that he is "so many days south" of his starting point this way.

The cross-country trip is also a good way for us to stay found.

Many wild places are marked off by highways or major roads. If you are left off on one and follow the compass faithfully in a single direction the other road will appear. It works every time. The topo map can show what lies in between the roads since there could be a 10,000-foot mountain to cross on the way from road one to road two.

A man who travels along a river or stream is going to stay found, too. And there is plenty of good hunting in such country. Often, a river or other waterway will lead into magnificent wild country, and getting lost becomes a small concern when that big shiny ribbon below is forever pointing the way home. Naturally, the perimeter of a lake serves the same function, and again, there is a lot of good hunting around lakes, as well as some remote and uninhabited country.

Landmarks are useful, and a big peak can keep a person going in the right direction. Hunting only one canyon can lead a man into vast expanses of country, as some canyons run for miles and miles and usually turn out to be fascinating places to hunt. Having a watch along is also helpful. I often watch my watch when I hike out. If I go into the sun for two hours, I have a pretty good idea that two hours in the opposite direction will at least put me back in the same area, if not the exact starting point. Naturally, up north, one has to be careful as winter sets in because the sun no longer comes up and goes down. It sort of rolls around the heavens right at the horizon in its short day, popping up like a bashful child hiding behind its mother's skirts, and just peeping out for a while and then disappearing again.

Another interesting way to hunt, and stay found, is to use railroad tracks as a guide. Up in Alaska, for example, there are iron trails through vast expanses of wild country. A man simply cannot get lost, yet he is on public property for the most part, and he stays off of any right-of ways. He simply uses the steel road as a map. Couple the tracks with a topo map and the lay of the land can be determined ahead of time and a hunter will know what he is going to encounter.

Backcountry black powder hunting puts it all together. It is like a state championship after a team has mastered all of the regular competition. The men, and it is suggested that at least two go together, are on their own. They have their skills tested often, but by carrying the proper hardware and decking out in the right software, chance for harm is quite small. My longest outing was 30 days in Sonora, Old Mexico. I had a river to guide my feet, and the country was as lonesome as any I have ever encountered. The hunt was pure recreation in the best sense of the word, re-creation. I felt like a new man and was certainly as healthy, if not healthier, at the end of the trek. The food was gathered wild mostly, augmented by what I carried on my back. It was a step back in time, and it would not have been complete without the charcoal burner along to add that last touch of nostalgia.

CHAPTER 14

What to Wear and How to Use Your Gear

An important facet of black powder hunting is being "set up" comfortably and adequately in the field with the proper outfit to get the job done. The powder horn that fits just right, the possibles bag that doesn't do a jitterbug while the hunter is hiking or stalking, pants that don't bind, shirts that keep the weather out, while holding body heat in, hats that repel the sun as well as the rain, and footgear that protects quietly, these and more are a must in order for the hunter to return from the woods in the same, or better, condition than he started out in. These attributes are important to all hunters, of course, smokeless as well as charcoal burners; but they are not as easy to come by for the modern black powder man because he is trying to combine intelligent gear with aesthetic appeal. It isn't that we can't survive as the mountain man did; in fact, times are easier in terms of living our days in the forest. After all, in the continental States chances of running across a marauding grizzly are, perhaps unfortunately so, rarer than finding a wad of money on the sidewalk of the city.

And there are no encounters with those who would like to offer an extra-close haircut either.

But at the same time, the modern hunter is not a product of the outdoors. He does not spend most of his time there, nor does he enjoy a day-to-day relationship with mother nature. Even those of us who make a living directly, or indirectly, from the woods and open spaces find ourselves more often behind a desk than leaning up against a pine tree in the middle of nowhere. We have to be prepared in wise gear and garb to make our hunts safe and enjoyable, as well as successful, both in terms of getting our game and in having a quality outdoor experience. Part of this success, in terms of black powder hunting especially, comes from our choice of clothing and packable gear.

For the most part, the modern black powder hunter ends up being a crossbreed between the old and the new, with a few rare exceptions. One of those rare exceptions is a modern-day mountain man who lives his whole life as did his forebears. His name is Ridge Durand to his white friends, "Tate Wakpa Wanbli," or Wind River Eagle to his Oglala Sioux Indian friends. He lives on a 3,000-acre ranch in the Never Summer Range of Colorado, remote country that looks across the Wyoming border. Durand, as described by one fellow, was dressed in a skunk hide hat, his long black hair making a pattern with the white stripes. His coat was made entirely of animal furs, wolf pelt for the front and back, with pine martin skins for the shoulder, raccoon sleeves and ermine decoration here and there. There were no boots on his feet. He had them wrapped.

Since preteen years the Wind River Eagle has spent his life in close approximation of the venerable mountain man he so honors, living a simple life in the woods, making most of his own gear, and doing personal art work in the little cabin that he calls home. The original part of his cabin dates back to 1874, and since other rooms have been added. The cabin is decorated with "mountain man art," necklaces carved richly, wood carvings, Indian designs on pelts. Ridge has even formed tools and traps, guns and gear from scraps.

The part of the fascinating modern-day mountain man that pertains to the average hunter who has taken to smokepoling is the fact that in his handmade and ancient gear the Wind River Eagle has trekked across the land on foot, ending up at his destination happy and secure. What he wore on his feet for these trips is not certain, but one "outing" took him from Vancouver,

Washington, to Laramie, Wyoming—on foot, 37 days and 1,200 miles. He again took a long trip with only his legs to carry him, this time from Missoula, Montana, back to Laramie, Wyoming, living entirely off the land as he went, or from what he could tote with him.

The moral of the story is that it can be done, even today, and the black powder hunter who wants to make his own garb from head to foot can do so, successfully. But this style is not going to fit the average man who reads the *Wall Street Journal* Friday and heads for the outback Saturday morning. Wonderfully comfortable moccasins at home around the fireplace and on the carpeted floor can become rags over broken rock, leaving feet looking like hamburger, and a rain-soaked animal pelt is no more than a soggy shroud on the trail. In a snowstorm or on the top of an Alaskan sheep peak a lot of the romantic gear of yesterday can become more of a burden than a boon to the modern man accustomed to thermostatically controlled heat in his city apartment back home.

With this in mind, and remembering that for the man who feels he wants to, and can, go full primitive we give our blessings, what should the modern "average" black powder hunter dress in and carry in his days afield? Starting at the bottom, there are the shoes, footgear. In warm woods on an autumn day, a thick-soled moccasin will work well, especially if the man is hunting from a base camp and can get back to it should a sudden shower dampen the country. A heavy moccasin, which can be purchased or handmade, is worthy of consideration. No longer will the hunter be divorced from the earth that he trods, but rather his feet will gain a new relationship with the ground. He will be a quieter hunter. And a comfortable one—in dry woods. An old trick to toughen the soles of the feet is to shun shoes and paint the bottom of the foot itself with neatsfoot oil. This is sticky stuff, but it dries hard and after going barefooted this way for a few weeks the feet will begin to callous and harden up.

In consistent cold and dry or frozen snow, the moccasin-type boot will also work well. After all, this is the footwear of the Eskimo, the mukluk, and few know more about warding off the cold than these resourceful and hardy people. When the mountain man wrapped blankets all around his feet up to and including the kneecap, he was contriving a makeshift mukluk. But these do get wet, and therefore are not very good in country that

The modern black powder hunter can make his own footgear, or he can purchase, readymade, a beautiful set of buckskin moccasins—or, he may elect to
wear modern footgear, such as these Lightfoots by Red Ball, which were
selected for the author's Dall sheep hunt in Alaska. It is up to the individual
and his requirements.

will freeze at night and thaw all day long, making muddy, wet conditions. In the far north when that sun finally goes down for the winter, it appears only as a shy visitor in the day and the grounds remain hard, not gooey.

Planning for a recent black powder hunt to Alaska where Dall sheep were the major goal, footgear became a concern, and finally three pairs of foot covering were selected for the hunt. First, a well-sprayed pair of modern waterproof boots was taken, these with the soft crepe sole, not the Vibram. The Vibram is a fine, fine sole and comes highly recommended, but it is hard, somewhat noisy, and it can be very tiring on the leg muscles. The softer crepe will wear out sooner, but it is quieter and easier on the legs. The second pair of boots was a modern lightweight arctic pack. These were designed for both armed forces use and the outdoor public. They are good to −30°F. and they weigh only 29 ounces, rather than the usual 70 ounces for this type of insulated pack. Feet are hard to keep warm because they are farthest from the heat pump, the heart, and they also gather cold right up out of the ground itself. Lightweight blown polyurethane is the secret behind these warm boots. Finally, moccasins did get selected for the hunt, heavy moose hide ones with pile inside, warm around camp, comfortable to wear all day when no hunting was going on.

Moving up to the pants, a heavy leather legging like the mountain man's will work fine, quiet to move in, comfortable, and good against the brush. Of course, these are selected more for art than practicality in light of the new brush pants of the day, but they do wear well, though hard to clean when soiled, and they will keep the legs warm, especially if the size is a bit large and longjohns or insulated pants are worn underneath.

The shirt can well be leather, and there is a good quality here, for leather is very windproof. A way to keep really warm when the weather demands it is to put on a soft undershirt, followed by a wool sweater, and then the buckskin shirt. This is a good combination, but the hunter must allow for a final covering of blaze orange where the law, or general safety, demands.

If the feet are hardest to keep warm, it is the head that most robs the body of its heat, being higher up and acting as an escape route. This is why the hat is so important, among other reasons, and a good tight felt "cowboy" hat will retain a lot of heat up on the dome. This type also serves to keep the sun out of the eyes, which is a boon to both looking for game and shooting.

The upturn on the cowboy hat is mostly for show. The flat brim is better for keeping the sun out of the eyes and the rain from streaming down the back of the shirt collar. Of course, it looks funny to flatten the brim of the old Red Ryder sombrero, but it often pays off, even if a few guffaws will be tossed at the hunter.

Scouting some whitetail deer country in the southwest one day my partner and I ran across a cowboy who was working cattle, or he ran across us. He rode up, pleasant, for a little jawing, but he couldn't keep his eyes off our hats, and finally he had to snicker a little. John, my friend, was wearing an expensive tan ten-gallon Texas hat that would sell for better than 50 bucks, and the cowboy started on him. "It pains me to see what you've done to your hat," he began. "Don't mean to be nosy, but why'd you flatten it out as if a freight ran over it?" He ended his question with an amused laugh.

John straightened him out quickly, however. "You're looking for cows," he began, "we're looking for deer. Cows stand out on the hills, all brown and white and big. Deer stay down on the ridges, all gray and ghostlike. If my deer were as easy to see as your cows, I'd wear my hat for the dance, too; but with looking for deer being so tough, I have to flatten this hat out to keep the sun out of my eyes." I don't know if that satisfied the cowpuncher, but he quit laughing.

Clothing turns out to be much the same as our other black powder hunting choices have been, a personal matter, with trial and error being the best teacher, albeit a sometimes very expensive teacher. The balance has to fall somewhere between appropriate gear for a modern buckskinner in terms of looks and utility. Looking like "Ole Gabe" is fun, and when the conditions allow for it, this type of Old West dress is also comfortable. But under harsh conditions where a normally deskbound hand is out in the great backwoods, a mixture of the old and new is often more fitting. We have to remember that the old mountain man had the best gear and garb of his day, but that was 100 years ago. And he mostly traveled astride his trusty steed, not on foot. When he did have to go afoot, which sometimes happened, more through accident than design, however, he was not known to have any immunity from being footsore, and some of our forebears did indeed die on the trail when the shelter most immediate to them, their clothing, failed to thwart the elements.

A couple other items popularly carried by the new mountain man as well as the old are the powder horn and the possibles bag. The horn is still useful as can be, and it comes in many styles. Two major types are the plain-end horn and the horn that has a built-in powder measure. Both work well, remembering that black powder can be successfully loaded in bulk, unlike most smokeless loads of a top-charge nature. The plain-end simply pours, and a cut-off chunk of horn can serve as measure; or an adjustable brass charger may be used. The handy horn with the built-in measure can be preset for just about any desired amount. Usually, the finger is held over the end of the brass tip and the trip lever is activated, filling the spout with powder. Then the finger is removed from the tip and the powder is poured home.

I was presented with a matched set of horns for shotgunning that has proved excellent. One horn is for powder, with a measure spout as just described. The other is almost the same, with an end machined for shot pouring, and it has changeable tips for any charge from 1 to 1½ ounces of shot. Mr. Starr, the old pro of black powder shotgunning, used a shot flask in much the same way. These are originals dating back a century and more and are now available in replica form, along with powder flasks. Of course a man can elect to go with the aforementioned "readyloads," eschewing any horn at all, but for those who enjoy the nostalgia of pouring powder and shot out of the old good-looking horns, there are many to choose from on the market today, or he can build his own, a fun project that takes neither much time nor money.

Possibles bags are among the most romantic of black powder gear and thanks to the artists of the Old West, as well as preservers who might have come across an original here and there, we know what the mountain man used as his own unique bag. The only trouble is that this bag does not necessarily work well for us today as modern hunters. Again, it is a matter of going on foot more than astride Old Paint that makes the difference. Artists, such as J.M. Stanley, who visited the 1830 camps of the pioneers, as well as the famous Frederic Remington, show us stout, heavy leather bags worn by our forebears of the Old West. Mostly, these large bags were not strapped on as such, but slung with a leather strip attached to the bag, something like a woman's purse today.

The large bags were excellent for the mountain man for two reasons. First, they held a lot of paraphernalia, and this was very important to a man who was living off the land, ranging miles and miles on his treks. He needed all the space he could get. Second, they were ever handy, easy to get into when gear was needed. The mountain man, once again, did not have to worry about carrying the bag, as such, since it was slung on him, but he was atop his horse; hence, the animal did the carrying. But more than that, he did not have to be concerned with the bag flopping along as he hiked because he did not, as such, hike. When stalking, the bag could be left on the horse, or packed along. After all, the stalk was slow and easy going, and again, the mountain man did not have to worry about his possibles bag bouncing along at his side, attracting the attention of game, or annoying him.

Not so the modern black powder hunter. The old slung bag can be bothersome. To be sure, on quiet stalks when little hiking is necessary, the soft pouch-type possibles is a pleasure to tote along. These are for sale widely, or can be made by hand easily in any particular type the hunter may like, including his own personal modification or a copy of one he may have seen someplace. They are adequate for day hunts, large enough, not cumbersome, bulky, or annoying. But for the hunter who plans to range, even for those one-day-away-from-main-camp hunts, these swinging pouches are not the answer.

While the hunter hikes, the bag bounces. It is annoying, attention attracting, and disconcerting even on a slow stalk. Hunting the river bottoms, such as for turkey or whitetail, this type will suffice, but going overland, there is a much better way. This is the belt possibles bag. Whether or not the old mountain man used this type or not is a moot point, but there are possible artistic hints of a hip-worn bag toward the latter part of the nineteenth century. The modern hunter, who will have most of his gear back at camp, in the pickup truck, or on his packframe, does not need a large possibles. He can more than get by with a small one that is attached to his person with a belt. This bag is ample for all the gear he will need, including extra caps, nipple wrenches, nipples, his short starter, ramrod jags, worms, screws, and any other small, but important, tools that should be handy on the hunt.

The belt bag does not flop around, does not sway at the side, and does not annoy. It does stay still, present itself readily when gear is needed, and hold plenty of extras. A special kind of possibles bag is more properly called a "possibles belt," for it is a wide comfortable belt with a permanent holster attached for the

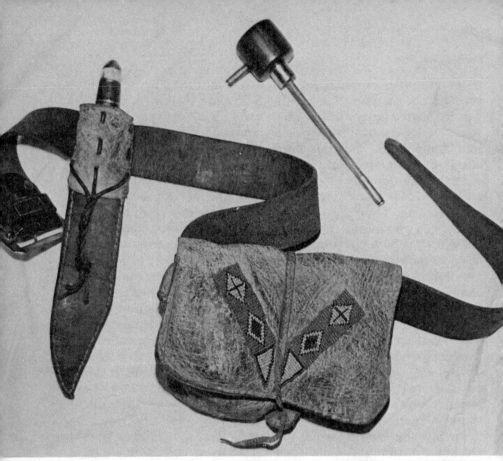

This is a possibles belt, small and light, but large enough to hold all of the necessities. It will not bounce around, or get hung up on fence crossings as easily as the "purse" type bag. Note excellent short starter, which fits into loop at the side of the bag. Knife is fully protected from loss by high sheath.

black powder six-shooter, as well as a permanent knife sheath. This practical arrangement works extremely well because different belts can be made for different purposes and rifles. All a hunter has to do, for example, is grab his .54 belt before he leaves the house and he will be assured that in it are all the things he needs to feed and care for his big game rifle. After tucking in his favorite knife and handgun, the man is ready to go. This is a good arrangement because by keeping that particular possibles belt loaded with the proper equipment, the hunter will not reach the field finding that his possibles is still loaded with quail shot instead of deer medicine. After a little bit of experience, the hunter will know just how to outfit his possibles belt for his own particular needs.

As this is written the possibles belt is still a homemade proposition, as no commercial model is available; but it is easy enough to make. A wide comfortable belt is the main ingredient. An old possibles bag, preferably one made of stiff leather, can be modified to fit the belt, or a special bag can be made, with belt loops, just for the task at hand. Many little attachments are handy on the belt. A small soft bag for carrying extra ball or caps can be added. A set of safety glasses can be placed on the belt. In this way, the hunter who does not wish to wear his shooting glasses while hunting can leave them off until it is time to actually fire the rifle. Then all he has to do is reach down, unsnap the glasses case, and slip them on his face. A small knife sharpener of the diamond-impregnated type, pencil style, can be worn on the belt. The hunter's own imagination will devise countless means of modifying the possibles belt for his own needs and the list can go on and on.

Outfitting for personal gear and garb is of top importance to any hunter, but is extremely essential to the modern black powder enthusiast, especially when he has been accustomed to self-contained cartridges, all kinds of Space Age aids, and present-day inventions. As long as the spirit of the hunt is not encroached upon, the mixing of the old and the new can result in a blend that is both pleasing and performing. A lot of these tools and clothes can be self-made, which is great fun. Black powder men are often do-it-yourselfers anyway, finding reward in making their own things, their way.

CHAPTER 15

Knives and Hawks for the Black Powder Hunter

Knives and hawks played a major role in the daily lives of the frontiersmen of the West. We conjure in our minds a picture of the mountain man as buckskin clad and Hawken toting, but that image would be incomplete if we did not see a knife and a hawk on his person, too. Cutlery, especially the knife, was personal to the mountain man and he gave names to his favorite blades, even when they were the cheaper "butcher" knives of the day, but especially if they were well-made models. Some knives were so personal that their reputation and deeds became spread among the buckskinners, and if a man somehow lost his favorite piece and it were picked up by another, it would be recognized and assigned to its owner by name.

The mountain man, of course, used his blade for more than camp work and dressing down his meat. It was a tool of war also. The popular model in Pre-Hawken days was, in fact, a war piece more than a hunter's blade. The blade was very long, and somewhat oddly shaped by modern standards, having a very crooked effect. In the heat of battle, the adventurers often held this knife in one hand with a tomahawk in the other, after having fired the single ball from their flintlocks. Indians called these early frontiersmen Long Knives in reference to these blades, and when pistols were introduced to the West it was a confusion to the Redman, for after the single ball was fired the pioneer then drew what appeared to be a knife and fired it. The Indian was quite taken with these men who could "fire one round with their rifles, then draw their knives and shoot again."

The Long knives, with blades of 10 to 12 inches, were fitted with deer horn handles and had a spear-point blade. This blade was not best for camp chores or meat dressing, but was just right for war. However, the mountain man soon found that he needed his knife for much more than warfare, and at this time the blade was made shorter and the "skinner" and other models came into play.

This transition began with another Long knife, but instead of the long crooked blade, there was a long straight blade, again 10 to 12 inches, and again with a spear point. Personalizing this model, the mountain man added a handle of deer horn, or he made the grips from the long bones of an animal. This model was still a combat weapon, but being straighter, it could double for camp chores and also skin out the buffalo and the elk, as well as the beaver pelt. Still, it was a long and cumbersome tool and further transition was in the wind.

The changes had to be gradual and thoughtful. We cannot experience the feeling, except vicariously, of having that single shot while facing either a formidable enemy or a charging bear. But this type of encounter often fell upon the mountain man. Therefore, his knife had to serve a dual purpose, that of skinner and meat dresser to sword in combat. The blade would often save the frontiersman's fat after his rifle was dry, or if the old smokepole failed to fire under adverse conditions.

As the knife style changed, it leaned more and more to a simpler design very prominent in about 1000 B.C. in Europe. Actually, many types were tried, including the folding knife, which dates back to at least 1715. One Indian grave contained a clasp knife with springs to keep the knife closed as well as helping to hold the blade in the working position, this find dating between 1781 and 1809.

The evolution of the knife in frontier times was not a clear historical growth. The "stabber," for example, hung on for a good while. This long-bladed, narrow fellow was really not much good as a heavy utility tool in the camp or field, but was really a combat weapon serving as a short sword. A knife that gained great popularity, however, was much more functional. It was called the "butcher knife," and it was fairly cheaply made at a forge, and not a handworked proposition at all. The mountain man often called this knife his "scalper," for reasons that are quite obvious. The butcher was made for utility, and it cost the manufacturer nine cents to produce. Back in the nineteenth century this nine-cent knife wholesaled out for double its price, or 18 cents. Of course, in the tradition of cheating the mountain man, it was sold to him for two dollars, and that meant two dollars in beaver pelt, which was turned into further profit by the businessmen who worked the rendezvous circuit.

In fairness, the knives were not junk. They did serve well, apparently, but they were certainly not the ultimate of the day, even though they did save a man's life from time to time, and they surely skinned out hundreds of pelts before they were rendered scrap. There were, in the era of the butcher knives, quite a number of specialty blades, too. Some of these were modeled for skinning primarily, others for fleshing the pelts down before stretching, and there were even a few surgical blades evident. There were many experimental types in the field, such as a crooked knife (bent) with an extremely strange blade that resembled a mountain road in curves.

Of the specialty knives, the Bowie has lived in history and remains a particularly prominent style today, though its use is mainly for show now. This type was often referred to as a "bear knife." The design itself was hundreds of years old when Arkansas blacksmith James Black made up the famous blade for Jim Bowie in about 1836. Bowie's death at the Alamo, with this knife still in his possession, furthered the legend. In truth, the type found limited use among the mountain men, and our carrying of a Bowie in pretended emulation of that breed of men would be inaccurate.

The Bowie knife did find service with the Army in the 1830s and 1840s; however, it was a modified version of the original named the William Jackson knife, smaller all around, with an eight-inch blade instead of the foot-long shank of steel of the Bowie. The model was very plain, with a bit of scimitar to the blade. The slogan attached to this chunk of cutting steel was "I surpass, try me." Again, this was not the mountain man's knife, though certainly some men must have used it.

If there was a mountain man knife, it would probably be that known today as the Green River, made famous by the buckskinners themselves. Its history is not thoroughly clear, but there are some good, and often verifiable, stories connected with this knife style. The Green River epithet was derived from the Green River area in Wyoming, where the mountain men often gathered for rendezvous. Rendezvous began in 1824, and it was rather logical that the Green River area be selected as one of the sites for this famous meeting tradition. The upper stretch of this river, quite unlike the lower portion which runs down into Utah, was cool and beautiful in the summertime when rendezvous was held, and it was a wonderful place to trap beaver as well.

The Green River captured the respect and covetousness of the mountain men, and someone named his knife after the location. We don't really know who. One story tells of the Green

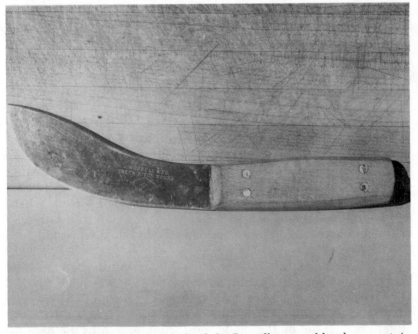

The original Green River Works knife by Russell, coveted by the mountain man, simple but capable, a skinner by style, but a general workhorse by trade.

River Forge in Massachusetts, and it contends that the knife was named after that company. Certainly, no Green River knife was ever manufactured in the Northwest. Another story, and one that has very high probability, says that the "real" Green River knife was made in Sheffield, England, by John Russell. The blade was stamped G.R. The mountain man, attaching his own interests to this knife, concluded that G.R. stood for Green River. As a matter of fact, later Sheffield knives sold in the Northwest had Green River spelled out on the blade. But those first G.R. knives quite probably did not stand for Green River at all, but rather for "Georgius Rex," or King George. That explanation for the G.R. on the early knives is certainly a reasonable one.

The Green River knife is of interest to us because it was simple, and its basic style and design are with us today in some of the most useable models ever to ride in a sheath. In this case, as in many others, going with the gear of the old mountain man really makes sense. The G.R. knife, much like the famous Hawken, certainly does not have a single model. Rather, it is a generic type. The blade is not a foot long, nor is the handle designed to break open a skull. It usually does not have a hilt, for a hilt, as found on the famous Bowie, was for allowing a thrust home of the blade, such as in an enemy's body, the hilt holding the hand back both for nonslippage and for power in the drive.

The G.R. was plain, not fancy. The blade was in the neighborhood of four to six inches long, and it had enough scimitar to it to allow for good skinning. In fact, these knives were skinners if they were anything at all. The knife had a point, which means it could be used well for the job of field dressing game, the point making initial cuts. With a blade of about five or six inches long, the knife did not have to be set aside when butchering was a task at hand. Steaks could be cut free with this length of blade, and boning jobs could be handled with skill and alacrity.

The blade became famous with the mountain men, and its fame outlived the mortals themselves who made history with them. In fact, there were special names given to G.R. knives, and special sayings connected with them. "To go up Green River" was to die by the blade, for example, and in the heat of battle one of the mountain men might yell out, "Give 'em Green River, boys!," which meant that the fight should turn to hand-to-hand combat using knives, not guns.

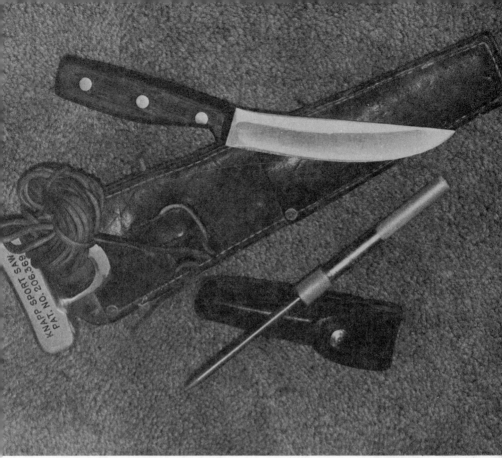

A modern kit carried by the author, a simple strong knife not unlike the Green River style, along with a saw to aid in cutting up meat for backpacking out of the country. The knife slips into the saw sheath. Note the strong cord tied onto the sheath, used on the pack frame itself, and the diamond sharpener, which keeps the knife honed to a keen edge while the boning process is in operation.

In recent times, the sheath knife, though very popular, lost much of its impetus to smaller folding knives and tiny skinners. The wearing and using of a big blade marked a man as "dude," though unfairly to be sure. For a time it was "in" to use the smallest knife possible for the largest jobs; and in an effort for one-upmanship, many a tiny toothpick blade whittled away at an elk carcass much to the glory of its user. The sheath knife that ran from belt loop about halfway to the knee cap was *out*. This trend, away from the really large knives, has remained, but a shift part way back has taken control.

Knifemakers and new interest in knives of and for themselves has allowed for the return of the medium-sized workhorses, the sheath knives. And many of these would darn well qualify as Green Rivers back in the old days because of their shape and their size. For those of us who live in moose country where a man can put down his winter's meat with a rifle shot, the return of the medium-sized knife is a blessing, and a fellow who wears one on his hip will not be considered a dude any longer. The selection of these knives is one of practicality and aesthetics. Today a black powder hunter can look into the old books and the work of the Western artists, pick out the type of knife he wants, and have a master build it for him. Dollars will be parted with, to be sure, but a one-of-a-kind knife will be enjoyed for life.

Aside from the custom, however, there are numerous ways to find a knife that will qualify for the modern black powder hunter. In fact, he can make his own Green River knife from kits now being offered, or he can buy one of the same basic models ready to go. The knife should first meet standards of labor. Will the blade get the job done with facility? That is the question.

One thing the black powder hunter may have to do is learn to bone an animal in the forest, taking out all the edible meat and leaving behind the skeleton for the predators to gnaw on. Bone, in terms of steaks and stews, has absolutely no value. It only takes up freezer space. The reason bone is left in on a steak in the grocery store is that we have to pay good money for them. So, leaving bones in the hills and taking out the meat makes good sense, and it is practical and legal. When cooking a soup, of course, some bone is all right, especially if they are to be cracked open for the marrow, which we seldom do in this culture, although the Eskimo knows the value of this inner meat and uses it extensively for Vitamin C and other nutriment values.

If a hunter is going to bone his meat, which will be an essential for the man who wants to take advantage of the backcountry outing, he will need a "real" knife. The little pocket models, useful for slitting the cavity and other chores, does poorly when real work is necessary. The Green River knife is just about perfect.

The animal is flopped over on its belly in this process. The first cut must be made right between the antlers, from one base to the other. Then, in the center of the skull, the sharp point of the knife is inserted and a cut made all the way down the backbone, just under the hide, and to the very root of the tail. Now four cuts are made, again using the sharp point of the service knife. These four cuts are on the inside of each leg on the animal, that is, all the way from the backbone slit right to the ankle. The hide is worked off now until the carcass ends up resting on its own clean pallet, in other words, the hide itself.

If the animal is going to the taxidermist, this type of skinning is excellent, for after making the long cuts from backbone down leg, the cape itself is worked back to the chin of the animal and the head is cut off, leaving plenty of extra hide for the taxidermist to work with.

With the body all exposed, as it were, and lying on its clean surface, free of dust and dirt, the meat is worked from the bones. First, the best part of the carcass is removed. These are the filets, or backstrap. It is easy to do. The knife is carefully rolled along the spine and the beautiful tender meat is worked free in a long continuous strip, one on each side of the backbone. The front shoulder blades are very easy to remove. With the longer blade, five or six inches, it is no problem to hold the leg out, thus lifting the shoulder, and cutting very close to the ribs. The shoulder blade will pop right off. The meat from the hind quarters is removed by cutting with a saw or a hatchet through the bone carefully so as not to hit the innards. Then the long blade is worked right to the bone with a rolling motion and the large chunks of meat are taken away in two to four main pieces.

Trying to form a picture in the mind of this process is a problem, but after a few field attempts the hunter is soon an expert at boning, and he finds that later butchering at home is quite simple when there are no bones to contend with. The hunter will soon devise his own methods of boning, and certainly this textual explanation is given only as starter advice.

The utility knife of roughly the Green River ilk is a combination tool. Its blade is thick enough to offer a wedge system. That is, during the cutting process the wedge effect of the blade forces the meat or hide away from the cutting edge. A whippy thin blade does not have this wedge effect and cannot be considered a good all-around knife for the hunter.

Next, the blade must have enough point so that initial incisions can be made cleanly. A rounded edge is fine for large skinning chores, but does not get the job done when punctures must be made. The wedge of the knife should drift away as it nears the point. In other words, it is thinner out toward the tip so that punctures can be made cleanly. Naturally, the blade has to be long enough to get the job done in boning. A short blade will certainly work; so will a sharpened letter opener—but a blade of four to six inches, just what the mountain man ordered, is excellent.

The knife blade must not be totally straight for best effect. There should be a bit of scimitar to it, that is, the rounded effect, a bit like the exaggerated swords of the Arabs which are highly bent upwards toward the tip. A reduction in drag is the result of the scimitar shape, which is very important because hide and meat are in effect trying to stick together and hold the knife fast in their grasp. With only a portion of the blade actually making full contact, this drag is reduced and the blade is allowed to pass lightly on to its work. About the same thing takes place in the drop point design, except that the pressure is forward rather then centered in the middle of the blade as with the scimitar.

Any knife of simple clean design with a blade in the four- to six-inch category can be our black powder hunter's sidekick.

Knives for the black powder hunter can be homemade or made by hand in a custom shop. Here a knife by Jimmy Lile is shown. Jimmy, the Arkansas master, will prepare a special knife for the black powder fan to his own specifications, as will most modern blade-makers.

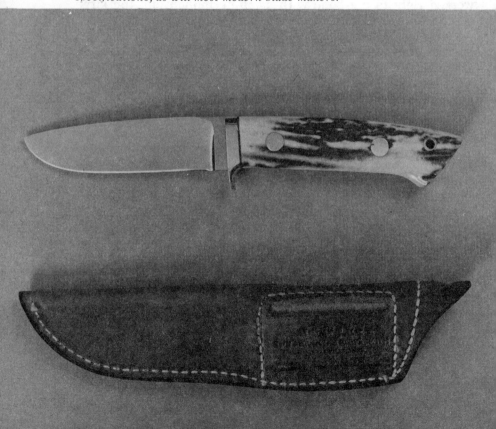

The nostalgia attached to the Green River replicas now available is a worthwhile one and enough reason to buy such a model. And having a knifesmith build a Green River is also very worthwhile for the man wishing to own something unique and willing to pay the price for it. And then there are many simple knives on the market, usually ranging from five to 10 dollars, which serve the modern day mountain man very well. They are for utility. They work hard and they work well. In a homemade sheath they fill the bill as a black powder knife.

The tomahawk, or simply hawk, of yesteryear was an essential tool for the mountain man. Whether it is for the modern day black powder hunter or not is open to question and to circumstance. The mountain man used as many tools as he could, and though we see him employing his trusty rifle in the thick of battle or the thin of putting meat in the pot, the truth is, he was skilled in more than firing a rifle. As a matter of fact, the mountain man was known to use the bow and arrow on more than one occasion. After a heavy battle with Indians, the buckskinners often used the bows and arrows of their enemy as a final means of dispatching the wounded. This saved DuPont and galena, powder and ball. Also, the mountain man was known to hunt with the bow and arrow. After all, it again was a saving measure, but it was quiet, too, and if he had invaded the domain of the Indian to trap beaver he did not want to announce himself with a blast rending the still air of the backcountry.

Another tool that the frontiersman came to know as an extension of his arm was the hawk. In the book *Joe Meek* by Stanley Vestal, about the mountain man of the same name, we find Joe confronted by a grizzly. "Quickly he jerked his hatchet from his belt, put everything into one desperate blow, and struck the bear behind the ear. He felt the blade crash through her skull into the brain." When a rifle misfired, or when the first shot was wide of the mark or not as effective as necessary, the two pounds of sharp steel in the hand was often the difference between eating or being eaten.

The long-handled hatchet, or hawk, was especially useful. It could be counted on to chop wood as well as skulls, and it was the standard beaver killer. The Green River was the Hawken of knives, but the trusty hawk or hatchet was often even more important than the famous knife. With a long handle, for leverage, it could be deadly, and naturally it was thrown with skill in battle, thus extending the reach of the arm. Best of all, it was a

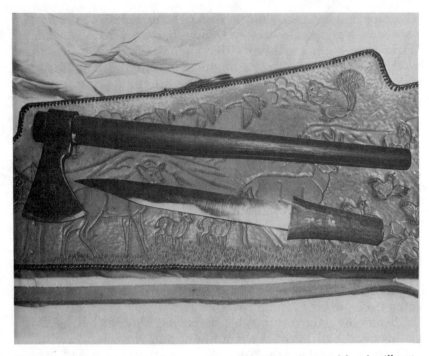

Here is a 'hawk that is useful as well as decorative. Its steel head will cut wood, or serve in the game field to help dress out a carcass. The knife is a homemade (from a file) model with deer-antler handle, mostly for decoration and conversation.

tool that could cleave the spine of an animal during the dressing process, and for that reason we still have use of the tool to this day.

In the backwoods a hawk of one kind or another can be a valuable aid and certainly a worthwhile part of the modern black powder hunter's kit. Should he knock down the big animal, such as the elk or moose, the hawk can be counted on to make short work of big bones. And it will serve to gather up a wood supply from a dry downfall for that evening fire. And though the notion is more romantic than practical, the good hawk can still be counted on to ward off some stout beast that has decided to make a meal of a hunter.

The main thing is selection of the hawk. The all-brass models are fine for hanging over the fireplace. But it is the steel types that must be sought for real work. Fortunately, these are still available. There is a kit which can be put together by the hunter, the product being quite serviceable.

Cutlery for the modern black powder hunter, then, can well be counterparts of the tools used a century and more ago. Naturally, with our live-and-let-live philosophy, the black powder man may select whatever cutlery he desires to work with in the field, be it a large folding knife, pocket knife, or Bowie longer than a warrior's arm. However, the key to selection is still the two main criteria, aesthetics and practicality, and a combination thereof is usually best—something that is both handsome to the eye and good in the hand.

CHAPTER 16

Make Your Own Black Powder Hunting Gear

Black powder hunters are by nature a do-it-yourself breed. Much of the reward and enjoyment gained from the sport comes from its hands-on aspect, from stuffing powder and bullet home in a single-shot barrel, to using any form of homemade gear from knives to clothing. The sport lends itself to homespun things. There is a special thrill in trekking the country and taking game with the aid of self-made things.

An entire book could be devoted to the things that a black powder hunter can make for himself; therefore, a chapter of this nature can serve only to whet the appetite of the buckskinner and give some hints about what can be done, how easy it is to do it, and how cheap. Relating the fun and the relaxation attending do-it-yourselfing cannot be accomplished here. The reader will have to find this out for himself by doing the projects. A list of gear and garb that can be homemade would run into hundreds of items, and surely something would be left out every time. The way to go about finding out what to build is to take a long look at the outfit that accompanies a man afield, and seeing what in it can be replaced with homespun tackle. Or browsing through catalogues can give many hints and clues as to what is necessary in the hunt, and which items can be made by hand.

All the clothing can be put together by hand, even the moccasins, which, as already stated, fit in well at least as camp wear if not field dress. There are stub starters made from yo-yo halves, powder horns, flasks, measures, storage buckskin bags, ball bags, speed loaders, loading blocks, loading leathers, patch cutters, wad cutters, possibles bags, possibles belts, rod tips, cappers, knives of all kinds from patch cutters to camp Bowies, pan chargers, vent picks, cleaning solutions such as moose milk, shot chargers . . . the list goes on *ad infinitum.*

A basic item that a black powder hunter can make for himself, however, and worth mentioning here, is the projectile. To be sure, both ball and conicals are for sale ready moulded, but the fun of doing-it-yourself on this project should be tried by all. Lest there be some misunderstanding, though the conical is provably superior in terms of sheer scientific physics, the ball should be a part of every frontstuffer's bag, unless he has a specially made rifle of quick twist designed to shoot only conicals, and some of these are being constructed now. The ball is highly effective, especially in large caliber, and the mountain man lowered even the mighty grizz with his round hunk of lead. Since more rifles are made to shoot ball accurately than are made to shoot conicals accurately, it makes sense to run your own ball at home. The old-timers called it that, "running bullets or ball," and it is basically a process of melting lead and pouring it into a mould to shape it.

Although it has been said many times before by many other writers and black powder aficionados, it is ever true that pure lead is best for making black powder projectiles, be they ball or bullet. In an exhaustive effort to disprove this, I tried dozens of different alloys of lead and tin; lead, tin and antimony; lead and antimony; and a few more exotic concoctions. They did *not* work. Of course, when we say "pure" lead, we mean the product we get from fluxing our supply. No lead that we can normally obtain will be 100 per cent pure; but we can come awfully close by fluxing.

Lead melts at about 621 degrees, and running bullets is usually best at about 700 degrees; though this depends on the mould being used, as well as other factors. Each shooter must decide for himself the temperature that works best for him. Lead that is too cold leaves a product that is more wrinkled than

100-year-old Chief Gray Horse, and too hot lead frosts over like a pumpkin with a glaze. So, getting the lead to proper temperature precedes fluxing *and* bullet making. I like about 700 degrees. After the lead is melted down and hot, I drop in a chunk of pure paraffin (wax) and stir it into the molten liquid. This is smokey, and best done outdoors. Of course, immediately lighting the abundant fumes with a match will decrease the smoke a lot. The stirring (I use an old large tablespoon) will result in surfacing a whole bunch of debris. Some of this is often dirt, but more usually it is antimony or tin, precious to the maker of hard lead bullets for modern guns, useless to the buckskinner. Every bit of it should be skimmed off and tossed away.

Starting with pure lead, of course, makes the task of cleaning it easier. Telephone cable sheathing, plumbing lead, radiology lab lead, and many other sources are available. But it all needs to be fluxed. If smoke and fumes of fluxing are a problem, a product called Marvelux is cleaner—no smoke. The pure lead is best for black powder shooting because it obturates well, that is, it upsets and forms a good seal in the bore. Compared with other metals, it is cheap. Lead is available, and not rare or hard to find. It is heavy, or more accurately, dense. Its high specific gravity means that for the volume there is much mass, and this mass means retention of initial velocity as well as high penetration. Lead is soft, but it is cohesive. It will not fly into numerous fragments on impact, but rather it hangs together and acts like a "bullet" should act. Lead oxidizes, but not like iron, and if kept in old tobacco tins, with their good sealing qualities, the ball or bullet of pure lead will remain bright and functional for years.

The process of making ball is easy, and it can be safe with precautions. First, a good pot is needed. I like such production-type pots as Lee makes; they are not expensive, and they do the job with temperature control. The spout may sometimes become clogged on any of these production pots, but since lead is so dense, this does not happen often. Most debris will float up, not sink to the bottom where the spout is. A basic pot over a camp stove will also work, and as a matter of fact, the simple lead dipper with spout is excellent for pouring ball, and often I use this even with production-type pots.

A hunk of clean, soft cloth or cardboard will serve to catch the ball as it falls from the mould. A moulder's hammer, such as offered by Shiloh, makes the process of getting the ball from the mould an easy one. A stubborn ball can be picked out with the sharp end of the hammer, though usually it will fall from the mould with a gentle rap of the softer end. Naturally, the sprue, or excess lead, is saved and remelted, but never allowed to get mixed up with the dross, which is the junk that was skimmed during the fluxing stage.

There are many facets to making good ball or bullets, and each black powder shooter will come up with his own formula eventually. But the simple means of finding decent lead, fluxing it clean, and then pouring at about 700 degrees will work for starters. I like to weigh my products, especially if they are going hunting. Air pockets seldom cause trouble, but can. Setting the scale, it is a simple matter and a fast one to slip each ball on the pan and see if any are light. Pure lead balls are accurate because they engrave so well, but if an extralight ball is fired among normal weight balls it will surely be off target, a real

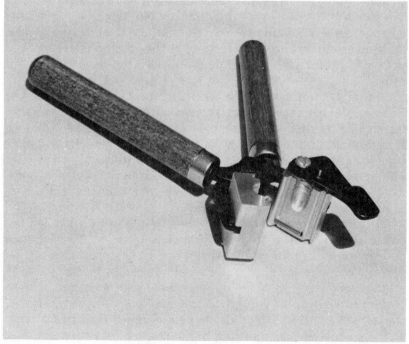

A relatively new type of mould is the aluminum, as offered by Lee Precision Engineering. This mould heats readily and often produces fine bullets and ball from the first sample. Easy to clean and work with, the aluminum blocks make very accurate projectiles. They must be cared for as abuse can damage the soft metal.

problem when a long stalk is blown because of a tiny pocket of air and a tad of hunter carelessness. Also, the pure lead projectile mushrooms well in game, and evenly, but it cannot be depended upon to do this job quite as well if it contains air pockets.

Safety in moulding is a matter of common sense. Haste may not make waste while running bullets, but it can produce a hell of a burn. Making bullets is a relaxing hobby, and fun. A rainy afternoon is well used in moulding a few balls for that sunnier day. There need be no reason to rush the job. Gloves will prevent burns. Leather shoes should also be worn. Lead may be fairly cool by the time it hits the floor should some spill, but still hot enough to scorch a bare foot, or a slippered foot. The place to mould is also very important. The kitchen stove is just not it. A good table is much better.

Taking care of moulds is vital. A chinked mould means a rough product, and moulds are expensive—they should be treated properly. After use they can be cleaned with a black powder solvent of isopropyl alcohol. When dry, a spray with a silicone base will help preserve the metal. Or Acra-Eez can be sprayed on the mould. This product burns off, and does not have to be wiped clean before the mould is used the next time, as oil must be.

Finally, some people like to swage their conical slugs. Ned Roberts, the old expert black powder shooter, was one who preferred this method. A swage is available in the proper caliber from Shiloh, and it is simply an accurate and smooth chamber that sizes the finished bullet. The bullet is slipped in at the top and rammed on through. This trues the projectile to a more exact size, somewhat reshapes it, and condenses the lead, all to improve accuracy according to Roberts and other experts.

I am not a qualified artisan, but in a way that is good because I have had to find the best way to be successful as a do-it-myselfer in spite of my two left hands. One thing which has allowed me to make good, functional homespun hunting gear is a bit of trickery in the form of *patterns*. I can make up my own leather breeches, if I want to, because of patterns. In this case, the pattern turns out to be an old pair of jeans. By cutting away at the seams and dismantling the pants, a pattern results. The two sides are laid on leather, traced around; the leather is cut out and then sewn together. The product is a little rough, but rough is all right as a flavor for black powder doings. Sewing, even leather of heavy thickness, is easy, too, with an awl. This

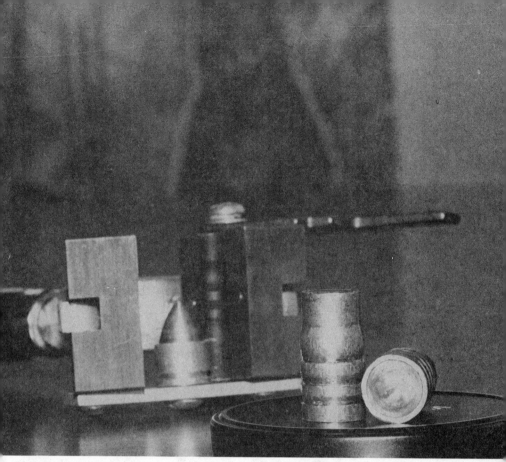

This Shiloh mould produces the ponderous .58 caliber Stakebuster, a slug which tips the scales at a full 610 grains, which was used by Val Forgett, president of the Navy Arms Company, on his African quest for big game. Note that the plug, which forms the skirt of the Minie, is hinged into the aluminum mould and does not fall out on use.

little tool is available in many catalogues, such as L.L. Bean, and it costs only a couple bucks. The best part is that the awl is mastered in a few moments, and it can use heavy nylon thread that lasts a long time under hard use.

If I don't have an original to take apart, I make my own pattern out of newspaper and cardboard. This is the key to easy possibles bags and belts, holsters, rifle scabbards and countless other leather goods. On making the holster for the black powder sixgun, for example, the gun is laid on newspaper and traced around carefully. Then the newspaper is cut out to form a mock holster. Probably, this model will be too small, so the mock holster is again placed on paper and a new larger one is cut out.

This one is pinned together loosely as a try-out. If it works, the pattern is placed on flexible cardboard, and a cardboard mock holster is made and modified with scissors until it is just what the hunter wants.

Then the cardboard pattern is placed on leather, traced around, and the leather is cut out. Simple, to be sure, but effective. The leather is sewn up either with the awl or by a shoemaker, who will have a heavy machine for this task, and the result is a personal, decorative, but highly useful product. A possibles bag or belt can be made the same way using paper patterns first, then cutting out the leather and sewing it together. These leather goods can then be decorated, stained or treated with any personal touch that the black powder hunter prefers. A knife sheath is easily formed this way. So are ball bags, tool bags, cap bags, flint bags, whatever is made of leather.

Some hunters will want to do it all in leather, starting with the collection of the skin in the field, and then tanning it at home. A coon, for example, can be turned into a fine hat, a do-it-yourself project from gathering up the animal right down to sewing the headgear together. The coon is skinned neatly and the fat and meat is scraped clean from the hide. There are special scrapers for this process and they don't cost much, and do last forever. A washing soda mixture is prepared and the fur is cleaned up, and cleaned again in a borax and water solution.

A simple tanning method is to pour a gallon of cold water into a bucket. Added to this water are a pound of ammonium alum, obtained from a chemical house, followed by a quarter pound of washing soda and a half pound of salt. This mixture will bubble like a witch's brew for a few moments. When it stops fizzing, the skin is dropped into the mixture and left there for about three days, stirring it a few times a day. After this soaking, the skin is washed in borax and water, then rinsed with clean water until free of the solution. The skin is laid aside, flat, to dry. When good and dry, pure bar soap is rubbed into it.

After the bar soap is rubbed in, a coating of neat's-foot oil is applied. This makes for good color as well as preserving. The skin is laid aside, and it will stiffen up. It has to be relaxed after about three days. A good stout work bench is good for the next move. By placing a protruding hunk of smooth wood shaped like a small ironing board from the top of the desk, this protrusion is used to soften up the stiff hide. Elbow grease is the secret. Rubbing the hide part on the wood will soften it up nicely.

I like to make the hat by use of my patterns again, forming up some good cardboard pieces until I have a basic hat, and then making my cuts on the hide so that they, too, will fold into place. The best way I know is to reverse the patterning process a bit by laying the coon hide down on the cardboard and tracing all around that hide, then cutting out the cardboard. Now any bending and cutting can be done on the cardboard, not the precious hide. When mistakes are made, a piece of cardboard is lost, not hide. And when that coon-shaped hide has been added to with other bits of cardboard, and when it has been cut to shape, then the coon can be dealt with, cut, and added to with pieces of leather until it is sewing time. Again, the awl can be employed.

Many wonderful knives can be made by the black powder hunter in his home workshop. The little patch knife can be cut from an old straight razor, but a fine utility knife can be hewn from a file, the mill type, flat. Since files are made of metal too hard for good knives, they must be tempered. It is laid in a bed of coals in the backyard barbeque grill and it will turn a series of colors. The first three are the important ones to watch for, and they are pale yellow, full yellow and dark straw. When the file approaches the color of dark straw it is immersed in cold water. Most knifemakers will want to grind all the teeth off the blade before this process, though it can be accomplished either way, tempering and then grinding or grinding and then tempering.

The knife profile is ground, and then the blade is sharpened. The Green River type is well advised, simple and useful. During grinding, the steel must not get hot. In fact, if it is too hot to handle with bare hands, it should be dunked in cool water from time to time. Grinding must be done with care. No way has been found to put metal back once it is knocked off. Final polishing should be avoided for the black powder buff. His knife should look homemade, with its tool marks in place.

The haft of the knife can be made of wood, bone, horn, or whatever unique material the hunter has in mind. This is a personal product and the hunter should do it his way, right down to the final carving of the handle. As for a cutting edge, the same holds true for the handmade job as the store-bought model—the edge should be sharp, but the very thin edges that resemble a razor often break off during work and are not necessary. Sharp enough to cut meat and skin without going through the hide and ruining it is sharp enough. The diamond-impregnated pencil-style knife sharpeners that operate as "steels" should accompany the hunter. He can stroke the blade a few times and retain a good, but not razor, cutting edge.

Making a powder horn is a lot of fun, a little messy, and highly rewarding. A horn is in a way spun hair, and is not antler-like or bony. Being hollow allows for its use as a container in the first place. The contents of the horn itself is a pulp that must be removed. Boiling is a good way to do this. The horn stinks when it is boiled, usually, so outdoors is the best place to accomplish this work. It is a good idea to clean the outside of the horn up first, even going to some light polishing. If it turns out to be an ugly devil under the outer crust, then it can be discarded before further work.

The horn has to be trimmed on both ends. A fine-tooth saw is needed, because the spun-hair nature of the horn can make it brittle; and heavy sawteeth can cause the horn to split. The horn is cut square on the butt. This end will later be plugged with a large cap. The other end will be the spout and just enough is cut away to allow for a reasonable pouring tip.

A hole is very carefully drilled into the tip of the horn, remembering that horns split easily. Drilling a little at a time will insure a clean hole from the tip into the cavity. The inside of the horn is scraped a bit in order to square it up and to make a good container for the fine granulation of the powder that will eventually reside there.

On the butt end, which has been squared up by sanding, a plug is inserted. Soft pine works best, about a half inch to three-fourths inch thick. This plug is inserted all the way into the base and kept there by small brads, decorative ones if you like. Now a nice piece of wood, cherry, walnut, whatever, is glued onto the soft pine plug. Wood glue is fine for this and will make a lasting bond. The wood should be allowed to rest firmly on the plug, but should not be squeezed down so hard that the glue is forced out and a poor bond results.

The plug can now be shaped after it is in place, sanded as it were, until it looks like a cap, rounded and smooth, fitted right to the edges of the horn itself. A little knob should be attached to the cap, either screwed in place or glued. This knob (the hunter can check photos of horns for different styles of knobs) serves to hold the strap of leather in place later.

The horn is shaped by filing. Really fine horns have been filed and then polished so thin that the powder supply can be seen inside the horn. The amount of work on this part of the project is up to the builder. The final smoothing is done with fine sandpaper, and the hunter may wish to decorate his horn with a woodburning tool, a scraper, dyes, or whatever his imagination comes up with.

Finally, the horn is polished. A cloth buffing wheel is best here, and as much time as the black powder man wants to invest is how long it takes to get a final polish. Sometimes an abrasive such as jeweler's rouge is used as the polishing is done to get a fine finish.

Naturally, this is a crude set of instructions designed to get the black powder hunter interested in making a powder horn (or

An example of the beautiful artwork created in the name of black powder is this exceptional powder horn made by an artisan who makes these scrimshaw delights on special order. A replica powder flask is shown with the horn.

shot horn), and many, many ramifications are allowed in producing really fine horns. Some of these are so fine that it takes literally months of effort before the final product is arrived at, and there are even horn-making experts who are able to use their skills professionally in handcrafting real beauties that are often engraved with awe-inspiring skill. These horns are the valued and cherished antiques of a future culture, made by modern day artisans.

All of these projects are samples, not step-by-step edicts. More how-to projects are found in greater detail in popular black powder publications.

There is one final muzzleloader-fan tool for hunting that must be mentioned, and in enough detail to provide the reader with all the knowledge he needs to produce one, and that is the aforementioned Moses stick, that fine walking staff that also serves as a shooting rest for that one good shot the buckskinner is going to have. The Moses stick is a walker's benchrest, as well as a signalling stick, a rattlesnake probe on those early season hunts when pit vipers are secreted in tall grasses. The stick has been used by hunters caught out in high country. By using it somewhat as a blind man uses his cane, the stick has revealed the edges of cliffs in the darkness, as well as craters in the earth or knee-breaking boulders. One of the major uses of the stick is a binocular rest.

These fine tools are made from light wooden staffs. Any strong and supple wood that is an inch or so across will serve, but the best of all are those of the agave plant, a sort of cactus that is often called a century plant. The hunter must not go around cutting one of these down for his Moses stick. This is wrong, and leaves the land denuded of a useful plant. Found mainly in the Southwest, the agave is best picked up off the ground after it has fallen over. Aside from the fact that this is grooming the land instead of denuding it, the staff will be better, for it is dry and cured.

Sawing it off, the stick should be about the height of its user, or an inch or two less. There will be leaves and branches protruding from it, and these are simply lopped off with a knife. At home, the first thing is to smooth up the staff, first with a knife blade, removing all of the knobs and rough edges, and then with coarse sandpaper. The stick does not have to be extremely smooth, but it should not put splinters in your hand.

After smoothing, the upper end of the stick must be fitted

with a nonslip, gripping, comfortable handle, and this means tanned hide, elk, deer, moose, hog—anything works well if it is soft. The upper third of the stick, all if it, should be covered with this handle. But first, it is wise to glue a thick chunk of foam rubber to the top of the stick. This soft rubber will serve later as a binocular rest, as well as guarding the hand should a hunter have to descend a steep wall, using the full length of the stick to help him come down. Sometimes two pieces of foam up top are best. They will compress very easily into place.

A small piece of tanned hide is glued over the rubber on top of the stick. This serves as a cap. Then the handle is wrapped around the stick. This large piece of hide wraps around the upper leather cap to hold it in place. The best means of attaching are gluing with a contact cement, and then tacking the full length with short brads.

That takes care of the upper end of the stick. On the lower end a rubber crutch bumper is put in place. The stick is whittled to size and the bumper is both glued and tacked in place. It won't fall off in use, and it will quiet the stick while it is serving as a walking staff, plus keeping the end from wearing away.

Finally, the exposed lower two-thirds of the stick are sprayed with just about any kind of finish, varnish, treated linseed oil, whatever. This will keep the stick from drying out too much as the years go by; it will weatherproof it, and such a stick will last the lifetime of the hunter. An agave stick is especially desirable because it is as light as balsa wood, but as strong as an oak tree.

A short starter can be made from a yo-yo half. The wood is drilled to accept a small dowel, which is glued in place, and there's a starter. A capper can be made from a piece of heavy tanned leather, cap-size holes either burned or cut into it and the percussion caps fitted in place on a long thin piece of the leather, which can be laid on top of the nipple, pressed on, with the cap going home easily. A loading block for bullets can be made by cutting a piece of wood to size, fitting a thong to one end for carrying, and cutting the proper caliber holes in the block, then inserting pregreased bullets. The block is laid over the muzzle, and with the short starter the prelubed bullet is forced from its resting place right into the muzzle of the rifle. Wads can be cut from stout cardboard with a properly sized and sharpened piece of pipe. Patches can be cut from cloth with a standard patch cutter or a homemade chunk of pipe, sharpened. A fine cleaning solvent that contains oil can be made by mixing water-soluble oil with water and dish detergent, this being Moose Milk.

The things that can be wrought from the hands of the modern black powder hunter seem endless indeed, right down to the artistic artifacts that can be carved from wood. Some modern day buckskinners are even returning to the art of scrimshaw, which technically is carving on whale teeth or bone, but loosely can be fine carving on other media, such as horn, with inked lines. I own a beautiful powder horn which is, in effect, scrimshaw-worked by its professional builder.

Do it yourself, black powder man, and add one more dimension to the fascinating sport of black powder hunting. During the off-season, a lot of interesting and relaxing handiwork can be accomplished. Later, these self-made treasures may well prove themselves in the field, to the satisfaction of their maker. And there is one more point not yet mentioned. Greenbacks are kept in the wallet by self-doing. Most projects are inexpensively put together. The modern black powder manufacturer is catering to his clientele today by putting many of his products in kit forms. Of course, this includes rifles, handguns and shotguns, as well as numerous accessories. They save time over starting from scratch, while also saving money.

CHAPTER 17

Care of the Smokepole

Advice on keeping black powder guns clean is related to advice on the common cold—it changes each season, and can reverse itself 180 degrees at any time, depending upon which expert is speaking. On one side of this fence is the all-out method, which requires tubs of water, hot and soapy, and the act of pumping gallons of that water up and down the barrel. The other side of the fence stands for moistening a patch with a touch of saliva or water, running it up and down the bore a few licks, and calling it good. As with most things in life, the Greek Golden Mean applies; in other words, the mid-point between these two extremes is probably best.

Talking about the necessity for cleaning black powder guns is a redundancy today. We all know that black powder is hygroscopic, that is, water attracting. And we know that every time a black powder arm is fired, it must be cleaned, the sooner the better. Old Ned Roberts used to list in order the details that the buckskinner had to attend to when he reached camp at the end of the day. Number one was to feed and care for the horses. Two, clean, oil, and reload the rifle. Then he ate supper, washed dishes, cut wood for the next day, and rested.

We're luckier than Ned was, though, because we have modern chemicals that aid us in the cleaning of our guns. But we can't count on these alone as yet, and there are some good reasons for this. A good kit, such as the Outers, designed for black powder, will contain solvent that can strip a lot of black powder residue from the bore. The main ingredient of this liquid is isopropyl alcohol, and the latter can be used to soften and remove fouling straight out of the bottle and at a good price. It should be followed up with good hard cleaning with a dry patch, however, and then a lightly oiled patch. A lot of chemicals that we put into the barrels are great for getting the gunk out, but tough, in themselves, on the metal. I don't know this to be true of alcohol, but I still recommend that it be removed after it has done the job.

Actually, there are two kinds of black powder cleaning: field and home. Home applies to camp as well as the hunter's house in the city. First, field cleaning. I especially like Moose Milk for this job because it lubes after it cleans. Moose Milk can be made in various proportions, but a good solution is to pour about a half pint of water-soluble oil, obtainable at a machine shop, into a quart container, followed by a tablespoon of dish detergent. The container is then filled with water and the result is a white liquid that resembles milk, hence the Moose Milk handle.

After enough shots to require cleaning, the Moose Milk goes to work. A patch is moistened thoroughly with the solution and the bore is swabbed out, as many times as necessary. Fouling is loosened, and the oil in the Milk offers some lube quality. Naturally, the last patch or two is run in dry so that there will be less chance of a misfire. A good trick is to take a tapered pipe cleaner at this point and run it into the nipple area. These pipe cleaners have a small end and they are absorbent. They will soak up any excess oils there and prevent the powder charge from getting damp.

Before going home the same treatment is given the gun. This beats heck out of letting the debris harden up and then having to scrub it loose at the camp or home. If shooting is done for the day, no dry patch is run down the bore after the Moose Milk is used, but rather, a coating of the liquid is left in the bore to continue working against the fouling and to protect against rusting.

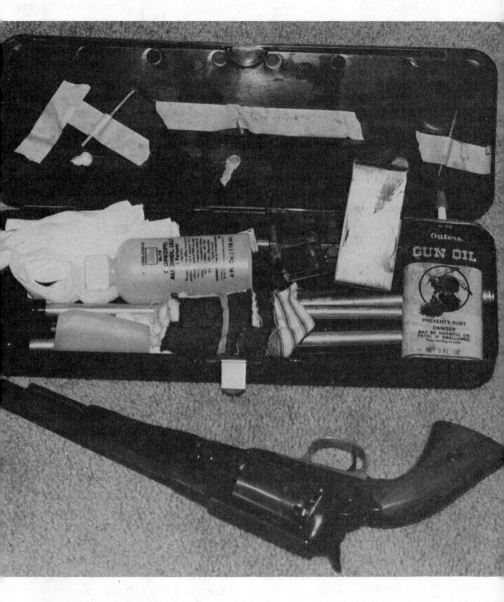

A simple black powder cleaning kit is the Outers model, this one modified by removing the inner rack so that more gear can be stowed away. Small parts, such as spare nipples, allen wrenches, screws, and the like, are taped to the lid of the box. Note the isopropyl alcohol, which is a fine cleaning agent. Purchased in the large bottle, this alcohol is extremely reasonable in price and will do the job of loosening up black powder residue in the bore of the gun.

At home, the barrel is removed from the wood and given a scrubbing, but not the buckets of hot water treatment. I still use hot water, very hot, because this gets the barrel good and hot and any water that may not get mopped up later in the gun someplace has a chance to evaporate. But a coffee can is enough of this, and I don't think adding soap does a thing; therefore, there is but one can of water used. The barrel is dunked down, breech-end first, and indeed, a rod with a tight patch is used to pump hot water up and down the bore. In a few moments most of the goo is gone. Then I run swabs of black powder solvent down the bore. This only takes a few swipes. Taking no chances on leaving chemicals in the bore, I give it the hot water shot for just a few seconds, and then allow the hot barrel to dry. One last patch is run home, very lightly oiled. Sounds time-consuming, but really, it only takes a few moments; it must be considered a part of the care and devotion given to the favorite and faithful muzzle loader.

What about removing the clean-out screw and the nipple in the cleaning process? We are advised that by taking these in and out constantly we stand to work the threads down and eventually bring on leaks of gas. But if we don't remove them, debris will remain in these areas and cause even more havoc. In a test, I fired a rifle and then a shotgun on several different occasions, testing for gunk left around the clean-out screw and nipple on the rifles, and the two nipples on the shotgun. No matter what care I took, when these were not removed, fouling was found in the threads of both clean-out and nipples.

Although in time the nipples and the clean-out will indeed stand a chance of getting sloppy by removal after removal, it is still best to do this, with great care, and then when they do finally get sloppy—and it will take time—oversize nipples can be inserted and an oversize clean-out screw. This is better than having those areas corrode.

Some cleaning takes place *before* the gun is fired. A light coating of petroleum jelly around the nipple before shooting will save the wood from burns and keep the fouling softer. The same applies to the six-gun, just a light coat of jelly in combination with a full patch of lube over each ball in each chamber. Also, a good grade of heavy lube, such as a silicone base, is wise to apply to the inner parts of the lock.

In the field, or at least at camp, there should be a good cleaning kit handy, either a commercial, homemade, or combination of both. In this kit will be the solvent, such as Hodgdon's, Hoppe's, or isopropyl, along with plenty of rags, a two-pound coffee can for holding the hot water, the tapered pipe cleaners, patches, a darn good long cleaning rod with a tip that will accept a cleaning jag as well as screws and worms, and a toothbrush for scrubbing away fouling around nipples and other tight areas. The toothbrush can be used later on with a light oil coating for applying oil to hard to reach spots, too. Some heavy lube, like Lubriplate, is handy to have. This is good not only for the already recommended lock maintenance, but also for a good coating on exterior metal as a final protection against the elements. The metal, still warm from the hot water treatment, will absorb the heavy oil to some extent, but it will also leave a coating to ward off water in the form of rain or humidity.

The black powder cleaning kit, such as Outers, often will have a small plastic bottle with a neoprene tube sticking from its mouth. These are very handy for camp and field. I fill this bottle with black powder solvent of the commercial types, or isopropyl, and attach the end of the neoprene tube directly to the nipple. Then by running a patch up and down the bore, the liquid in the bottle will run up and down the barrel, then back into the bottle, very neat and clean, and effective.

A wise inclusion to the gear going along on an expensive backwoods hunt is the complete black powder cleaning and care kit, which includes all of the above and much more. Packed back in, it is wise to have a back-up rifle, but even with this precaution, it is very nice to be able to repair small problems that may arise, thereby allowing the continued use of the hunter's favorite rifle.

We have already mentioned the ramrod being used for more than pushing bullet and ball down the barrel. With a proper tip, a cleaning jag can be screwed in when it is needed, as well as the screw to remove a ball or bullet, and a worm to go after a patch, or shotgun wadding. Once in a while a ramrod will need some help, especially when trying to pull a stubborn ball free. Then a two foot leather thong is mighty welcomed, for it wraps around the rod and can be tied to a tree. Pulling on the gun with the thong in place will provide the straight-line power to free the stuck rod. This is especially useful when the rod gets stuck on the fouling ring, that spot just ahead of the ball in its loaded position within the barrel. This ring is normal, and a rod can get hung up on it. The trouble is that the ramrod will be all the way down, scarcely anything left showing above the muzzle to grab onto. Then the long leather thong is most helpful indeed.

Naturally, a nipple wrench must go along with the field care and repair kit, and extra nipples. There should be a nipple pick, too. A hat pin will work here, or a piece of fine, strong wire. The tapered pipe cleaner will normally remove junk from the nipple, but sometimes the obstruction is a hard piece of cap that can't be budged by the softer pipe cleaner. Then the pick does its work.

A few good short-handled screwdrivers *that fit* the heads of all screws on the guns that have gone on the hunt is a must. As for extra parts, it is wise to have along a hammer spring; these break once in a while, and adhering to Murphy's Law, it will be at the worst time, such as on an Alaskan trip. A sear spring is a wise addition, takes up very little space, and can save the day. Of course, sear springs have been jury-rigged from safety pins, but it is nice to have the real McCoy along. And an extra sear wouldn't hurt.

A mainspring cramp is nice to have so that the big spring can be held in place while work is performed on the lock. A small three-cornered file is nice to have for working on sights and other small problems that need tuning up. A replacement screw for the clean-out *is a must*. These get lost. One associate was fiddling with his near the campfire. Yep, in it went, and he did not have an extra, nor could we find a screw out there in camp to thread into its place. Ramrods break. This caution does not necessarily apply to the steel or fiberglass rod, but many fine rifles, especially the customs, have wood ramrods. A spare one is wise to have on hand.

A wiping stick, this is the longer "ramrod" used for wiping between shots on the range and for heavy duty cleaning in camp, is very useful, and each hunter should have one along, rather than sharing. This way, if one snaps, there will be another one to take its place. A spare front and rear sight is a good addition for the pack train trips where the gunshop is more than a five-minute drive to town. Rib screws can fall out. A few extra take up almost no space at all.

After a few long treks into the outback, my pards and I have come up with what we call a "possibles box." It is perhaps an unfair trading on the name possibles, but it is possible to find darn near anything we want in it. All of the above paraphernalia is included, and more. The more includes a first aid kit. It is appropriate, we think, to have the fixins for our bodies in the same place as the fixins for our guns. A few quick-rivets are included since they are handy for repairing leather goods. A hunk of wire is also there for whatever use it might be called to serve. There is a needle and thread, as well as the ever-handy awl and its heavy nylon thread. A chunk of acid-core solder is there, though it takes a pretty handy fellow to make really good use of it. We even toss in a few extra balls and patching in a small metal tobacco tin.

A small can of silicone spray is in the box, and a few assorted fishing hooks and some line. Worse comes to worse, we'll tie this onto the end of our ramrods and catch a bass if we get hungry. There is some kind of fire starter, or a can of lighter fluid. If a man falls into cold water and rushes back to camp he won't have to rub two sticks together to get a blaze going. There is a sharpening stone, too. This is not only used for the obvious knife-edge work, but also to hone up a broken sear that needs dressing.

Caring for the sootbelchers is a labor of love, and there really is not that much hard work involved. Each "expert" is going to tell black powder care and cleaning his way, of course, and the reader has to soak it all up, sort it out, stay with what works for him and falls upon his mind as accurate, shun the rest, and finally end up with a modified personal method that keeps his guns in top working order. When in doubt, the hunter should carefully field strip his arm so that the fouling is sought out, located, and gotten rid of, in spite of a little extra time involved. The handgun is the biggest chore, of course, as it requires more stripping than the rifle, and it is wise to go the whole way and do it right.

Someday there will be a bulk powder that gives results similar to black. It might not smoke. It might smoke. But it will be a safe substitute in place of the original charcoal. The purists will cry, moan, and foam at the mouth when this stuff comes out, but it will be invented. After a day of shooting with this powder, the frontstuffer will be wiped down as a modern arm is and stuck back in the closet. Those of us who love the smell of soot burning and the delicate veil of black powder smoke hanging on the air won't use it for hunting, won't even use it for matches, even if it is allowed at these affairs. But when we are all wrapped up with our daily lives, it's going to be fun to get Old Betsy out, especially those handguns, load 'em up and shoot them all we want without having to come home and toss them in a bathtub or stink up our wives' kitchens. Hopefully, technology of this vein will not overrun the sport and render it defunct in terms of its original spirit.

The extent of use given the newfangled stuff will, of course, rest with the individual black powder enthusiasts, as well as the letter of the law in hunting and the rules levied in the black powder shoots and contests.

CHAPTER 18

Off-Season Fellowship and Shooting Matches

The annual days of hunting do not last forever for the modern black powder hunter, and when the season is over, he will want to occupy himself in some facet of his sport until next year. Fortunately, there are a host of interesting things which can be done between hunting seasons. A few of them are mentioned here as starters.

One of the most interesting nonhunting events in black powder is the modern-day rendezvous. A really excellent get-together of this nature is held annually in the Pinedale, Wyoming area, and it attracts people from many, many states, some who try to travel to Wyoming as primitively as possible. Why Pinedale? The reason for this locale is a rather obvious one if a man will study a road map. Pinedale is next to the upper part of the Green River. It is in the same place that the most famous of the original mountain men rendezvous took place, and this one is still called the Green River Rendezvous.

Aside from the main interesting events and sights at the Green River Rendezvous, a buckskinner can meet many of his own kind. This is especially fun for the newcomer, who can learn a great deal from the old pros who gather in Pinedale annually. It's a sight to see. Many of the participants are dressed the part, with buckskin from head to toe, scalp locks dangling from their belts, some original guns, and countless look-alike possibles, or originals that will fascinate any black powder people.

Pinedale is a friendly place all year, but exceptionally so during the Rendezvous. It is in high country in the western part of Wyoming and can be quite cold any time of the year. Though the general surroundings of the city seem somewhat open, with sagebrush rolling hills and antelope flats, the fact is, Pinedale is the gateway to high timber country; and it has been known to snow in the month of June there, though certainly only a flurry. So, the visitor should go prepared with an extra blanket for the cool nights spent in his tepee.

It seems that one rendezvous spurs another, and now there are many all around the country. In 1974 the first annual Fort Bridger Muzzle-Loading Rendezvous was begun, following the pattern set by the Green River and other meetings. Plains-style Indian tepees were erected, and many of the enthusiasts came out of the Midwest, West Coast, and numerous places in the western U.S. Even the ladies came in frontier garb, buckskin dresses, and Indian clothing.

Typical of other rendezvous there were many shoots and prizes. One interesting feature of the Fort Bridger meeting was a blanket shoot, where contestants each laid a prize on an open blanket on the ground, and then the man who shot best took away his first choice, with the second man taking second choice, and so on. There were knife and 'hawk throwing contests. A contest in flint 'n steel fire starting was held. Belt gun (pistol) shooting matches were held. One of the main events had nothing to do with black powder guns and gear, but did relate back to the mountain man's era, and that was a liar's contest. Trading took place in some of the tepees.

For those who might feel closed-in at the larger meetings, such as the Green River and Fort Bridger rendezvous, there are the local clubs, which often hold similar gatherings on a much smaller scale. These are groups of friends who get together once or twice a month as a regular black powder club, and then often, especially in the summertime, hold shoots and camp-outs. Clubs

The black powder hunter in the off-season may entertain himself by joining the local soot belcher's club and getting in on the fun. Here, a member of a black powder club joins in an informal shoot after enjoying a club picnic with the whole family. This kind of practice pays off when the hunting season opens up again in the fall.

can be a great deal of fun, and again, good places for the beginner to learn his sport.

Another social event for off-season black powder hunters is an even less organized outing, the family picnic, with the smell of black powder on the air to give it a new flavor. A couple families can get together and find a lonesome place where they can set up some safe shooting. Between fried chicken and pie a lot of practice can take place, and any of the regular rendezvous events can be tried, from 'hawk tossing to stake busting.

Then there is the N.M.L.R.A. This stands for National Muzzle-Loading Rifle Association, and they stand for "Understanding of and ability in marksmanship with early American

muzzle-loading firearms," and "Match promotion for the purpose of advancing fine accuracy . . .," and "Greater safety with
all firearms, especially with muzzle-loading rifles, pistols, and
shotguns." All of the N.M.L.R.A. platform is well established,
especially the last section. Although this book has not singled
out safety in each chapter, the undercurrent and destination of
every word has been with safety in the background, and there is
no man who is too careful. No hunter, old-timer or newcomer,
practices all that he preaches, or does what he knows to be right
at all times. We know that safety glasses are a must, but we do
not always have them on. And black powder safety is nothing
new. Lewis and Clark, on their famous expedition, had plenty of
trouble in relation to safety practices, and they were always
trying to keep their crew safety-minded.

In fact, Lewis ended up getting shot on their long trek across
the West. A near-sighted fiddle player returning from an elk
hunt apparently saw something moving and fired a .52 ball from
his 1803 Harper's Ferry Rifle. The ball hit Captain Lewis. Fortunately for both the fiddler and the captain, the wound was not
serious enough to hold up the travel. Sometimes the men in the
far west were forced to use their guns improperly in order to save
their lives. Captain Lewis records that on July 15, 1806, a man
named Hugh McNeal broke his musket while clubbing a charging grizzly bear, and many a mountain man was known to
wreck his rifle while using it as a club.

So it is that the N.M.L.R.A. states boldly that one of its main
reasons for existence is promotion of safety. However, the group
does even more. Located at P.O. Box 67 in Friendship, Indiana
47021, they are headquarters for the most important major
black powder shoots in the country. Two of the biggest are the
"Spring Shoot," and the "Fall National Championship Shoot."
The latter is what we know as the "Nationals," and is, probably,
the chief black powder shooting event in the world. N.M.L.R.A.
holds these shoots in its home area, Friendship, about 75 miles
south of Indianapolis. Hundreds and hundreds of shooters
gather in Friendship for these and lesser meets each year, carrying with them every kind of black powder arm imaginable, from
old originals to modern tack-drivers made by hand in custom
shops.

There are more events at these matches than can be mentioned here, including the Seneca match, probably the most
popular of all, though only a few men take part in it. The entrees

for the Seneca must be dressed in original garb, buckskin dress and beaver hat. Competitors train for it all year in many cases, because the match contains more than shooting. The match consists of a 300 yard run, and it is a run, through a course that contains many obstacles, and while covering this 300 yards the contestant must shoot at five targets, loading safely as he goes. There is a possible 50 score, and many of the top men end up with high 40s on this run, taking no more than seven to eight minutes to cover the ground, load, and shoot.

The N.M.L.R.A. does more yet, including helping clubs form all over the country. They are the citadel of record-keeping and organizing for the black powder shooter.

There is also the historical type black powder gathering, such as the North-South Skirmish, where hundreds gather dressed in Civil War clothing and ready to compete against each other. This is a totally friendly gathering, as a matter of fact, and not a memorial to war, but rather a memorial to history. The participants have a great time and make many new friends among both blue and gray uniforms.

The primitive matches are also great fun. Using fixed sights, there are often interesting targets set up at various ranges. One match has an iron skillet at 80 yards, a clay pipe at 30 yards, and a cut feather at 20 yards. A really interesting event is splitting the ball. An axe blade, sharp, is set up with the edge facing the shooter. His task is to hit the blade dead on, thereby splitting the lead ball in two. But that's not all. The two halves are now directed to break two clay birds that are hanging behind the axe blade. These are fun matches that can be duplicated at any shoot.

Aside from the organized shoots and outings, from small family gatherings to the big N.M.L.R.A. matches, the off-season black powder hunter has a number of things that he can do to occupy his time and further his knowledge and interest in his sport. During the few weeks prior to the opening of the season, big or small game, he can scout. This has been mentioned before, but is worth repeating, for scouting before the hunt often makes the difference between success and failure in terms of filling the pot. Also, scouting gives a chance for practice. There is great practice value in finding game and stalking it, even though no shot is fired.

When the old mountain man was not on the trail, he holed up for winter and did his chores, such as repairs and rebuilding

In the off-season, testing and practice is a must for the modern black powder hunter. Here the shooters are testing new all-lead projectiles by shooting them first into a target for practice, but trapping them in a clay bank behind the target so they can be unearthed and studied. (Nick Fadala photo)

of his gear. The modern black powder man is well advised to do the same. Repairs and modifications can be attended to during the slack season. Naturally, this is a good time to build black powder gear in the home workshop, as well as modify existing tools and repair things.

A lot of experimenting can be accomplished in the off-season. The club chronograph can get a workout and a buckskinner can prove to himself the true speed of the load he has carefully and safely worked up. Not only that, but new gear can be broken in and tested, too. It does not have to be a hunt, and shouldn't be one, to find out if a pair of boots is going to pinch the foot, or a new jacket bind the shooting act.

Finally, when the season is closed a fellow can catch up on his reading. There are many good periodicals that can be sifted through. Sometimes the reader will want to make photocopies of some of this information, or put together a black powder notebook filled with useful hints on loading techniques, do-it-yourself projects, or hunting hints and tricks. A part of the reading can be the fascinating history of the fur trade, as there are numerous good books and articles on this subject. The modern hunter gains an appreciation for his sport by learning more of the men who did black powder hunting for a living. There are books which contain the work of frontier artists, and in them a hunter can find authentic drawings and paintings of frontier days, as well as the gear used back then. In fact, a fellow enthusiast has looked into prints by Remington and other artists of the period and has tried to duplicate some of the mountain man tools and clothing that he has seen there. One product was a beautiful buckskin gun case that looks an awful lot like that carried by an old mountain man over a hundred years ago.

The black powder season is never really over. The focus simply changes. A lot of planning and enjoyable black powder activities take place when the hunt is closed down. There is much learning that can be gained. And when it again becomes time to roam the hills and fields for game, the man will be refreshed, better equipped with know-how and tools, and ready to go at it another time. Closed season is not really closed season for the man who wants to enjoy his sport all year. And if he wants a taste of the "real thing" from time to time when game is not open, he can turn to varmints and predators, for often these will remain in season when everything else is closed down.

CHAPTER 19

The Outlook for the Sport Today

One of the finest adventures remaining in our country awaits those who are willing to enter the woods and fields carrying black powder guns and gear. Daily, the ranks of these "primitive" hunters grow, and looking at a crystal ball that shows the future of hunting in America, we can assume that there will be even more old-style hunting in times to come. As the number of hunters grows, while the habitat of the wild animal shrinks, doing it the old way may well be the new way, and a trend is already starting in that direction. State after state initiates special seasons for the primitive hunt and its hunters, as shown in the survey presented in Chapter Twenty.

There are some opposed to this trend, mostly the uninitiated and self-appointed experts. These fellows claim that there is no difference at all between black powder hunting and modern arms hunting. To those boys we all echo the challenge, "Come try it!" Anyone who thinks that there is no difference between hunting with a modern repeating, or even single-shot, cartridge rifle with precision barrel and telescopic sight and a single-shot, front-stuffing, low-trajectory muzzle loader is not thinking at all. I have encountered a few of these men who would oppose the sport and I have offered this challenge—come shoot with me. I'll set up a target at 200 yards, shoot at it with my 7mm Frank Wells custom, and you shoot with any frontstuffer prepared for the hunting field. If you win, you can have my 7mm Mag. No takers on this offer yet.

Black powder is also a wonderful way to start the young hunter. This does not mean that we do not wish our young shooters to learn modern arms. Far from it. Not a word of disparagement has been cast on modern arms in this text, nor on modern weapon hunting. In fact, in many places where a high harvest is a must, the more difficult muzzle loader is probably not the best tool in the hands of the average hunter. But black powder is an excellent teacher of youth.

First, the loading technique is more precise and involved. The young shooter gets a chance to understand a very basic principle of the load itself: where the ignition, the powder charge, and the projectile are. He must learn safety not only in terms of how much powder to use behind each ball or bullet, but also how to be certain that each and every load is firmly against the powder charge. He also learns such techniques and principles as putting proper pressure on the ramrod so that the more compressed load will burn its powder charge better.

There is more hands-on procedure with the black powder gun, not only in the slow loading process, but also in clean-up. A youth has to learn how to field strip his piece and clean it carefully and responsibly. Each time he goes through this he finds out more about his firearm and comes to respect it more. He has a lot of time invested in that shooting iron, more than he would have in a smokeless arm that can be fired, wiped down, and laid back into the closet. The black powder gun requires more care, and it develops the responsibility of the young shooter because of it.

I also like the fact that there is no chance for rapid fire in black powder shooting. Surely, there may be a value in repeated fire later on, but the newcomer need not involve himself with this process. He is better off with the attitude that he has one shot, only one shot; and that single bullet must go where it is aimed, for a second chance will be darn slow in arriving.

This one-shot attitude moves into the field with the young hunter. He finds that he must not rely on banging away at a

Starting a youth with a black powder firearm has many advantages, including a good sense of responsibility in loading the single-shot arm for each and every shot fired, and cleaning up after the outing. Here, the author's son, John Fadala, has his first cottontail with a breechloading .22 black powder rifle at age seven.

game animal because he is not capable of it with a frontstuffer. I think this will make him a more careful hunter and shooter later on when he takes to cartridge guns, too. He cannot fire upon animals far across a hill with any hope of consistent success. And this, too, is good. He learns that stalking is a great part of hunting. Finding that game animal before it locates the hunter, and then figuring a way to get close to it, becomes the byword. He shouldn't trudge along in hopes of kicking something out then knocking it down when it shows itself a few hundred yards up the ridge. Again, this is not to toss rocks at modern hunting. It takes great skill to drop an animal cleanly at long range, and I don't care what modern flat-shooting scope-sighted rifle is in the play. But we are talking about youth here, and it seems better to me to have the new hunter work close and put that one shot right where it belongs. He will learn a lot about game this way, especially finding out just how well equipped most animals are to see and hear man in the outdoors. Finally, I have a suspicion that a young hunter taking his first game with the basic firearm is going to enjoy a somewhat higher level of appreciation for his sport.

Another plus of black powder guns has been fewer restraints on their use. After all, the government has recognized, even though some folks have not, that these are primitive by modern standards. Black powder guns, as this is written, may be shipped. A hunter can feel free to order from a catalogue if he so desires and receive in the mail a black powder firearm.

Of course, there are hassles, but so far they have not deterred the black powder shooter from enjoying his sport. Black powder has been restricted as to shipment policy, and there are those forces which would have it banned. There has always been trouble of this nature afoot. Back in 1865 Ned Roberts relates a ploy used by powder shippers. Due to restriction, there was a bit of smuggling going on. A 25-pound can of powder was shipped in a 50-pound can of lard with a false bottom. The inspectors were known to have probing sticks that reached down into the lard buckets, and the smugglers set the black powder just one inch below the level of these probes so the Government man would feel only lard, and not propellent, when he poked down into the can.

In the age of genetic engineering, space travel, and computerized tax returns, many eyes have turned back to a quieter America for a form of recreation that was once a livelihood to an amazing breed of men gone West. It is a sport that can be approached in many different ways, individually, and its rewards are often very personal. Modern black powder hunting is back from the past to stay and destined to gain an even more prominent foothold in the American hunting future.

Remaining are two chapters that can prove valuable to the buckskinner as well as to the novice in the black powder hunting scene. First, there is a rundown of hunts and regulations for black powder in the U.S.A. Then, in the final chapter of the book, there is a brief listing of manufacturers of black powder guns and gear. Used as a reference point, both of these chapters can be a time-saver for the reader, as well as a source of information.

Until we meet on the black powder hunting trail, keep your eye shining for that big buck, your powder dry, and your face ever in the wind. Good Hunting!

CHAPTER 20

Rules and Regulations
For the Fifty States

Day by day, black powder hunting gains more devotees, and in recognition of this, the game departments of the country have responded by offering special seasons for the buckskinner, or if not allowing him this privilege, at least acknowledging his sport by allowing the use of his primitive arms during regular hunting season. Below, is a compilation of the 50 states and their attitudes toward black powder. Addresses are given for each state because the hunter can use this section as a guide, deciding where he wants to hunt and what game he wants to pursue; then he must write for full details, including any possible changes in the law since this information was compiled.

Looking at each state, it becomes obvious that all 50 have had to say something about black powder, even those states which have not as yet offered special seasons for the sport. Alaska, for example, while having no special black powder hunts, has made the statement that black powder hunting is acceptable and legal, with no restrictions as to caliber, powder charge, type of ignition, barrel length, or any other criterion.

Of course states have always varied widely in their ballistic requirements for hunting and types of guns allowed for the chase. In black powder terms some of these laws are difficult to understand, but they exist and must be obeyed. The reader will be puzzled by some of the requirements, such as bullet length and exposed ignition versus exterior ignition. The rules, however, apply, and most of them are sensible and worthwhile. Some states will outlaw the telescopic sight for the special primitive season. If we look for a moment we can understand this rule, for the spirit of the hunt is essentially thwarted by changing the old-time nature of the frontloader.

On the other hand, while hunting with the cartridge shooters a black powder hunter may use a telescopic sight in most states. This is also reasonable. After all, he is competing with long-range repeaters with glass sights. Certainly he should be allowed to use magnification on his slow-loading single shot. The double-barrel rifle is often legal on primitive hunts, but not always. The percussion is almost always legal for these special hunts, but not always. Sometimes the hunter is limited as to the projectile he can shoot, round ball or Minie, but not always. The many nuances of law make it necessary for us to look at the 50 states collectively to decide where we want to go for what, and then write to that state for all the information we need, including dates of the hunt, game management units open and closed, bag limits, and hunting fees. Today, it is becoming a common practice for hunters in various states to get together and share their hunting knowledge. This is a "hunter's trade society," where a man in one state learns his game and uses the buddy system to help his out-of-state friend bag a limit. The favor is returned when the man who played host first time around becomes guest. A hunter's seasons are doubled by this method.

Black powder hunters are a friendly breed. And they usually form some sort of club. This fact is especially helpful to the man who wants to hunt out of state, but knows no one who can advise or "guide" him. By looking at the 50-state compilation below, deciding what game is to be hunted in what state, and then writing to the game department for information, the hunter can often obtain the address of a state black powder club. The president of this club will be happy to help set up a black powder hunt trade most of the time if not always. A man sitting in Tennessee boar country may write to a black powder hunter residing in Montana elk country and the two can get together and exchange hunts. Better yet, by writing to the National Muzzle-Loading Rifle Association, whose current address can be found in any recent issue of *Muzzle Blasts,* black powder hunting clubs' locations can be learned.

Finally, the listing of black powder hunts and laws for the 50 states is fun to browse through even if the hunter does not intend to become a nonresident hunter. The future is going to bring more attention to the black powder hunter and his game. As habitat decreases and hunter population increases, the quieter and simpler style of primitive hunting is becoming more appreciated.

ALABAMA
Department of Conservation & Natural Resources
Game & Fish Division
Montgomery, AL 36104

"The state of Alabama, with a variety of game running from alligator to whitetail deer, allows the use of black powder during the regular hunting season, and also offers special primitive weapons seasons in most of their game management units," explains Dalton Halbrook of the Division.

Calibers are restricted to .40 and over, but no other regulations are stated for black powder weapons.

ALASKA
Department of Fish & Game
Subport Building
Juneau, AK 99801

"Alaska big and small game regulations make no distinction for the black powder hunter. We do not restrict caliber, bullet type, or weight, nor do we have special hunts. Current regulations do, however, preclude the use of muzzle loaders for taking marine mammals," says Donald McKnight, Research Chief.

All nonmarine wildlife may be hunted with black powder in Alaska in accord with the regular hunting laws.

ARIZONA
Game & Fish Department
2222 W. Greenway Road
Phoenix, AZ 85023

"Each year we are experiencing more interest in the sport and more people are becoming fascinated with not only black powder hunting but the ability to build their own guns from kits . . . Once you put the kit together, what else is there to do but take the gun out and use it?," says John Russo of the Department.

Arizona does have special black powder hunts for deer and javelina. Restrictions simply state "muzzle-loading rifles" for big game. And for turkey and javelina the black powder man may use a pistol of .36 caliber or over. Muzzle loaders may be used during regular hunting seasons.

ARKANSAS
Game & Fish Commission
Game & Fish Commission Building
Little Rock, AR 72201

"Black powder weapons are legal for all hunting in Arkansas as long as the black powder weapon used is the same type as the allowed modern weapon . . . shotguns for turkey, black powder handguns for rabbits and squirrels, and .40 caliber or larger arms on deer. There is a nineday permit muzzle-loading deer hunt . . .," says Lew Johnston, Game Biologist.

Arkansas welcomes the black powder hunter, who may use his basic arms during the regular, as well as special hunts.

CALIFORNIA
Fish & Game Commission
1416 Ninth Street
Sacramento, CA 95814

Muzzle-loading rifles and shotguns may be used on all game in California, but no special seasons are open for the black powder buff. The state has an estimated 1.5 million mule deer, but hunting conditions keep the percentage of success low, about 10 to 15 per cent.

"The nonresident may hunt bear with his muzzle loader, as well as deer, waterfowl and all small game," explains Leslie Edgerton of the Department.

COLORADO
Colorado Division of Wildlife
6060 N. Broadway
Denver, CO 80216

All huntable game in Colorado may be taken with black powder arms, and there are special seasons on elk and deer for the muzzle-loading fan. Furthermore, if the hunter is unsuccessful during these special primitive hunts, he may buy a license for the regular season.

Caliber .50 or larger must be used on elk. A .40 or larger is legal on deer and antelope. The rifle must use iron sights, be of single barrel, firing a ball or a bullet "the length of which does not exceed twice the diameter."

CONNECTICUT
Department of Environmental Protection
Wildlife Unit - Room 252
Hartford, CT 06115

The state of Connecticut is clear and concise on black powder. As Timothy Linkkila, Supervisor, says, "There are more and more sportsmen turning to black powder in Connecticut. All game may be taken by black powder, and we have a special one-week muzzle-loader deer season."

No mention of restrictions on black powder weapons is given.

DELAWARE
Department of Natural Resources and Environmental Control
Division of Fish & Wildlife - D Street
Dover, DE 19901

There is a special combined archery and black powder deer hunt in Delaware. Normally, game in this state is hunted with shotgun due to population, but a frontloader is legal as long as it is caliber .42 or over and the barrel is 30 inches or longer. The BP shotgun must be 10 gauge or smaller.

FLORIDA
Game & Fresh Water Fish Commission
Farris Bryant Building
Tallahassee, FL 32304

"In Florida, as elsewhere, there is an ever-increasing interest in black powder shooting. It does not appear that this interest has topped out yet. The commission tries to provide the maximum recreation in keeping with the best interest of the resource. Each season during the past three years, the primitive weapons hunters have been given more opportunity. I presume this will continue. Small game may be taken with a handgun as long as specific management area regulations do not state otherwise," says Maurice Naggier, Editor of *Florida Wildlife*.

Uniquely, Florida opens several species for the primitive weapons hunter, including boar (wild hog), deer, squirrel, quail, and rabbit. Muzzle loaders for deer must be at least 20 gauge, but not larger than 10 gauge and a rifled bore must go .40 or over. Muzzle loaders capable of using any type of self-contained actual cartridge are not allowed.

GEORGIA
Department of Natural Resources
270 Washington Street, S.W.
Atlanta, GA 30334

"The future of primitive weapons hunting in the state appears good. Deer hunting on our wildlife management areas with primitive weapons, mostly muzzle loaders, is very popular. We do not have an exclusive hunting season for black powder hunters," says Carroll Allen, Biologist.

Although there are no specific black powder hunts, there are "primitive hunts" in which bows or black powder can be used. The muzzle loader must be caliber .44 or over using iron sights only; the ML shotgun must be 20 gauge or more. Small and nongame may be hunted simply with "muzzle-loading firearms."

HAWAII
Department of Land Resources
Division of Fish and Game
1151 Punchbowl Street
Honolulu, HI 96813

"We do not permit the use of such hunting arms on state-owned or controlled lands; however, there are no restrictions on its use on private lands. At present we do not have any plans to implement this type of hunting. The people who use these arms are for the most part hobbyists," says Noah Pekelo of the Department.

Obviously, the use of black powder in Hawaii is not encouraged, but may be employed on private property, and has been for boar, axis deer, blacktails, mouflon, and upland birds.

IDAHO
Fish & Game Department
600 S. Walnut Street
Boise, ID 83707

"There is little question that the sport of black powder shooting and hunting is destined to increase in popularity and opportunity over the coming years. In this day, with the demand for hunting on the increase and the vital ingredients for more game on the decrease, it is essential that hunters look at the total experience rather than hunting solely for meat or trophy. Black powder hunts lend themselves to this philosophy, and I see no reason why they won't be utilized to a greater extent in the future," says Jerry Thiessen, Big Game Supervisor.

Idaho does have special seasons for the black powder enthusiast, including a new special antelope hunt by drawing. The rifle must be over .40 caliber, loaded from the muzzle with black powder or equivalent and iron sights only are allowed on the special hunts. Revolvers are okay as long as they meet the standard requirements.

All game legal for modern weapons is legal for black powder including waterfowl and upland birds.

There are seven special hunts for buckskinners currently, including a fine season in September that allows for deer, elk, and bear on the same outing.

ILLINOIS
Dept. of Conservation
605 State Office Building
400 Spring St.
Springfield, IL 62706

"The future of black powder weapons seems to be fairly promising in this state. We are initiating steps to determine how many muzzle loaders attempt to take deer during the Illinois shotgun season. We do not have any special black powder hunting seasons; however, we do have specific areas for muzzle loaders during the deer season," says Forrest Loomis, Biologist.

Shotguns are used for deer hunting in this state, but the muzzle-loading fan may use his rifle if it is caliber .38 or more and has a barrel at least 26 inches long, shooting black powder only with flint or percussion ignitions.

INDIANA
Department of Natural Resources
State Office Building
Indianapolis, IN 46204

"In Indiana hunters may use any black powder firearm for taking any game species with the following exceptions: wild turkey, only muzzle-loading shotguns of 20 gauge or larger loaded with pellets; deer, muzzle-loading rifles of .44 caliber or larger loaded with single ball or elongated bullets; and waterfowl, only shotguns no larger than 10 gauge. We feel that black powder weapons are here to stay and encourage their use during regular hunting seasons," says Edward Hansen, Chief of Wildlife.

Indiana does not as yet have any black powder only season, as such, except for a special one-day hunt on Jefferson Proving Ground.

IOWA
Conservation Commission
Wallace State Office Building
Des Moines, IA 50319

"I believe that black powder shooting and hunting has a great future in Iowa. Each year there are more people hunting with the muzzle loader and attending the rifle shoots," says Charles "Butch" Olofson, Hunter Safety Officer.

Although there are no special BP seasons, the buckskinner is free to hunt alongside his breechloading friends if he uses a smooth-bore or rifled arm of caliber .44 or larger with a maximum shotgun bore of 10 gauge (.775). No deer, turkey, or waterfowl may be hunted with BP handguns, but other game apparently may be.

KANSAS
Forestry, Fish & Game Office
Box 1028
Pratt, KS 67124

No special BP hunts, but all game including deer and antelope may be hunted with BP arms of .40 caliber or more. The nonresident may not hunt large game in Kansas. Only small game.

KENTUCKY
Department of Fish & Wildlife Resources
Frankfort, KY 40601

Hope Carleton, Director for PR of the Department, says that any normally hunted game in Kentucky can be pursued by legal black powder guns. "We have a special area known as the Pioneer Weapons Wildlife Management Area." This area is open only to the muzzle-loading enthusiast or archer.

The rifle must be .38 and up in size.

LOUISIANA
Wildlife and Fisheries Commission
400 Royal Street
New Orleans, LA 70130

There are special black powder hunts in this state. The gun must be single barrel, .44 or larger, or single barrel shotgun under 10 gauge firing single ball, no buckshot. Percussion or flint may be used, only iron sights, with ignition system exposed to the elements.

MAINE
Department of Inland Fisheries & Wildlife
284 State Street
Augusta, ME 04333

"In the State of Maine we have no special black powder hunting season; however, any animals or birds that may be hunted, can, if the hunter so chooses, be taken with a black powder firearm," says Alanson Noble, Chief Warden.

No black powder restrictions are listed.

MARYLAND
Fish & Wildlife Administration
State Office Building
Annapolis, MD 21401

A special BP season is listed on the Eastern Neck Wildlife Refuge. Muzzle loaders may be carried where modern arms are legal if they are .40 to .775 in caliber, and they must be loaded with at least 60 grains of powder.

MASSACHUSETTS
Division of Fisheries and Game
State Office Building
Boston, MA 02202

Although no standard rifles may be used for deer hunting in this state, the muzzle loader of .44 to .775 with a smooth-bore barrel may be employed. There has been a special three-day primitive arms hunt in Massachusetts.

MICHIGAN
Department of Natural Resources
Box 30028
Lansing, MI 48909

Robert Timmer of the Department says: "It appears that black powder hunting is gaining in popularity in Michigan . . . varmints can be shot with black powder firearms and handguns, also small game."

There is a special muzzle-loading season for male deer and a shotgun or rifle can be used, but the rifle must be of caliber .44 or larger, shooting a round ball with black powder. Bear may be hunted with black powder, too.

MINNESOTA
Division of Fish and Wildlife
390 Centennial Building
658 Cedar Street
St. Paul, MN 55155

"Muzzle loaders have always been legal for taking game in Minnesota," says Leroy Rutske, Wildlife Specialist. And there is now a special deer season for the black powder enthusiast, acquired in 1977. The arm must be at least .40 caliber if it is rifled, or at least .45 if it is a smoothbore. Flintlocks or percussion are allowed. Small game may also be hunted with frontfeeders.

MISSISSIPPI
Game & Fish Commission
Box 451
Jackson, MS 39209

Regulations vary by county. BP shotguns and rifles with single ball or slug without scopes are legal for hunting deer and turkey. No special seasons.

MISSOURI
Dept. of Conservation
2901 N. Ten Mile Drive
Jefferson City, MO 65101

"Missouri is a state where competition shooting and hunting with black powder arms never did die out. There have always been a few persons who utilized black powder guns for these things. In recent years there has been an upsurge in black powder, both for pleasure shooting and hunting," says James Keefe, Information Officer.

The state has "historic weapons" only seasons in which mostly muzzle loaders are used. They are on permit and always oversubscribed. "Thus there is no doubt as to the popularity of such events," states Mr. Keefe. Muzzle loaders may also be used wherever legal modern arms are used.

MONTANA
Department of Fish & Game
Helena, MT 59601

"Montana laws do not address hunting with black powder or primitive firearms. Therefore, the laws and regulations apply to all firearms hunting. We do not have black powder only hunting seasons," says R.H. Bird, Chief of Safety and Training.

Montana has no caliber limitations, other than shotguns being no larger than 10 gauge. Therefore, it follows that all hunting in this state is open to black powder arms, including predators and varmints, which are open all year without license and bag limit.

NEBRASKA
P.O. Box 508
Bassett, NB 68714

"There are no restrictions on muzzle loaders for small game or unprotected species, except that game birds may not be taken with a rifle or pistol. For deer and antelope, only muzzle loading rifles of .40 caliber or larger are legal. We have one area, the De Soto National Wildlife Refuge, which had deer hunting for muzzle loaders only. Another small area will probably be added next year for muzzle loader only deer," states Karl Menzel, Big Game Specialist.

NEVADA
Department of Fish & Game
P.O. Box 10678
Reno, NV 89510

"Nevada law currently allows the taking of big game animals, e.g. mule deer, antelope, bighorn sheep, elk, and mountain lion, with black powder *rifles* if they meet this specification: 'Use of Muzzle-Loading Rifle; a muzzle-loading rifle, either flintlock or percussion, of .44 caliber or larger, shooting a lead ball or conical bullet is permitted.' In addition, state law allows the taking of mountain lion with a muzzle-loading black powder pistol," relates David Rice, Information Officer.

Small game may also be hunted in Nevada with BP guns, and so may waterfowl. There are no special BP hunts right now in Nevada, although the black powder hunters in the state are asking for one.

NEW HAMPSHIRE
Fish & Game Department
Box 2003
34 Bridge Street
Concord, N.H. 03301

Lee Salber, Information Officer for New Hampshire, says "Our muzzle loader season has been received enthusiastically ever since it started in 1963. Muzzle loader license sales have increased steadily. We have a special ten-day deer and bear season for muzzle loaders that runs prior to the regular rifle season. Only single shot muzzle-loading firearms of .40 caliber or larger may be used."

Small game in season is open to BP, too. Waterfowl may be taken with BP shotgun.

NEW JERSEY
Division of Fish & Game
Box 1809
Trenton, N.J. 08625

Although this urbanized state has good game populations there seems to be no organized interest in black powder hunting to date and nothing on primitive arms is mentioned. No rifles allowed.

NEW MEXICO
Department of Game & Fish
Santa Fe, NM 87503

Jesse Williams, Chief of Public Affairs, says, "As in most states, muzzle-loading hunting is becoming more and more popular and I see no reason why this will not continue."

New Mexico is asking hunters to choose between modern and primitive arms as this is written, and once the hunter has a license for one type he cannot switch to the other. There is a special deer season for black powder only. The rifle must be at least .40 caliber, and for BP small game in this state a 28 gauge is the smallest allowed. Muzzle loaders may be used on all game, but black powder pistols may not be used on javelina, although modern handguns are allowed.

NEW YORK
Division of Fish & Wildlife
50 Wolf Road
Albany, NY 12201

Where gun hunting is permitted, the black powder arm is also allowed. There are no special seasons for primitive hunters. The arm is supposed to be .44 or larger for BP, loaded with at least 60 grains of powder, but not over 120 grains.

NORTH CAROLINA
Wildlife Resources Commission
Raleigh, NC 27611

"Shotguns and rifles using black powder are legal and there is a three-day special muzzle-loading only season for deer prior to the regular gun season," says C.J. Overton, Assistant Chief of Enforcement.

No special caliber provisions are mentioned.

NORTH DAKOTA
Game & Fish Department
Bismarck, ND 58505

"Deer hunting is permitted with muzzle-loading rifles of .40 or larger during the normal gun season. We have no special black powder only seasons or special areas where only muzzle-loaders are used. No such special seasons are contemplated in the near future," says C.G. James, Biologist, who adds, "I think black powder hunting will slowly grow over the coming years."

OHIO
Department of Natural Resources
Fountain Square
Columbus, OH 43224
"There is a growing interest in primitive weapons hunting in our state as evidenced by the yearly increase of hunters who participate in the special primitive weapons hunting season for deer," says Kim Heller, Information Officer.

Ohio hunters may take small game with BP, including handguns, but handguns cannot be used during the regular deer season. There are no animals classified as varmints in Ohio, but all game may be taken with BP if it is also open for smokeless. There is a special primitive season for buck deer, and a black powder arm of .38 or larger using a single projectile is legal.

OKLAHOMA
Department of Wildlife Conservation
1801 N. Lincoln
Oklahoma City, OK 73105

"Black powder hunters in Oklahoma have very few restrictions," writes M. Frank Carl, Western Regional Supervisor. "They are permitted to hunt with muzzle-loading shotguns for all upland species. Black powder rifles may also be used on turkey, squirrel, and rabbit. There are no restrictions as to type of muzzle loaders used in either predator or varmint hunting."

The state does have a special BP season, an either-sex deer hunt. Flintlocks or percussions are legal, .40 or larger, firing a single slug or ball, black powder, or Pyro only, iron sights. In this state a black powder handgun is legal for dispatching a game animal wounded with a rifle first and down.

OREGON
Department of Fish & Wildlife
506 S.W. Mill Street
Portland, OR 97208

Ken Durbin, Oregon Information Officer, says that "Black powder hunting in Oregon is practiced by an ever increasing number of hunters. And, in fact, there seems to be an increasing interest in all types of primitive weapons, anything that handicaps the hunter and puts more challenge in his hunt."

Oregon has four special hunts for deer, with a new BP elk season coming up. Right now the state has energy limits on the rifles allowed for elk, being 1,220 foot pounds retained at 100 yards. Since this is a kinetic energy figure, some black powder loads would surely fall short of the mark.

On other game, but not elk and sheep, the muzzle loader must be of .40 caliber and does not need to meet the energy requirement. It must be single barrel, flint or percussion, using black powder or Pyro, loaded from muzzle only, iron sighted with exposed ignition and a barrel at least 26 inches long.

PENNSYLVANIA
Game Commission
P.O. Box 1567
Harrisburg, PA 17120

Glenn Bowers of the Department says: "Black powder guns have always been permissible for hunting in Pennsylvania with only three restrictions," and he names them as these: first, the rifle must fire only one lead projectile. Two, during the special season, only a .44 or larger may be used, *flintlock*, with iron sights. And, three, the black powder guns must meet the same crimes codes rules as any other arm.

The special muzzle loader season was initiated in 1974 and has increased in popularity.

RHODE ISLAND
Division of Wildlife
83 Park Street
Providence, RI 02903

No special BP hunts. No rifles. Smoothbore and muzzle loaders are allowed with deer being major big game.

SOUTH CAROLINA
Wildlife and Marine Resources Department
P.O. Box 167, Dutch Plaza, Building D
Columbia, SC 29202

"There is a special deer hunt for the BP enthusiast," reports W. B. Conrad, Chief Game Warden. "No changes or additions are contemplated at this time."

The black powder shotgun must be 20 gauge and up, and the rifle must be at least .36 caliber with open sights only. No revolvers. No pistols, and the ignition must be primitive only, percussion cap or flint, firing black powder only.

SOUTH DAKOTA
Department of Game, Fish & Parks
Anderson Building
Pierre, SD 57501

Ken Moum, Information Specialist, reports: "We allow hunting for all game animals with muzzle-loading weapons." The state does have one special BP only hunt for deer.

Handguns must have a muzzle energy of over 650 foot pounds, but the rule that they must fire factory ammo automatically excludes the BP type, it would seem. Rifle must be .42 or more in bore.

TENNESSEE
Wildlife Resources
Ellington Agricultural Center
P.O. Box 40747
Nashville, TN 37204

Michael O'Malley, Information Supervisor, says: "Muzzle-loading cap or flintlock rifles with rifled barrel(s) of .40 minimum are permitted for taking deer, bear, and hog during all big game hunts where rifles are allowed. Muzzle-loading shotguns and rifles are also legal for taking small game and game birds."

The ML shotgun is legal for waterfowl in this state, too, 10 gauge or smaller. But BP pistols are not legal for any game. There are many

238   **Black Powder Hunting**

special primitive hunts in Tennessee, and Mr. O'Malley says further that "Muzzle-loading hunting is increasing in popularity each year."

TEXAS
Parks and Wildlife Department
4200 Smith School Road
Austin, TX 78744

G.A. Boydston, Technical Programs Coordinator for the Division, stated that while they do not have a special black powder hunt at this time, there is enthusiasm for such a season. At this time, experimental hunts on two wildlife management units are being conducted to evaluate muzzle loaders in terms of efficiency and success for hunters.

There appears to be no specific restriction on the use of black powder during regular hunting seasons, other than those applied to smokeless guns. The state of Texas is game rich, and the black powder enthusiast will find much to keep him interested.

UTAH
Division of Wildlife Resources
1596 W. North Temple
Salt Lake City, UT 84116

"The future of muzzleloader hunting looks very good if we can keep it a 'primitive' sport and not let it get contaminated with substitutes and modern gadgetry. Seasons are getting more liberal; membership in muzzle loader clubs is booming," says A. L. Robertson, Training Specialist.

Any gun may be used on nonprotected small game, such as jackrabbit. A black powder shotgun is legal for all upland game. All big game may be taken with black powder rifles of over .40 caliber, but no shotguns. Black powder must be used, only iron sights. There is a special hunt for deer.

VERMONT
Agency of Environmental Conservation
Department of Fish & Game
Montpelier, VT 05602

"In Vermont we have nothing special on the subject of black powder guns. They can be used the same as any other gun under our laws," says Walter Cabell, Chief Warden. Mr. Cabell goes on to inform that there are objections to any special seasons for BP from landowners who already have enough pressure.

VIRGINIA
Commission of Game & Inland Fisheries
4010 W. Broad Street
Richmond, VA 23230

A consensus of the law on black powder is extracted from the Virginia regulations as follows: "Hunters using muzzle-loading guns (single-shot flintlock or sidelocks percussion weapon) may hunt deer only on Jefferson National Forest. Weapons must be at least .45 caliber, fire a single projectile loaded from the muzzle end, and propelled by a minimum of 50 grains of black powder. Telescopic sights are prohibited."

WASHINGTON
Department of Game
600 N. Capitol Way
Olympia, WA 98501

Black powder is popular in this northern state. There are many special seasons, as well as BP hunting allowed during the regular season. There are restrictions on the ML rifle that may be used, however. It must be a single- or double-barreled rifle of original-ignition design with that ignition exposed to the elements. Black powder and ball must be loaded from the muzzle. Caliber .40 is minimum, and the barrel must be at least 20 inches long, iron sights only. Percussion caps are all right, as is flint, but no other devices for ignition. Further, only one barrel of a double can be loaded during the special primitive hunts, though both can be loaded during the regular season hunts.

WEST VIRGINIA
Department of Natural Resources
Division of Wildlife
1800 Washington Street East
Charleston, WV 25305

Susan Taylor of the Division states that there is no special season for black powder fans in her state. But black powder is allowed during the regular season.

WISCONSIN
Department of Natural Resources
Box 7921
Madison, WI 53707

Frank Haberland, Supervisor of the Big Game Division, says: "Wisconsin allows the use of black powder firearms without any special restrictions except for caliber size . . . a smooth-bore muzzle loader must be at least .45 caliber and a rifled muzzle loader must be at least .40. Muzzle loader hunters may hunt all species with these weapons."

Black powder handguns are not allowed. A brand new primitive hunt was instituted in Wisconsin by popular interest in order to "evaluate the attitudes, experience, and abilities of muzzle loader hunters. This is being done to gain more knowledge of the muzzle loader hunter and may lead to an expansion of special seasons in the future."

WYOMING
Game & Fish Department
Cheyenne, WY 82002

Bill Brown, Information Director for Wyoming, says: "The future of black powder (frontstuffers) in this state is golden. I think we're just starting to get into it really big."

Mr. Brown goes on to say that the liberal general season, in which the frontloader is used at will, has apparently satisfied the Wyoming hunter for there have been no large requests for special seasons. The law is clear on which arms may be used. A rifle of caliber .40 is legal, but it must be loaded with at least 50 grains of black powder; Pyro is illegal at this time. Upland game may be hunted with black powder, too—all game may, and some grouse may be taken with black powder handguns legally. Any gun may be used to take predators and varmints.

CHAPTER 21

List of Suppliers

Catalogs are always fun, especially when the reader browses through a Wish Book shopping for the objects of his passion, in this case black powder guns and gear for hunting. A listing of various black powder companies with addresses appears below. Some of these dealers offer free pamphlets and catalogs; others have expensive productions and they have to charge for them in order to break even. There is usually enough good reading in these to merit the price.

A few short years ago the space permitted in this chapter would have been ample to include all of the serious black powder manufacturers and importers in the country. Not so today. The black powder march has developed such interest that company after company has joined in producing and selling the guns and gear that make possible black powder hunting. The inclusions below represent a sample only of the total population of dealers. These were selected as fairly as possible on the basis of current advertisements in black powder interest publications, and the exclusion of any company was in no way calculated.

Selections were made at random from reading current black powder literature and not on any other basis, including quality of product or popularity of firm.

The Armoury, Inc.
Route 202
New Preston, CT 06777

A complete line of kits and finished guns for the black powder hunter.

Catalog available.

Atlanta Cutlery Corp.
Box 33266M
Decatur, GA 30033

Makers of finished Green River knives at reasonable prices. Also, knife blades.

Browning Arms Company
Morgan, UT 84050

Manufacturers of the Jonathan Browning Mountain Rifle in .45, .50, and .54 calibers with single-set trigger.

Catalog available ($2).

The Buffalo Bull Shop
Box 8
Marion, OH 52302

Leather clothing for the buckskinner, including gun cases and kits.

Catalog available.

Butler Creek Corporation
P.O. Box GG, Dept. SIA
Jackson Hole, WY 83001

Makers of poly-patch plastic sabot for ball shooting.

Centennial Arms Corporation
3318 West Devon Avenue
Lincolnwood, IL 60659

A complete line of kits and finished guns for the black powder hunter.

Catalog available.

E. Christopher Firearms
P.O. Box 283F
6818 State Road
Miamitown, OH 45041

Quality hunting bags, deluxe bullet starters, bullet bags, and special powder measures.

Connecticut Valley Arms
Saybrook Road
Haddam, CT 06438

Distributors of the original Green River works New England knife dating to 1834. Life-time warranty. Also complete line of muzzle-loading guns and gear.

Catalog available ($2).

Colt Industries
150 Huyshope Avenue
Hartford, CT 06102

Reproducing their own 1851 Navy Squareback and Third Model Dragoon.

Catalog available.

Dixie Gun Works
Union City, TN 38261

A huge 521-page catalog featuring a complete line of black powder tools, firearms, clothing, and supplies. ($2).

Eagle Arms Company
River View Drive
Mt. Washington, KY 40047

Home tanning kits, Lee-Mac capper, quick loader for ball, and special pan primer.

Catalog available ($2)

Euroarms of America
14 West Monmouth Street
Winchester, VA 22601

Reproduction black powder firearms.

Catalog available ($1).

Firearms Import & Export Corporation
2470 N.W. 21 Street
Miami, FL 33142

Sellers of flintlock and percussion Kentucky rifles plus other black powder guns.

Forster Products
181 East Lanark Avenue
Lanark, IL 61046

Makers of Tap-O-Cap, homemade #11 percussion caps as well as muzzle-loading accoutrements and kits.

Catalog available (25¢).

Golden Age Arms Company, Inc.
14 West Winter Street
Box 283
Delaware, OH 43015

Special Douglas ML barrels, curly maple stock blanks, Hawken pre-carved stocks, and a tomahawk kit.

Catalog available ($1.50).

Green River Rifle Works
Roosevelt, UT 84066

Manufacturers of excellent reproductions of the trade rifles.

Catalog available.

Harpers Ferry Arms Company
Berkley Plantation
Dept. MB
Charles City, VA 23030

The Maynard carbine in .51 caliber, historical guns, uniforms and accessories.

Free brochure available.

Harrington & Richardson, Inc.
Industrial Row
Gardner, MA 01440

Manufacturers of modern style reliable black powder firearms.

Catalog available.

The Hawken Shop
3028 North Lindbergh Blvd.
Dept. GK/12
St. Louis, MO 63074

Hawken rifles and a complete line of replica gear.

Catalog available ($2).

B. E. Hodgdon, Inc.
7710 West 50 Hi-Way
Shawnee Mission, KS 66202

These are distributors of Pyrodex and Scottish black powder, as well as black powder arms and a black powder loading manual for $1.00.

Catalog available ($2).

Hornady/Pacific
Box 1848
Grand Island, NE 68801

Manufacturers of swaged round ball for the black powder shooter.

Indian Ridge Traders
P.O. Box 869
Royal Oak, MI 48068

Do-it-yourself knives.

Iver Johnson Arms
109 River Street
Fitchbuer, MA 01420

Black powder handguns.

Catalog available.

Jimmy Lile Knives
Route 1
Russelville, AR 72801

Custom knifemaker producing individual blades for the most discriminating black powder hunter.

Lee Precision Inc.
Highway U
Hartford, WI 53023

Makers of lead melting pots and bullet moulds of many designs for the black powder hunter.

Catalog available.

Log Cabin Sport Shop
8010 Lafayette Road
P.O. Box 275
Lodi, OH 44254

General black powder shooter supplies, including leather.

Catalog available ($2).

Lyman/Sierra
Route 147
Middlefield, CT 06455

Sellers of a complete line for black powder guns as well as manufacturers of bullet moulds and accessories, almost all black powder calibers.

Catalog available.

Michaels of Oregon
Box 13010
Portland, OR 97213

Makes powder measures and a host of black powder accoutrements for the hunter, including excellent sling swivel kits.

Mowery Gun Works
Box 28
Iowa Park, TX 76367

Sell 1835 Allen and Thurber rifle, plus many other excellent longarms.

Brochure available.

Navy Arms/Replica Arms
687-C Bergen Boulevard
Ridgefield, NJ 07657

Manufacturers of the fine Hurricane/Hunter American made big game hunting rifles, as well as a complete line of all needs for the black powder hunter including handguns.

Catalog available ($1).

Numrich Arms Corporation
West Hurly, NY 12491

Manufacturers of the Hopkins and Allen underhammer as well as a Kentucky rifle, a shotgun, a boot-pistol kit, an over-under rifle, and black powder parts.

Catalog available ($2).

Orlfh Hulvey
406 East Dewey
Normal, IL 61761

Handmade tomahawks.

Outers Laboratories
Box 37
Onalaska, WI 54650

Makes excellent black powder cleaning kit.

Ramrod Gun and Knife Company
R. R. 5, State Road, No. 3 North
New Castle, IN 47362

Trail boots, buckskin outfits, building supplies for custom guns, and black powder hats.

Catalog available ($1).

Richland Arms Company
321 W. Adrian
Blissfield, MI 49228

Sellers of the .50 caliber Wesson rifle as well as a complete line of rifle and handgun kits and black powder accoutrements.

Catalog available.

A. G. Russell Company
1705-B8, Highway 71 N.
Springdale, AR 72764

Custom knives for the black powder hunter.

Catalog available.

Sharon Rifle Barrel Company
P.O. Box 1197
Kalispell, MT 59901

Kits for the J&S Hawken half- and full-stock rifles, an English percussion shotgun kit, locks, and custom barrels from .50 to .62 caliber.

Shiloh Products, Inc.
37 Potter Street
Farmingdale, NY 11735

Manufacturers of electric casting furnaces as well as complete line of casting accessories and high quality black powder bullet moulds in unique designs.

Speer Products
Box 896
Lewiston, ID 83501

Makers of round ball for the black powder shooter.

Sturm, Ruger & Company, Inc.
Southport, CT 06490

Makers of the Old Army black powder six-shooter, a magnum among primitive-type handguns.

Catalog available.

Sublette County Historical Society
P.O. Box 666
Pinedale, WY 82941

Sellers of the 1832 Green River trade knife.

Swede's Forge and Gun Works
4301 North Iroquois
Tucson, AZ 85705

Makers of custom Hawken rifles for right- and left-handed shooters. Also, manufacturers English fowling guns, single barrel, in 10 or 12 gauge. Will build custom guns to the shooter's demands.

Tecumseh's Trading Post
P.O. Box 369
Shartlesville, PA 19554

Authentic and completely handmade buckskin frontiersman outfits, shirts, pants, moccasins and boots sinew sewn, hides of buckskin, rifle cases, etc.

Catalog available ($1).

Tingle Manufacturing Company, Inc.
1125 Smithland Pike
Shelbyville, IN 46176

Make muzzle-loading shotgun wads in gauges 8 through 20, with many odd sizes in between.

Catalog (28¢ in stamps).

Thompson/Center Arms
Rochester, NH 03867

A complete line of black powder hunting guns including the .54 Renegade and a lightweight .36, or .45 Seneca. Also makes moulds.

Catalog available.

Track of the Wolf Company
P.O. Box Y
Osseo, MN 55369

Distributors of complete black powder hunting guns and gear.

Catalog available ($2).

Ultra-Hi Products Co., Inc.
150 Florence Avenue
Hawthorne, NJ 07506

A complete line of finished guns and kits as well as a unique replica air rifle of a Kentucky muzzle loader.

Catalog available.

Index